MW01051413

IOWA IMAGES

DUTCH IMMIGRANT HISTORY ILLUSTRATED

IOWA IMAGES

DUTCH IMMIGRANT HISTORY ILLUSTRATED

IRENE KOOI CHADWICK

© 2004 Irene Kooi Chadwick

All rights reserved. No part of this book may be reproduced in any form or by any electronic or mechanical means, including information storage and retrieval systems, without permission in writing from the publisher, except by a reviewer who may quote brief passages in a review. For information address:

Pie Plant Press
PMB 192
1700 McHenry Ave. 65-B
Modesto, CA 95350-4336

Chadwick, Irene Kooi.

Iowa Images: Dutch immigrant history illustrated / Irene Kooi Chadwick. — 1st ed.

390pp 8$^{1}/_{2}$ x 11 inches 22x28 cm.

ISBN 0-9642725-4-7

1. Subject 1 (History). 2. Subject 2 (Iowa). 3. Subject 3 (Farm life). I. Title.

Printed in the USA by Parks Printing on acid-free archival paper.

Cover by Staudesign

Front cover photographs (clockwise from upper left): Terp Hogebientum, Friesland, 1995; Verna Mae Kooi (now Vicki Peterson) as baby, 1932; Well-worn klompen of Piet de Groot, Friesland, 1995; Six youngest Kooi children on horse: Verna Mae, Milly, Irene, Elmer, Stan, and Glenn, 1942.

Back cover photographs (clockwise from upper left): Illustration from Holy Bible of Geertje and Peter Kooi, 1870; Bregtje Sybesma, Franeker, Friesland, 1903; Garfield Township District No. 8 School near Lebanon, Iowa, 1905.

Visit our web site at www.iowa-images.com

And, you know, whoever has once in his life caught perch or has seen the migrating of the thrushes in autumn, watched how they float in flocks over the village on bright, cool days, he will never be a real townsman, and will have a yearning for freedom to the day of his death.

Anton Chekhov in "Gooseberries"

Ida Sybesma takes niece Bertha Bierma to school three miles from
the Bierma farm. Faithful Prince was a vital part of the family for 27 years.
Sioux Center, 1912.

MEMOIR FOR MOTHER

Contents

PART III: THE OUTSIDE WORLD

APPENDIX

Introduction

Until I was age ten, I lived in a place so isolated and protected that the everyday language was different from the ordinary language used today. This place was a farm in Sioux County, Iowa, seven miles from the nearest town. "Sex" was a word I never heard or saw. Neither did I know where babies came from. I had not seen Santa Claus, liquor, or advertisements for it. Jails were something I knew existed but had not seen. Strict rules isolated us: no dancing, gambling, or watching movies, and no wearing of makeup or revealing clothes. No mixing with the outside world—in other words, with heathens, because the Bible said, "Ye are in the world but not of the world." Books and magazines were church approved. The music came almost entirely from our singing of songs found in the *Psalter Hymnal* or *The Golden Book of Favorite Songs*, accompanied by a piano or organ or sung a cappella. We went to church services twice every Sunday and mid-week to catechism. Social life revolved around programs at church or school, visits with relatives in their farmhouses, and occasional weddings or funerals. Winter holidays were celebrated at church and summer holidays at the park in town. School picnics on Memorial Day and Labor Day marked the beginning and end of summer vacation from school. The religion was Christian Reformed, and the farm families were, like us, from Dutch-immigrant stock.

Mother left the farm in 1945 when I was eight. Around this same time, my four oldest siblings, and then the fifth and sixth, left the farm to go to war or to start their own lives. Even though I attached myself to Pa during this time, he was more or less emotionally unavailable. Subsequently, most of what happened between 1945 and 1947, between the ages of eight and ten, were forgotten—until 1984. After Mother's funeral on February 6, 1984, I wrote twenty-seven pages of eulogy, "She Held Us All Together," and sent it to my four children, nine siblings, and the uncles and aunts in Iowa. They corrected errors and added their thoughts. From that beginning grew these recollections.

Over the years, four of us sisters shared our photographs and writings about Iowa. We discussed gathering these records into an *anthologia*, from Medieval Greek meaning "gathering of flowers." Such a collection of poems, stories, and photographs could be a bouquet to honor our parents. For me, this idea began to be realized when I lived in Israel with my daughter during the fall of 1989. Here, during the *Intifada*, there were many similarities to my childhood on the farm during World War II. On subsequent journeys to Israel, Iowa, Michigan, Colorado, and Friesland, I gathered family documents, photographs, and letters, and recorded oral history.

Memory is a leaky sieve through which the particulate matter of experience gets strained. Each stream runs down hill into a river, eventually blending into a sea. And so, even though I researched dates, places, and events to make them as factual as possible, errors will be found. The categories of fiction and non-fiction sift and shift, one into the other. And so, who is to say where fact ends and fiction begins? "Your siblings will be quick to point out where fact ends and fiction begins," sister Vicki reminds me. In fact, readers closer than me to the actual events portrayed in this book may say that such and such never happened. Everyone remembers their own childhood from his or her unique perspective. I am responsible for what I have recalled, not others in the past who could not have known what effect they might have had on me. Several people described here are still alive and may dislike my portrayals of them or of others. I have no wish to hurt anyone's feelings, but my goal has not been to be nice, but rather to be true to my experience of childhood on the farm and a way of life now gone. Recording a lifestyle that has now disappeared is in keeping with an ageless aural tradition: The only stories that have lasted 10,000 years are those that were told by aboriginal Australians to their children.

Many people contribute to the creation and production of any artistic, musical, or literary work; and for a book, the reader is the performer. Errors of fact will undoubtedly be found. Readers are invited to send corrections, additions, or comments to the author at the publisher's address. These will be acknowledged and either used in a second edition or passed on to the next generation. This book could not exist without the generous and continuing contributions of countless others. However, the author acknowledges responsibility for its final form and content.

—IKC

Permissions

For "Ralph," by Harold Aardema, originally published in the Doon Press, May 4, 1989. Copyright © 1989. Reprinted by permission of the author.

For poems and stories by Bernice Afman: "Death in an Iowa Farm House," "An Oak Table," "Market Day," "Peddle Wagons," "One Room School," "Huis Bezoek," and "The Drought," printed by permission of the author.

For excerpts from "Bierma, Watse Family," by Syne Bierma, from *The Centennial History of Sioux County*. Copyright © 1991. Quoted by permission of the author.

For excerpts from "The Dutch Among Us" and "Letters from Lucy," by Dena Boer, from *Stanislaus Stepping Stones*, volume 10, #3. Copyright © 1986. Quoted by permission of McHenry Museum & Historical Society.

For "Grandma's House," by Gladys Gritter. Copyright © 2001. Reprinted by permission of The Banner. For other poems and stories by Gladys Gritter: "My Most Unforgettable Character," "Childhood's Passing" from *Pen Queens 1979-80*, "Our Family Register," "Journal #1: Kooi Name," "Our Trip," "Gophers" from *My Memories*," "On Saturday Afternoon," "Where Babies Come From" from *Journals of Gladys Gritter*, and "Letter from Abbey Hengeveld," printed by permission of the author.

For excerpt from "A Remembrance of Jennie Haverhals given by John Haverhals, March 8, 2000," printed by permission of John Haverhals.

For excerpt from *Still Life with a Bridle: Essays and Apocryphas*, by Zbigniew Herbert, translated by John and Bogdana Carpenter. Copyright © 1991 by Zbigniew Herbert and John and Bogdana Carpenter. Quoted by permission of HarperCollins Publishers.

For "Lesson #1, This Is Skin," by Rebecca Tannetje Houwer, from *poems at the curb* (Toronto, Ontario, Canada). Copyright © 1999. Reprinted by permission of author.

For excerpt from *An Informal History of the German Language*, by W. B. Lockwood. Copyright © 1965. Quoted by permission of W. Heffer & Sons.

For excerpts from *Netherlanders in America: Dutch immigration to the United States and Canada*, 1789-1950, by Henry S. Lucas. Copyright © 1955. Quoted by permission of University of Michigan Press.

For excerpts from *Siouxland: A History of Sioux County, Iowa*, by G. Nelson Nieuwenhuis. Copyright © 1983. Quoted by permission of the author.

For poems and stories by Vicki Peterson: "Drown Proof," "Lineage," and "Green Is a Color," printed by permission of the author.

For excerpts from *The Netherlands* by Max Schuchart. Copyright © 1972. Quoted by permission of Walker Publishing Company, Inc.

For excerpts from *The Netherlands*, by Sacheverell Sitwell. Copyright © 1945, 1974. Quoted by permission of Hastings House Publishers.

For "Washday," by Durk Van Der Ploeg, from *The Sound that Remains: A Historical Collection of Frisian Poetry* (bilingual ed.), translated by Rod Jellema. Copyright © 1990. Reprinted by permission of Eerdmans Publishing Co.

For excerpts from *Pocket of Civility, A History of Sioux Center*, by Mike Vanden Bosch. Copyright © 1976. Reprinted by permission of the author.

Acknowledgments

The creation of any song, picture, or story comes from many antecedents. Without the generosity and support of such ancestors, this book could not have been conceived, born, and grown into print. Especially, I wish to thank my sisters, Gladys Gritter, Bernice Afman, Vicki Peterson, and Mildred Kooi for their significant contributions of letters, stories, records, poems, journals, documents, photographs, memorabilia---plus their loving care. Their unique voices enlarge the scope of the book, as does the history contributed by my brother, Raymond Kooi. Additionally, Vicki Peterson gave careful readings of each chapter, as did my husband, Douglas Chadwick, son Brent Chadwick, and Paula Theno. Their encouragement and criticism was invaluable. The genealogy charts exist because of the expertise and generosity of Don Sanford. My sons, Tim and Eric Chadwick, gave invaluable computer help at crucial times, and without the unique perspective of my Israeli daughter, Nanette Chadwick Furman, there would be no book.

In Iowa, the late Jennie (Kooi) Haverhals, deserves special mention for sharing genealogy records, photographs, documents, letters, and oral history. The late Margaret (Mike) Kooi, Bertha Vander Lugt and George Kooi are among the many relatives whose acts of generosity are printed on my heart, also Mike's husband, Bill Kooi, Terry Kooi, Henrietta Bierma, and many of the other Iowa Koois and Sybesmas who are first, second, or third cousins, uncles or aunts, nephews or nieces.

Grateful acknowledgement goes to strangers in foreign countries met by chance, such as Karin Zuiderhoek in The Netherlands, also to second cousins, Rinske de Boer, Klaas vander Schaaf, Tietje and Pieter de Groot for photographs, documents and translations. Contributions came from: Dena Boer, Denise Metzger, Arlene Figueroa, John Haverhals, Catherine De Bie, Jerry Fondse, Penny Williams-Ramos, and members of the Modesto Chapter of the National League of American Pen Women.

For illustration, grateful acknowledgement especially goes to Gladys Gritter, Vicki Peterson, Margaret Vander Stoep, and Kathy Schreurs for finding, lending, and reproducing old photographs; and to Tim Chadwick for scanning and printing images and genealogy charts. Snapshots of us thirteen on the farm (1940-43) came from Vera (Van Walterop) Scheeper as a surprise package in the mailbox. To each and every person mentioned goes a red rose for her or his contribution to this bouquet of flowers gathered to honor Dutch immigrants to America.

Part I

FROM ISRAEL
TO IOWA

1

War Zone

A bomb shelter lies below the building where my daughter and I are living in Israel. Children descend the dark stairs to the bomb shelter when they find that the door has been inadvertently left unlocked. I climb four flights of stairs to our apartment, enter, and pull on the string that turns on the light bulb dangling from the center of the ceiling. A breeze comes from the Negev Desert to lift the curtain of gray gauze over the window. Air moves into the room and twirls the crocheted loops held by the lampshade's wire hoops around the bare bulb. The light projected through the wire-framed loops casts moving patterns around the room and mixes darkness with light. Around the walls of the room race circles, stars, triangles, trapezoids, ovals, and rectangles—elongated, widened, misshapen, then sharpened into the familiar patterns of the crocheted doilies I remember in the Iowa farmhouse.

The blank shadows of linked paper dolls cut from a single piece of paper march around the walls and attach themselves to memories of early childhood. I am climbing steep wooden stairs, negotiating them one by one, going upstairs to bed. Oval shadows along the walls lengthen as daylight changes into night. In the narrow hall above me is a long string dangling from a light bulb. Even when I stand on tiptoes, the string is nearly out of reach. I miss. It swings. The floor is cold, the dark is scary, but I must reach the elusive string to pull on the light before a ghost grabs me from behind.

Time passes. Gradually the dangling string becomes several threads, frayed, growing into the fuzzy colors of family, each member's fabric unraveling stitch by stitch. Bouncing off each other are times when light and darkness mix sections of farmland with city squares, bomb scares with exploding stars, an Oriental Mideast with an American Midwest. Memories of Iowa during World War II reverberate off the reality of living in Israel during the *Intifada*. Over and over on continents on opposite sides of the globe, wartime austerities, patterns, and practices reveal remarkable similarities. In

2

both kitchens, the same spoke is missing from the back of a wooden chair. Walking up Eilat's streets, I pass kitchen windowsills where glass jars of preserves are lined up, sunlight singing through the rich reds, purples, and golds of harvest. Light bouncing off the Red Sea illuminates the door to a bomb shelter—a storm cellar below the farmhouse in Iowa. In the dusk, I stare at peaches, pears, tomatoes, and beans swimming in Mason jars lined up on wooden shelves next to a bin of potatoes.

During the autumn of 1989, I lived with my daughter, a marine biologist working in Eilat, Israel, located at the northern tip of the Gulf of Aqaba on the Red Sea. Here coral reefs attract marine researchers, also scuba divers, snorkelers, and water sports enthusiasts. Eilat is a winter resort for vacationing Europeans and Asians, similar to the Caribbean for Americans. It is situated on the Great Rift that once separated the land mass of two continents. Between mountains, desert, and sea, Eilat lies on a slope, its shoreline shared with Egypt, Jordan, and Saudi Arabia. The four countries lie so close to each other that their ancient conflicts seem to shake the ground under foot. Mountains of stone rise up as treeless ramparts, closing in and turning the four countries toward the Red Sea. Pink with coral beauty and crystalline clarity, the Red Sea reflects the distant red hills of Jordan, carving shadow from light.

In 1989 an estimated 6,000 Arabs without licenses to work were living underground in Eilat. They helped to keep the luxury hotels afloat, earning better wages than they could get in the occupied territories of the West Bank or the Gaza Strip. Ever since the Intifada began, however, tourism has been down and terrorism up. Fewer hotels are full, and more Arabs are out of work and on the streets. Israelis have become used to making a wide detour around the paper bag, that might hold a bomb, left on the sidewalk or street. Security is tight; children, especially, are protected. Elementary schools are often recessed in the ground and fenced, their gates locked and guarded. At age eighteen, all Israelis become soldiers for three years. From age twenty-one to fifty-five, the men disappear into the military for three weeks each year, their families not knowing where they go. A man in every apartment building is in charge of the rap on the door at night that means GO NOW. On the street, one out of ten is in khaki; at home, one out of ten is dead from the recurrent conflicts between Arabic countries and Israel.

On the streets of Eilat, pairs of soldiers wander past, guns slung loosely across their backs. My shoulders carry only the weight of doubt. To enjoy a cup of coffee, I select an outdoor table in the tented Shalom Plaza Shopping Center. Positioned next to a busy Kodak store and other small shops, this is a good place to watch people. At the next table, gun across his lap, a khaki-clad man reads a Hebrew newspaper to friends. Four Americans share news with newly found friends. People with backpacks hustle past baby buggies. Young locals mix with a diverse crowd coming in from the airport across the street. Men, young and old, smoke and watch the parade of adolescents walking by, advertising their assets. Girls have colorful hair bands holding their long hair straight up, letting it fall from above their heads in a cascading fountain of fuzz. Boys wear Jewish skullcaps. I notice that these yarmulkes are as obvious an identification as the tribal marks cut into the faces of native West Africans.

Loud music competes with the roar of jets landing alongside the hotel strip. From their fat bellies, the jets disgorge Arabs, Jews, Americans, Europeans, Orientals, and Africans. They collect their bags and wander by, taking in the newness of this place that is neither black nor white, but varying shades and tones. Asia meets Africa at Eilat and at the nearby towns of Taba in Egypt and Aqaba in Jordan, all sharing a common coastline on the Gulf of Aqaba.

Since Eilat is a small town, everything is within easy walking distance. Climbing hills behind tall apartment buildings under construction, I find a sign marking the entrance to an archeological site and ascend to caves hidden by weathered burlap flaps. I find bunkers. On the next walk into the hills, there are more cave entrances blocked by twisted balls of barbed-wire. Clearly visible are the lights and smokestacks of Egypt, Saudi Arabia and Jordan. In the Gulf of Aqaba are fleets of gray gunboats at anchor. In the distance are the dark holes of more bunkers in hillsides. All of Eilat is easily within view of her enemies.

The area is steeped in history. Near to Eilat in the Negev Desert at Wadi Timna are the remains of King Solomon's copper and iron mines. Excavations have uncovered the ruins of metal foundries from that time. Eilat (Elat) was then called Elath or Ezion-geber on the Gulf of Aqaba, and excavations carried out in the area from 1938-1940 show that these were successive names for the same

4

place. It was one of the encampments of the Israelites on their journey toward Canaan after Jehovah had parted the Red Sea to let them pass through to escape an Egyptian army hot in pursuit. The Israelites wandered in the deserts of Sinai for forty years before reaching their "Promised Land." As regularly as manna came from heaven to feed the Israelis, Pa's Bible reading followed every meal on the Iowa farm. And so, we also criss-crossed the Sinai Peninsula, chapter by chapter, through Exodus, Leviticus, Numbers, Deuteronomy, and Joshua.

During Biblical times, the Gulf of Aqaba was a crucial commercial artery for Arabia, as well as a military seaport for the whole of Arabia. King Solomon extended the borders of ancient Israel down to Ezion-geber. He based an overseas trading fleet there and the port became a heavily defended export center. The goods traded included ebony, sandalwood, gold, silver, ivory, myrrh, panther skins, peacocks and apes. After Solomon, Judean kings ruled, then the Persians, Greeks, Romans, Moslems, Crusaders, Turks, and, more recently, the British. Today, the Gulf of Aqaba remains the only gateway to the Indian Ocean for Israel and Jordan; their sea-going trade with the Orient occurs at the adjacent seaport towns of Eilat and Aqaba.[1]

Modern-day Eilat came into Israel only fifty-six years ago, after World War II, when the United Nations created the State of Israel. In 1949 Israel sent their convicts to build Eilat. It was a cost-effective measure to send law breakers away from the populous north, down to Eilat at Israel's southern tip, a place so remote that jails were not necessary. As the convicts laboriously carved the road to the Red Sea out of the desert, mile by mile, guards had to be posted to protect the law-breakers from the Bedouin. When the first group of convicts finally arrived at the Red Sea, they found only three abandoned huts on the beach—no shelter and no food. Jordan had moved the borders of their ancient town of Aqaba a few yards up the beach and

[1] John Bright, *A History of Israel* (Philadelphia: Westminster Press, 1972). Index: Plate III is map titled *"The Exodus from Egypt,"* showing criss-cross wanderings of Israelis across Sinai Peninsula, also trade routes. Additional trade routes in *The Bible as History*, page 218, Figure 37, by Werner Keller (New York: William Morrow, 1981).

had abandoned the three-hut, Turkish police station called Um Rashrash. The convicts stayed and became the first citizens of Elat, assuming its Biblical name but adding an "i." Between the sealed borders of Jordan and Egypt, the town quickly grew to 24,000. Its rapid construction was watched and continues to be watched with suspicion by the Arabic countries. In 1989, Eilat was so close to Aqaba that anyone could walk into Jordan except for the armored patrols that prevented entry for any Israeli, or for anyone passing through Israel.

On the street I am approached, at different times, by two long-time pawns in the Israeli system of justice. They want me to write their stories. Both are being detained in Eilat by rabbinical courts. The Iranian man was, at various times, the late Shah's aide, a Los Angeles lover and importer, and an Argentinian businessman with a Jewish wife. He says he is being detained without chance of deportation. His story is intriguing. We set a time for coffee the following day when he will bring documents; the next day he does not appear. The Russian woman claims that the Israeli husband she is divorcing has absconded with their children. Apparently she has the money, he the children. In any event, she is a woman dressed to attract attention, lively and fun, pursuing pleasure while the court takes its time.

Israeli law decrees that for every ten school children away from the confines of the school for any reason, an armed adult must accompany the group. We are at Ein Gedi, on the shore of the Dead Sea, with our daughter. As we climb the trail to King David's Cave, along comes a teacher with ten emotionally disturbed kids. On the rough terrain we stop to chat with the teacher and watch the antics of the out-of-control adolescent who carries the gun.

"Why this kid?"

Pulling the bullet clip out of his pocket, the teacher laughs. "That kid needs to be in charge of this hike."

After living in Israel for a while, I grew nonchalant about guns and bomb scares. In the streets I was among the curious who would stand and watch demolition teams come and go. Once, I was entering the Post Office when a young soldier who was waving his gun around, instantly saw that I did not understand the meaning of his shouts. He frantically motioned me to use another door, "Leave, leave, get out of the square!" In mere seconds

6   the cavernous old Post Office and the adjoining square were empty. People react to crises such as this bomb threat with speed and discipline. I did not expect to meet such an emotionally expressive people with such argumentative natures. Perhaps there is a strength and courage that comes from acting bold, and loud talking is a way to cope with adversity. In any event, during their long history of surviving against all odds, Israelis seem to have become more resilient than other peoples.

In the night sea, patrol boats search for depth charges. On the beach, my daughter makes a routine call in her newly acquired Hebrew to the Israeli Navy, letting them know that she and her research partner will do another night dive to record data from the coral reef. No dice—until her Israeli partner arrives and makes the same call in his deeply familiar Hebrew voice to the Israeli Navy. While they dive, I stand on shore and watch the dark ghosts of patrol boats slip silently over the Red Sea. Sea depths call up childhood on the Iowa farm during World War II: submarines, and depth charges, white sailor caps, the U.S. Marines and the Army Air Corps.

One of my older brothers was a B-17 belly gunner, flying weekly bombing missions over Germany in 1944. During the summer days of that year, I was seven and one of the five youngest in a family of eleven children ranging in age from three to twenty-two. On hot summer nights, some of us slept on the rickety tar roof of the wide front porch and watched stars dive through the sky. In the afternoons, we little kids might walk the half-mile on the dirt road to the mailbox on the corner, hoping to find mail that our brothers in the Army Air Corps and Navy would send to Mother.

Memories keep pace with the back-and-forth tramping of my feet as I walk the shoreline of the Interuniversity Institute for Marine Research, waiting for my daughter and her diving partner to surface. Waiting in the dark, an inscrutable, deep-under world seems to threaten. I shiver as a wind comes up and I hear the angry command of an Egyptian standing guard at the border town of Taba a half-mile down the beach. I keep waiting for my daughter and her diving partner to emerge from the Red Sea. Soon I hear the sound of flapping fins and am glad to see two black heads above distant waves. Once they are on the beach, my daughter secures the collected data and stows her dive gear. She shivers. Our chatter is light and easy as she rinses off sea water and changes into street clothes. "It's getting chilly." I don't mention the threatening voice of the border patrol, and my memories of World War II are missing in action as we prepare to drive home. The flashing of red lights at the border recedes in the rear-view mirror as we drive north around the curving sea toward Eilat and falafels.

Back in our living room, however, the whirling lightshade creates patterns of shadows on the walls that call to mind guilt, a crazy quilt falling apart like the doilies on the arms and backs of the davenport in the front parlor of the farmhouse. How could I, at age six, have felt the collective guilt of countries sending off their young to war? Mystery floats in shifting perceptions. Something is missing from this kaleidoscope turning round and round, displacing and replacing pattern after pattern. Lights and colors scatter and change as asymmetrical figures in lopsided wheels lope away. Stars turn round and round and then disappear into the ground. The spokes in the wheel of the wheelbarrow whirl around into the muddy distance and then disappear into thin tangles of embroidery thread.

It is December 7, 1991. Yesterday my oldest brother turned seventy. A voice on the radio announces that this is the two hundredth birthday of Wolfgang Amadeus Mozart and the fiftieth anniversary of the bombing of Pearl Harbor. I had just turned five when that news came into the farmhouse. A large floor radio was located in the front room next to the front door.

We little kids are playing on the floor. We have taken dried corncobs from the wood box and are lining them up to make roads, farms, and houses. Tractors and dolls litter the landscape. Pa is anxiously turning the two knobs near the top of the radio, one to control the volume and the other to find a station. He leans closer to tune in a news bulletin while half-turning his body and lifting his left hand to warn us to quiet down, but the straining urgency coming through the static has already lowered the volume of our commotion. The radio crackles and the voice of the newscaster grows louder, becoming fixed in my mind as an incomprehensible danger. No matter what hour that news actually did come into our lives, to me it will always be one o'clock, with snow outside and Pa sitting in the wooden rocker, his stout gray hair bristling straight up two inches from his red forehead, his strong body

8   slumped toward the large old radio. Suddenly he cocks both ears forward and cups them with his hands. The room grows still. An alarm is sounding to bring an early end to the sheltered life of the thirteen of us on the farm.

As our daughter guides us—her father and mother—we visit Bethesda, an archeological site of five-columned porches around a pool of spring-fed water. During Biblical times, Bethesda was a wellspring of life for the sick and crippled who came to lower themselves into the pool "when the waters were troubled" by the rising, hot mineral springs. Above the Sea of Galilee, we climb a mountain and sit in a vineyard to read The Beatitudes to each other. "Blessed are the poor in spirit, for theirs is the kingdom of heaven. Blessed are those who mourn, for they shall be comforted" (Matthew 5:3, 4).[2]

I close my eyes and see the large black family Bible resting on the windowsill next to Pa's chair at the head of the kitchen table in the Iowa farmhouse. At meals the older brothers sit on a bench under the only double windows in the hot kitchen. Both windows are open and a breeze is moving the curtains into the room.

---

[2] The King James Version of the Holy Bible is the version of the Bible that is cited here and throughout this book.

2

Summertime

Touring Israel at Capernaum, our daughter reads to us from the Bible. For her, Sabbath has become Shabbat. She has been drawing nearer to an Israeli boyfriend, pushing aside Western teachings and her American parents, although she continues to seek understandings from her patriarchal past. It appears as though she actually can hear my strict father, who is one-fourth of her genetic heritage. She never saw her grandfather when he was on the Iowa farm reading the Bible and saying long prayers—but somehow she seems to. Maybe she can hear the repeated banging of the screen door as we small children run from the farmhouse kitchen to go play in the grove. Maybe she can see the doorsill, sloped toward its worn middle below the banging screen door and flies buzzing at the barrier.

On the front stoop is the worn-down pattern that soles make on wooden steps. A dirty towel twists around a spinning, wooden roller held by rusted pins above the basin of wash water used by workmen. Memories are pockmarked by the rhythmic coughing of the pump over the well in the front yard. Nailed to the kitchen wall in Eilat is a Hebrew calendar; to the kitchen wall in Iowa—a Farm Bureau calendar. Repeated patterns, country-wide austerities, and striking similarities come around, over and over again. How can this place NOT call to mind Mother's housekeeping habits—wartime on the Iowa farm? Jars of rationed sugar saved for Sunday's cake. Then and now, here and there: dishes in the drainer, dishpan on the hook, chipped plates, no two glasses alike. Worn patterns in the oilcloth covering both kitchen tables. Homemade clothes and wartime habits: use it up, wear it out, make it last, or do without. Monday washday, Tuesday ironing, Wednesday sewing, Thursday cleaning, Friday baking, Saturday's bath in the round tin tub upon the kitchen floor, Sunday church. These worn patterns nail down war-torn pages from the book of childhood.

Barefoot until dark in summertime, we stay far enough away from the house so as not to hear Mother calling us inside to do chores. We live on 160

10

acres of black soil on which Pa and the older brothers grow corn, oats, alfalfa, and some rye or soybeans in the slough if it isn't too wet to plant. Hospers is seven miles away, Sheldon the same. In the summer of 1942, I am five and one of the "five little kids" stretching from ages eleven to two—from Verna Mae to Milly, myself, then Elmer and Glenny. Within nineteen years, Mother gave birth to twelve children so that, naturally, each one is expected to look after the next one younger in age. Verna Mae is eleven and no longer outside watching us as much as she used to. In fact, she really isn't considered a little kid anymore, but neither is she considered one of the older six. She is right smack in the middle. Glenny is only two, still babied and often kept inside the house, watched by the older girls. Verna Mae (who later changed her name to Vicki) recalls that Mother's favorite line for her was, "Now, Verna, you take Milly, Irene, Elmer and Glenny and go outside to play. That would be such a big help."

> Reluctantly, I would head for the kitchen door followed by Milly, Irene, Elmer, and Glenny. You knew your pecking order! Mother's last words as we were leaving would always be the same. "And be sure to watch the baby!" We usually went to play in the grove. Periodically, she would stick her head out the back door and holler "Verna, where is Glenny?" I would yell back, "He's right here!" as I looked around to see where he might be.[3]

Usually it is only Milly, Elmer, and myself playing together outdoors. Both of them are shy and quiet, so it falls to me to be the ringleader. Being the loud one I stand out, and sometimes get in trouble. Bossy, I have learned ways to stand up for myself—or stay out of the way. Since last summer I have been old enough to be responsible for Elmer outdoors. Mother is clear: "You see after Elmer now." This is no problem since he has just turned four, and by that age we pretty much watch out for ourselves. From time to time, all of us will hear plenty of "watch outs" from those who are older—when we're within hearing distance.

"Watch out for walking too close behind a horse."

---

[3] Letter from Vicki Kooi Peterson to author, 1999.

"Stay away from the tool shed, the pig pen, and the tank of water in the middle of the yard where the horses drink. Remember, you could drown in there." But its green-scummy surface feels cool; its mysterious depths tempt us to touch it, to float and sink stick-boats, to fish for what lies underneath.

"Don't climb up the windmill."

"Never climb into the haymow," comes with an emphatic, "especially during haying." They must know that we climb into the haymow as often as we can without being seen. Listening this time, I emerge from the habit of ignoring big people with their tiresome litany of watch-outs and ask, "Why?"

"You could get buried alive." Intriguing idea.

"How?"

"Well, why of course, when they dump a load of hay through the hayloft door, they can't see you little kids in the dark down there."

"Oh, really?"

"Don't play around the well or carry off that board over the hole. It's there to keep out dirt *and you, too* until Pa gets to town to get the part he needs to repair the pump. If you fall into the well, maybe you'll never get pulled out." Feels like this could be so. We don't play around the well.

Way-deep-down-things get covered up, but little kids pry up every board to see what's underneath and examine each black spot on the orange backs of ladybugs. Shadows emerge from underneath things. Warnings nail down pages torn from the book of childhood: Keep quiet about that. Don't be a tattletale. Better not tell.

"Watch out for the tractor going through the yard." Walking through the yard, I see the large heads of Pet and Dewey poking out of the Dutch door of the barn. We are allowed to ride these gentle old horses because they are too old to be used as workhorses.

"Never leave the barn door open. Your head could be cut off if the horse bolts for the barn. You're too little to halt a horse heading home into the barn for hay." Entering the yard on the back of Dewey, I panic as the out-of-control horse races for the barn.

"Whoa! Whoa!" somebody yells and races to grab the reins and hold the harness before Dewey gets to the barn door. We stop in the nick of time, right before the door, Dewey pawing, snorting, jerking to get free, my heart racing.

12   Gladys recalls that:

> On the farm it happened fairly often that horses were "spooked" by
> something and ran away. Actually, they always ran back to the barn—
> but it was a dangerous business. We'd hear the noise, the men yell-
> ing, and Mother would run out, "Oh no, oh no, where are the chil-
> dren?" Her next concern, "Did Pa (or the hired man) get off the
> cultivator (or whatever) safely?" No one ever got hurt in these run-
> aways that I can remember. That was due, I think, to the fact that Pa
> was so safety conscious. I can still hear him say, "Never tie the reins
> around your hands or body."

Stalls for horses line one side of the barn; stanchions for cows line the other side. In the heat of summer, flies swarm around the cows being milked. As they swish their tails back and forth, trying to get rid of flies, their long tails swish into the faces of brothers hard at work milking. If I loiter in the barn, I will be told to hold the cow's tail or to braid it to keep it from swishing into the face of a brother, leaning into the sweaty flank of a Holstein cow, pulling milk out of the four teats, two at a time, alternating between the front and back teats. Cow poop stinks, flies bite; waves of heat intensify composting hay, the barn smells. Chewing cuds echo the rhythmic squirt of a stream of milk hitting the side of a metal pail. Underfoot, mewling kitties and snarling cats lap at spilled milk streaming down the gutter. A tired brother directs a squirt of milk at a cat to scare it away. The cat yowls and runs. My brother laughs.

Cows are milked twice a day, and a metal pail of milk is carried to the kitchen. Milk is poured into white pitchers that are set on either end of the table to be passed around during meals. Cream sits in a pitcher next to the sugar bowl in the center of the table. In the barn is a separate room with a cement floor for the shiny cream separator. Tall metal cans of cream are picked up by the cream hauler from the creamery in Boyden. Back comes some of our cream in the form of butter that is always on the table for breakfast, dinner, and supper, as well as for lunches at nine and three. Next to the butter dish there is usually a Mason jar of jam, jelly, or apple butter put up during canning season by Mother and the older girls. Apple butter tastes the best, but plum jelly is nearly as good.

At busy times such as planting or harvest, Pa hired men to help in the fields. Mother also hired help in the house during times such as births, canning, corn shucking, haying, baling, and always at threshing time. The hired girls and men often were cousins, such as Frank, Bertha, Catherine, or Betty from one of the family farms in Lebanon, Iowa, South Dakota, or Minnesota. Ray, the oldest in the family, recalls that, "Cousin Bertha Fiekema was our hired girl on the farm before Gladys and Bernice became old enough to be the 'hired girls.' Bertha, then about sixteen, once sat on my head when I misbehaved. I called her 'fatty,' other things too." Aunt Mattie, or a neighbor, Mrs. Bonnema, always came to be with Mother when she gave birth. For one of the babies, Aunt Mattie arrived late and as she rushed into the bedroom, she moaned, "Ach Ietje, ach, my, and you all alone, ach." All hired girls or men, whether family or not, were treated as family. However, when the older six in our family were little, so were many of the cousins. Then Pa had to hire outsiders to help.

"My Most Unforgettable Character" is Gladys' memory of one of the hired men on the Lebanon farm:

> In my child's-eye view, he was always old. He was also deaf and strange, and he limped. "But he's sure reliable," Pa said. "When I get the plow oiled and the seedcorn ready, he's here." He would come for the first plowing of the fields, stay through the last picking of corn, and disappear until spring. He was our hired man through the years of the Great Depression. He didn't drink or smoke. But he chewed big wads of brownish slime that he spat out as he walked past the woodpile. We kids thought the woodpile grew caterpillars from the slime, and we kept away from it. He never talked to us. When we did something he didn't like, he glared. We thought that was why his last name was Glerum. We stayed out of his way. Mother would say, "Now you kids be nice to him; he won't hurt anyone." But we didn't believe her.
>
> Once we heard that he had tried to kill himself. After that we tried smiling at him. He never smiled back. Even the fact that he was old and not married made him different. Older people were married people–fathers and mothers. We didn't know any other kind. We never saw him read or write or visit. In the evening, when the day's work was finished, he would sit against the haystack, watching the sunset, chewing on his everlasting wad of tobacco. We kids would sneak around the haystack, daring each other

to peek at him. But one penetrating glare from him and we'd run, scared to death of what he might do. We imagined almost everything about him-and knew almost nothing. One spring he didn't come back. So Pa got another hired man and that was the last we heard of Pete Glerum. Many years later I asked Mother about him, and she told me the true reason Pete Glerum left.

"Oh," she said, "One fall morning I went upstairs to make his bed and found he had ladies clothes among his things. I went out to tell Pa. He brought Pete back to town. We never saw him again."

Everyone on our eight-party line listens in when Pa phones for help. He handles the receiver as though it were a loaded shotgun about to go off. Swiveling the black mouthpiece of the wall phone up close to his mouth, he shouts. "Hello Gert! Fred! It's Fred at Hospers! Bad connection, ja. Hang up, I'll try again." The second time his voice races higher, "Ja, good weather here at Hospers, ja," then softens and saddens, "Ja, Ida's feeling some better." His voice lifts. "Ja, canning peaches next week, I guess." Then he pauses. "Say, is Pete there? I'll be needing another hand next week. Ja, I'll wait then. Tell Pete to ring when he gets back from Ireton."[4] During the next pause, he half laughs at Gert's question, "Ja, well, guess there's always somebody here, you know." He looks around as he listens. Now his voice winds down with, "Ja, okay then. Say hello from us to Opa, Fannie, Adeline, Dreaka too." Intently he listens, obviously eager to hang up and get back to the fields, nervous about this new delay, yet knowing he had better do whatever his sister asks. "Ja, ja, I'll tell Ida. Well, goodbye then."

Slowly he cradles the black, horn-shaped receiver into its hook on the side of the wooden telephone hanging on the wall near the kitchen table. He turns away, head bowed. Aunt Gert is his oldest sister and probably a lot like their Ma was. At the beginning of the conversation, his voice carried an air of excitement, and then a rarely heard affection emerged through the rising and falling tenor of his voice. As he turns to go out the screen door, a bittersweet sense of nostalgia lingers.

---

[4] Pete would be asked for one of his sons to "help out" for a few days. Then, Pete would send Pa another hand. The cousin "helping out" was not asked, just sent. Sister Bernice was first sent to "help out" at age fourteen or so.

Aunt Gert's iron-grey hair is pulled back severely, plastered straight against her skull, and held tightly in a small, coiled bun by long metal pins. She is a no-nonsense woman, seeing to a big family on a large farm near Lebanon. Her husband is cigar chomping, red-cheeked, genial Uncle Pete. The two old men who live with them are Opa, his father, and his father's brother. We know all eight cousins: their faces, their gait, how each one acts and looks, smiling or staring. Aunt Gert's countenance makes me wonder about Pa's parents, the grandparents I never knew, who appear stern in old photographs.

The farmland in Sioux County is set and measured into sections, the roads run straight around each square mile. We live an orderly and predictable life on a farm where things are kept neat, each fork, knife and spoon stacked straight in its wooden stall in the forks and knives drawer. Mailboxes stand six in a row on an intersecting corner of four dirt roads that go foursquare, straight around each square section of 640 acres of land. We live on the northwest quarter section of one square: 160 acres of rich black dirt. All the envelopes in our box say: Fred Kooi, Rural Route 1, Hospers, Iowa. Most of the time the R.R. 1 is missing, but it doesn't matter; the mailman knows who we are. Sometime after the sun goes over the top of the sky, a newspaper comes to the box from Sioux City, fifty miles to the southwest. Halfway to the mailbox is a pasture where a dozen cows graze. At certain times, Pa keeps a big angry bull on the other side of a barbed-wire fence. Maybe he borrows the bull from the Houtsmas, the family on the farm at the mailbox corner. From their driveway, vicious dogs come running out to bite at our legs and clothes when we walk to the mailbox.

Sometimes a cow or the bull breaks through a fence and gets into the next field, and then there's trouble. Pa's face gets as red as the bull's eyes. He commands Mother, "Keep those little kids in the house out of the way."

"Why?" I ask Mother.

"A bloated cow can die fast-faster than any vet could get here. Stay out of Pa's way."

"What does it die from?"

"Guess the cow eats too much green oats too fast, just like your eating too many green apples gives you a tummy ache."

16

"But we don't get big and die."

She ignores that but then explains, "Well, maybe there's air trapped in the cow from all that green oats."

Ronald Jager describes the securely regulated life of his childhood on a Michigan farm.[5] Similarities to the Iowa farm life we knew abound. We too, heard the harsh squeak of the rusty windmill, twisting to catch the fickle wind. We never went out to eat or on a vacation trip. Babysitters were unheard of. Life was square, spare, regular, and insulated from the wicked world we heard about from the preacher on Sundays. The Iowa we knew was clean and structured. Discipline was admired and order prevailed. Until World War II, we existed in a microcosm as secure as moths in cocoons. The effects of this isolation and rigid structure showed up in later life to give positive as well as negative qualities, not only to bind, but also to free us. Many of our cousins turned out to be doers, goers, energetic adults with imagination and curiosity. Our spouses tell us that we are extremely individualistic and have strong personalities.

The life jackets worn by servicemen in danger of drowning were called Mae Wests. What filled them out, according to Mother, was the light-as-air silk that blows from dried milkweed pods. According to the bigger kids, it is something else. Maybe it is their puffed-up fantasies. Each August in the ditches alongside the road, silk unwinds from long brown pods dangling partly open on tall brown stalks of milkweed. In the kitchen, Mother hands us a gunnysack to collect the shiny-smooth, silky-white stuff that clings to the black seeds in the pods. We march out, slamming the screen door behind us, proud to be important in "the war effort." Walking to the mailbox to get the daily paper and the occasional letter or card, we spin out fantasies and fears while gathering the soft stuff. The slender strands are hard to unwind from the sticky seeds; they drift around, lift on the breeze, and float away. Although we manage to catch some silk, there is never enough to fill the gunny sack.

No matter. We collect and save everything: scrap metal, rubber bands, the worn-out rubber soles of old shoes, tin cans, and old clothes, then haul the collection to town when there is a drive. Everyone wants to contribute what he or she can to "the war effort."

---

[5] Ronald Jager, *Eighty Acres, Elegy for a Family Farm* (Boston: Beacon Press, 1990).

Five oldest children with Mother:
Ray, Clarence, Peter, Bernice, Gladys Kooi,
Lebanon Farm, 1930.

18

Back: Milly, Stan, Verna Mae. Front: Irene, Elmer
in water tank below windmill, Hospers farm, c. 1942.

Five Little Kids: Verna Mae, Milly, Irene, Elmer, Glenn Kooi
in front of kitchen window, Hospers Farm, 1945.

3

The House of Childhood

A freight train lumbers slowly across a high trestle over the river below our house in California. Boxcars overloaded with produce from the fertile San Joaquin Valley shake the wooden scaffolding that descends to the belly of the river. The ground underneath sends out ripples. The trembling earth echoes the fast-receding intensity of dreams. As the reel of the last dream unwinds, my body remains buried, underneath covers, rocking awake to faint rhythms and vibrations. Last night I fell into a deep sleep brought on by desire completely satisfied. Now, my muscles still feel drugged—dead in another place. As I begin to come alive, I am quickly pulled back under the swirling current of the river, hugging one shore, cradled by another. Pillows of water fall forward to cover my head. Underneath is warm and safe, until I begin to hear the faraway whistling of another train coming closer.

In the dream, the frame house is big and old with porches. My children and I have just unlocked one of the four doors with a ring of old keys. Two of the keys are from a bunch we found buried in the crevice of a growing tree where we nailed those keys decades ago. Now they come to light after we have raked a narrow path from the tree clean down to the street. Oh, the work of it, my child, oh! We are on the far edge of the yard where the gently swishing branches of the cottonwood tree send silver-dollar leaves to the ground. Behind us the dark house emerges empty and old. The ring of old keys dangles from the metal plate under the knob of the front door. Trees and groves surround the house. I look into my hands as they grow into the branches of a tree, keys—safety from lockout. Keys once lost, now unearthed.

Ordinarily, I awake from dreams bathed in the half-light of dawn, rising up in synchrony with the sun coming up and moon going down. Ordinarily, I fall asleep as the tipped bowl of the big dipper of stars appears. The regularity of natural rhythms anchors and comforts, but this morning the sun is already up and I am still half asleep, clutching at dreams and hearing distant rumblings. I shield my eyes from the force of bright sun hitting white walls.

In reality, the house of childhood is painted white. Two stories of clapboards go all the way from foundation to roof. The trim around the doors and windows is painted a deep blue. Four windows are on each side of the house. From the dirt road running in front of the farmhouse, the black eyes of two upper windows look out from a square face, much like the pencil drawing that a child might make, before adding a lopsided chimney as an afterthought and tacking on three porches. Although narrow windows adorn all four sides of the upper story, the lower story has wider, double windows. In the summer, screens cover the windows and doors in a vain attempt to keep out flying insects and creepy critters. In winter, storm windows provide an additional barrier against the hard cold from the unremitting snows. Icicles form outside the windows, growing longer during successive freezes to become heavy stalactites.

Leading into the farmyard from the graded dirt road is a driveway that runs parallel to the house, then ends in a large farmyard. Running the length of the house parallel to the driveway is an open porch that is supported by five pillars. Wide steps go up onto this front porch. The front door has an oval window in its upper half and is always unlocked. Above the pillars is a balustrade to protect children from failing off the roof of the porch. Under this roof sits a wooden rocking chair and an old glider that is pushed back and forth by shuffling feet. On summer nights hot air rises into the upstairs bedrooms and the stifling air cannot escape even though the windows are open. So, we kids climb out the bedroom windows to sleep on the roof of this porch, even though Mother warns against doing this. "Don't go out there. That roof isn't safe to walk on."

Trees tower over the house in the surrounding yards, protecting it from farm animals on all four sides. A wire fence with gates encloses two of the yards. The other two yards are closed in by stands of trees. A two-hole toilet sits beyond the clotheslines that run along the side of the house that is protected by a grove of Chinese elm.

Before moving to the Hospers farm in 1939, we lived on a farm near Lebanon. Gladys tells about the cob house and the toilet on this farm:

> The first job I did was "picking cobs." About twenty feet behind our Lebanon farm house was the cob house. This was a small, square, red-painted building filled with corncobs. After corn-shell-

ing time the cob house would be filled and each day, morning and evening, I would have to pick cobs. We kids would fill two or three baskets or old tubs with cobs, carry them to the kitchen, and set them near the wood-stove.

They made excellent fuel. They were light, dry, started easily, and quickly made a hot fire. As we picked cobs we played many games. Sometimes we counted how many cobs went into a basket, sometimes we threw them at each other—anything, I suppose, to break the monotony of the job. Probably what made this job hard for a three-to-eight-year-old was that the tubs, when filled, were heavy; the cob house was bitterly cold in winter, and the cobs tended to make our hands sore.

Behind our cob house was the toilet. Oh, that toilet! What a lot of memories go with that white two-seater. The second seat was lower and smaller. We never had hinged covers on our holes, like some farm families had. There was a hook on the door (too high for small kids) which could be hooked if one wanted privacy. No one below three feet had privacy! Toilet paper—I never heard of. The out-of-date Sears or Montgomery Ward catalog, or the *Sioux City Journal* worked very well. Besides, these made excellent reading material! In the winter it was so cold I didn't linger long—but in the summer if the flies and the smell weren't too bad I could read, or dream, or just get away from the rest of the kids for a while.

Every so often the toilet was moved to a new hole. The old hole was covered over. Our toilet must have stood in several different spots over a period of time—perhaps it ended up in the same spot after a few years—I don't know. My Pa and the hired man took care of the moving. My Pa called it the privy, but we called it simply *the toilet*. Ours was usually in good condition, unlike some others I'd see. Some were terribly old, leaning, with holes in the floorboards. I can remember being scared to go into a relative's toilet for fear the whole thing would fall over. Except in extremely cold weather, even in the winter, we ran out to the toilet. We put on a coat and cap—ran like mad—sat on the icy hole—did the job more than quickly and flew back to the house. At night, in the winter, there were pots in the house.

The front of the Hospers farmhouse appears to face the road, but this really is the back of the house. We little kids often play in this back yard, making up games to amuse ourselves. The yard slopes slightly downward toward the row of trees. The grass is scant and the ground caked dry.

It is the perfect place to line up side by side, take down our pants and yell, "Get ready, get set, go!" as we watch our streams of pee wiggle down the slope through the fine dust coating the uneven ground. Which yellow stream will go the greatest distance and win? Of course, it is always one of the little boys with their handy little handles giving them a leaping start. "No fair!" yell we little girls and refuse to play again.

We are not supposed to play on or under the small porch held up by two pillars. This door into the front parlor is never used and the small space below this porch is a perfect underground hiding place. No one can see us, but we can hear anyone coming to look for us and gauge the relative urgency of anyone calling us into the house. Anyone older than age six is not able to squeeze under the porch. We crawl under and lie in the moist dirt to probe secrets in the dark, undressing and poking parts of our small bodies, trying to see where babies come from, or where a baby might grow. Sometimes we find kitties or other small animals under the porch, sometimes living, sometimes dead.

Once, when we were playing in the grove, we heard the cries of kitties. We crawled under the porch to investigate and found a dripping wet gunny-sack of kitties tied tightly shut with twine. It had been held down in the water tank and then tossed into the grove. In the grove, the mother cat must have found the wet gunnysack with her kittens imprisoned, and clawed and bit at the twine to get them out. Not succeeding, she dragged the sack under the porch to hide it, and then, finally exhausted, slunk off.

The shock and confusion of finding kitties in trouble threw us into action. A kitchen knife, large and unwieldy, was borrowed from the kitchen to cut the twine. An older kid cautioned, "Don't let anybody find us doing this." Under the porch in the dark we worked with speed, afraid of being found out. If an adult called us to come in, or we heard footsteps approaching, a single finger would fly up in front of each pair of lips. "Shhh!" We whispered, furtive eyes searched for other eyes. Silence was maintained until the danger faded away. When we got the sack open, some of the kitties were dead. A shoebox was needed for each kitty's burial. Kitties still alive ran away as fast as they could, but if someone could grab one before it escaped, then carrying it to the mother cat in the grove was the trickiest job of all—for the biggest and strongest one of us, surely not for me, scared and trembling.

In 1990, my sister Vicki Peterson, read her story, "Drown Proof," to her fifth-grade classes.

The Iowa farm where I was born and raised had many animals. The usual, of course, pigs, cows, chickens and horses, plus a few ducks were fattened for Thanksgiving dinner. We also had pet animals, dogs and cats. One spring when we had an overabundance of kittens, I was given the unpleasant task of doing away with some of them. We never had cats or their kittens in the house. The mother cat, with her nest of newborn kittens, was usually found nested in the haymow in the barn. My father said, "Some of those kittens will have to be killed. There are just too many of them."

I knew the procedure. I got a brown gunnysack from the hen house. It had just been emptied of milled, cracked corn that had been used to feed the chickens. Going into the barn, I climbed the vertical ladder to the haymow. With the help of a shaft of sunlight coming through the open door, I found a nest with three baby kittens in a far corner. The mother cat was not around, and I carefully put the kittens into the scratchy sack. Their tiny, sharp claws dug into the skin on my arm, and their soft, fuzzy fur was warm and downy-like. "Lay still," I said, more out of anger and frustration than anything else. I carried the sack across the yard to the large circular water tank. Holding the gunnysack under the water, I counted, "One ... two ... three ...four ..." My father had said, "Hold it there for three minutes." It seemed like an eternity.

Job done, I carried the now-still sack into the grove behind the house and dumped it into the farthest corner of the wooded grove. It wasn't until a few days later that I was helping my older brother put oats in the feed bins in the barn that I heard a strange sound coming from the haymow. It was not just one cat meowing. It was many. I climbed the ladder and peered through the dusty sunlight on the second floor of the barn. Following the meowing, I saw a sight that turned my stomach. The mother cat had found the gunnysack in the grove with her baby kittens in it. Somehow she had untied the twine-enclosed top. The kittens lay in the nest. Two were well and healthy. Unbelievable! They were climbing all over the place. I stared. A third was half-alive, or half-dead. I poked at it with a piece of straw. It moved feebly. The mother cat snarled at me.

How had she ever found her babies? And how had she untied the sack? She must have dragged the sack with her half-dead kittens inside, all the way from the grove, up the ladder, and into the hayloft. The next year there were not as many baby kittens. Besides, I was a year older, and the detestable job of doing away with any over population was assigned to another sibling."

Vicki's students would ask questions. "Why didn't you just give the kittens away?" Answer: Neighbors had this same over-population problem. "Why didn't you have the mother cats fixed?" Answer: Money was not spent on unimportant things like that on the farm—not in those days, anyway.

The real front of the house—and the life of the farm—faces inward toward the yard enclosed by the barn, machine shed, tool shed, garage, chicken coops, hog house, corn cribs, pig pens, barnyards full of manure, the windmill, farm machines, junk yard, and the groves. In the center of this large interior yard is a tall pole. At its top is a yard light that bathes the farmyard in yellow light at dusk and stays on all night.

Foot traffic leaves the house from the kitchen door and goes through a small, enclosed porch called the wash porch that holds the wringer washing machine, washtubs, clothesbaskets and clothespins. Hooks in the wall hold dirty overalls, coats, and hats of men coming into the kitchen for meals. Out the door is a stoop that descends to a front walk going past the well. To the right side of the stoop is the well-worn path to the toilet.

Halfway to the front gate, an iron pump stands over a deep well. A pail stands under the spout and a dipper with a long handle hangs over the spout. Water drips from the bowl of the dipper. Down the walk and beyond the gated fence is a large farmyard, surrounded by buildings, farm machinery, and groves. Beyond the farmyard are fields—and a cow pasture with a creek running through it.

The groves hold the pleasures and freedom of childhood: playhouses, tree houses, swings, and the junk pile. Mother's vegetable garden with the grape arbor and fruit trees has its own grove running next to the road, but we rarely play in this grove, preferring instead the two groves nearer to the farmyard. Against orders, we play in all the farm buildings and borrow what we need from the tool shed. Outdoors, the groves contain our love and imagination, but indoors—if only one room could contain childhood—it would be the kitchen. Here, boxcars of memory are loaded with the freight of sensory experiences recorded on our blank, infant brains, before the train of words begins chugging along, and language is learned.

Rubbing sleep from my eyes, I slowly make my way down the stairs one at a time, open the door, and step into the warmth of the kitchen. Everyone is ready to start breakfast. The baby is in the highchair next to Mother. I look up at light coming through the windows, down at my feet, and up to Mother.

Steaming Lump

Blue crystals glinting off
Jack-frosted storm windows
My small feet bare on cold linoleum
Her gentle chiding
What? No sox? No shoes?
As she puts a lump of brown sugar
Into my hot bowl of Cream of Wheat
I look up to her, then down.
Under my uncertain spoon the lump
Melting, begins to wear a smile.[6]

The heart of the kitchen is the black cast-iron cookstove, near the door to the stairs going up to the bedrooms. Nearest the door is a wood box holding sticks, dried corncobs, and perhaps, some lumps of shiny coal. Behind the wood box is a battered bushel basket that has some thin slats gaping from the wires girdling it. Old newspapers stick this way and that from the basket. At the other end of the cookstove is a reservoir that holds water gradually being heated by stray heat from the stovetop and oven. To stoke a dwindling fire, tinder is used. Kindling my memory is a can of kerosene kept high, out of reach. A little kerosene is half poured, half thrown from this tin can onto tinder laid just so on the cold ash. Before anyone strikes a match to light the stove Mother warns, "First, put the can of kerosene back on the shelf." Repeatedly, she tells us about the little cousin who was poisoned after drinking a can of lye, thinking it was something good. "Did he die?"

[6] Irene Chadwick, "Steaming Lump," from *Dawn Pearl* (Modesto, California: Ietje Kooi Press, 1994), page 3.

28

"No, but his throat got terribly burned."

"Which cousin?" I think it was Marlin.

"Wasn't the can up high, out of his reach?" Don't know, maybe he climbed up on something.

"Could he go to school the next day?" Seeing that her warning has hit home, Mother answers with vague generalities, then turns away to go and do something else.

Near the can of kerosene placed high above us hangs a match holder. A box of Diamond Kitchen Safety Matches is inserted into the top of the match holder. Single matches drop into the rounded trough at its base. Frequently in use, the match holder hangs slightly crooked, swinging on the six-penny nail that holds it to the wall. It is always up there, out of reach, a safe distance from the hands of we small fry who stand watching.

The routine of lighting a fire becomes written on our small minds before we learn to speak. We frequently hear Mother ask someone, "Have you laid the fire?" And, before someone lights the fire, she cautions, "Be sure the flue is open first." Swiftly a match is taken from the match holder and quickly struck against the cold stovetop, then tossed into the stove. The kerosene flares up, lighting our faces. Flames leap up. The door is quickly lowered, its hinge always making the same creaky sound. A corkscrew handle dangles from the latch, shaking and shining attractively. Tongues of red leap up and can be seen through the black grating of the door. As the fire grows, heat starts to radiate throughout the kitchen. The flue is open in the fat black stovepipe that carries the fumes up through the ceiling.

The wood box also serves as our only wastebasket. Today it seems unusual, even odd, for a house to have no wastebaskets, but I recall none. Only a few scraps of food are left over after meals. Into the slop bucket for the hogs go potato peelings, husks, apple cores, pea pods and so forth. Eggshells are used some other way. If there are any scraps left in the frying pan, they go into the big pan of meat and water on the back of the stove. Nothing is wasted. The rare tin can goes to the dump in the grove. An old car tire is used for a swing. By summertime, when we search the dump for items to use in our playhouses, winter has rusted the tin cans a chestnut brown. Now they are the prized containers that we use to carry water and dirt to make mud pies. After World War II, we had more disposables, and the flour may then have come in paper bags rather than the cloth bags that had been used to make dishtowels or clothes. Well-used Kleenex went into the wood box. Seeing a child wad up a half-used Kleenex and throw it in the wood box, Mother would admonish, "Use all of it." Then, she would see that it was retrieved and entirely used before being tossed. "Waste not, want not," was the eleventh commandment.

I sit on the cold linoleum to pull on socks and shoes. Mother is handling a pan of hot oatmeal, a frying pan of eggs, or a pot of coffee. A big sister pours milk in glasses for each little one and then places white pitchers of milk on both ends of the table where they can be easily reached. A patterned oilcloth covers the table that is pulled out from its place against the double windows so that the bench under the windows can be used as a seat. The big boys have just come in after milking cows. One at a time they ease themselves onto the bench and sit down, their long legs stretched out under the table, waiting for Mother to finish lifting food from the stove onto the table. When everyone is seated, Pa will say his opening, first prayer. In 1941 all thirteen of us are still at home on the farm. When the oldest leaves, the front porch will hold the chair that no longer is needed around the kitchen table.

Always on the table for six-thirty breakfast, lunch at nine, noon dinner, lunch at three, and supper at six, is a plate of freshly cut bread next to the butter dish. After Pa's long prayer, everyone waits while each small child, from older to younger, in turn, says, "God bless this food for Jesus sake, Amen." Mother coaches the youngest, helping each one to learn it by heart. This is easy to do since we hear the prayer said three times a day by four or five others. The older we are—or hungrier—the faster we say the prayer, until the blurted words blur together, "Ga-bless-this-foo-for-Jesus-ake-amen." Saying it too fast wastes time because one parent is sure to insist, "Say it over, slowly this time."

Bowls of food circle the table. We pass each bowl the same direction, taking enough but not too much. Nothing should be left on our plates when we are done. Second helpings can be taken. After the meal, what remains on the center of the table is a cluster of things used at every meal—sugar bowl, tumbler of upside-down teaspoons, salt and pepper shakers, toothpicks in their holder, the butter dish and jar of preserves. In summer there is also a cruet of vinegar for leaf lettuce from the garden. Between meals, the table is put to other uses.

After breakfast Pa takes jugs of water out to the field for the long, hot morning of work. Summertimes at nine, Milly and I carry the big black dinner pails (currently called lunch boxes) to a field where the men are working. A heavy quart thermos of coffee is held up above the bread and jam by a jingly wire, and sometimes there are cookies. Mother sees to it that we eat lunch before starting out, so we will not be tempted. "Don't stop along the way to play. Don't snoop in the pail."

Standing in my city kitchen, I am helping my little children with this and that while I prepare dinner. I stand at the sink, peeling off potato skins so thin that even my thrifty Dutch Mother would approve. "Make the peeling so thin it doesn't break. See?" In my mind's eye, I see Mother holding up a very long, curling potato peeling. I am plucking out eyes as fast as I can with the scoop end of the potato peeler when I remember big sister Gladys coming to get the big pan of potatoes to put on the cookstove to boil. Dinner on the farm was always at the same time with the same foods, which included a heaping bowl of fluffy mashed potatoes. As I am poking at stubborn eyes that are hard to pluck out, I see through the red potato eyes into black ones. Through the black pupils I see into a bin of dirty potatoes in a dark storm cellar, and then faraway into another kitchen where a little tyke is running through the screen door, screaming.

The potato patch is beside the deeply rutted path the men take to the fields. It is located behind the fenced barnyard that holds the cows before they are let into the barn to be milked. At planting time in early March, or later if the ground is still frozen, Pa or an older brother disks up the brown-stubble potato patch. Then this small patch is plowed, harrowed, leveled, and planted on the way to do that same kind of work in bigger fields beyond the potato patch.

By August Mother is using several ways to get rid of us when we hang around, tugging at her skirts, whining for something to do. Usually it is work of some kind.

"There's nothing to do."

"How would each of you like to earn a penny?"

Jumping up and down we demand, "How? How?"

"You know what potato bugs look like?"

"What?" I ask.

"Ya know, you seen 'em," says Milly.

Shaking my head I object, "Huh uh, never did."

"I know. I'll show you," says Elmer.

To stop our bickering, Mother smiles and says, "I'll give you a penny for every hundred potato bugs you can pick off."

"A hundred?" Elmer asks.

Milly chimes in with, "That's a lot of bugs."

I say, "We can do that easy. C'mon, let's go," and start to push the screen door open.

Elmer thinks differently, "Aw it's too hot out there. Ain't gonna go."

But Milly is thinking about this offer and says, "Well, five pennies buys an ice cream cone in town on Saturday afternoon."

Mother is drawn to the yeasty smell of bread dough rising in the round dishpan on the windowsill under a damp dishtowel. Suddenly she shoos us out the door. "Go run play now."

We mess around the pump, trying to pump up water, when suddenly I stop. "Is that a hundred bugs each?"

Milly gives me a look. "Of course, dummy. Didn't cha know that?"

For a moment I feel beat, hot and hesitant—but there is nothing else to do, so we reluctantly make our way out the unlatched gate, past the tool shed, through the farmyard, past cow pens, groves, and chicken coops to start out. We wander in the deep ruts made by the tractor, wagons and horses, the hayrack, and the wheels of various machines on their way to the fields. I stop to watch the horses, old Pet and Dewey. Milly lolls behind, and Elmer wanders off to a playhouse in the grove, but pretty soon we three all get to the potato patch.

The fence that separates homecoming cows from the potato patch is made of four lines of barbed-wire. As they amble to the barn to be milked twice a day, cows try to poke their heads through the lines of barbed-wire, weakening the wires. Other wires sag from age and some are knotted where they have been fixed. First, we wander along the fence, looking for a hole

32   big enough to climb through. All the bigger holes have been repaired. We will have to find another way to get through. We try climbing over, then try crawling under, but cannot do it. Where a post is leaning part way over, we find weaker wires. Milly braces herself against the post, holds the two top wires up with both hands, and steps on the lower two so I can ease myself through the hole she is making. She tries to keep the hole big enough so my dress won't catch on the barbs. I make it through.

Now it's my turn to hold up the two upper wires, and at the same time step down on the two lower wires. Getting through barbed-wire fences always takes quite awhile to negotiate. After Milly goes through, I wait for Elmer. From watching Milly and from fussing with the wires for a while, I figure out a way to hold the barbed-wires so the barbs can't puncture my skin. Soon, though, I get tired of waiting. Mad, I holler at Elmer, "Hurry up! I can't keep this up all day." Elmer's nature is to take his own sweet time. I must see that he gets places on time—to meals, and later on, into the car to go to school while Pa waits, honking the horn.

Milly shows us where the potato bugs hide under the low, flat leaves, where they race to when we lift a leaf, and the trick to picking them off. Under the August sun, Elmer wanders off to play under the barbed-wire fence, lying on his back and gazing up, spearing bugs on barbs, pulling himself under the lowest line of wire and watching how barbs rip clothes and skin. He lies still then, examining something. I rub the fuzz from a weed off my leg and shove a pincher bug away. Nettles puncture my skin and raise bumps on my kneecap. As I run away from the bugs, I squeeze through the rusty barbed-wire too fast. Red welts from bugs and nettles rise up, smart, then really hurt—but nothing like the long scratches made by the sharp barbs of the fence that rise up louder and faster.

Yelling with pain, I run home from the potato patch to Mother. Elmer is not far behind. He ambles into the kitchen, examining the curious pathways blood is taking around his kneecap before it runs down his leg. I howl, holding onto my hurts. Mother looks up from my knee to his leg. Her scolding scalds me. "Stop crying now. Look at Elmer's. Shame on you." Sniveling I jab at dirty snot and tears, and stare in silent awe at Elmer's calm indifference, his pooling blood congealing, our different skins—mine so hot and thin, his so calm and cool. Quick shame pierces me as I hold onto my hurts—

mere scratches compared to his.

Mother, with always too much to do and never enough time to do it, took notice of our different skins. By reading her face we learned many things. One of her many great-grandchildren wrote this poem.

Lesson #1, This Is Skin

this is skin
my skin, not yours
see the difference
mine is a little darker
and the pores are
spaced further apart
my freckle pattern
is less random
and i have a scar
just below
my right thumb
this is how you can tell
how you can be sure
this is where i start
and you begin [7]

[7] Rebecca Tannetje Houwer, "Lesson #1, This Is Skin," *poems at the curb* (Toronto, Ontario, Canada, 2000), page 12.

Farmhouse of Fred and Ida Kooi Family, Hospers, Iowa, 1939-1947.
(Photo by Margaret Vander Stoep, 1947).

Summer view of farmhouse from driveway. On right is small front porch that
faced the road that went to town, Hospers, 1946.

Winter view of house facing farmyard shows wagon, storm cellar doors,
stoop and wash porch, Hospers, 1945.

L-R: Milly, Verna Mae, and Irene, with Elmer in wagon,
playing in the grove. Toilet is behind the fence.
Hospers, 1940.

After decades of disuse, the toilet remains standing
on Hospers farm, 1995.

Tool shed on Hospers farm also remains standing, 1995.

4

Playing in the Grove

Standing in my city kitchen, my little boys tugging on my skirt, I reach down to pick up one of them. I am trying to get dinner on the table, thinking there is always too much to do and never enough time, when I hear Mother's voice, "Irene, set the table now." I begin to wonder how Mother was always able to get meals on the table on time. Out the windows is a high sun in a wide sky. I see the men in the fields glancing up at the sun straight up in the sky, the men coming into the farmyard, washing up on the stoop outside, banging through the screen door, and placing their weary bodies in their usual seats around the table. Pa lets his head fall forward as he starts to pray.

I begin to wonder how Mother found time to write in her diary and remember her answer. "I made work of it." Her oldest daughter, Gladys, recalls that, "For fifteen years while I was growing up, Mother kept a Line-a-Day. She called it that too. I didn't know what a diary was. Often she would say, 'Gladys, get me my Line-a-Day. I have to write in it.' I thought it was a special name and one word: linaday."

Each Line-a-Day leather cover is gold-stenciled: Five-Year Diary. Allotted to each day is an inch of space and five faint lines, with four days on each four-by-five-inch page. In her steady, small, handwriting, Mother recorded births, deaths, how many acres planted, jars of apple butter put up, metal cans of cream taken away by the cream hauler, pickle crocks put to cure in the cellar, who visited the farm, and so forth. Vicki notes that it is interesting how the birth of a baby was often an addition to telling about something else. "I remember anxiously looking up my birth date and finding it as a footnote to what the men did!"

Apr. 21, 1932: Pa planted corn, the hired men ... our baby daughter was born at 1:30 this P.M.

Son's birth: May 3, 1925: Nice day, some showers. Baby was born at 7:20 P.M. Mrs. Bonnema and doctor were here, also John and Mattie. Mrs. B. stayed here all day and night.

40

We had slews of cousins since our parents' many siblings had many children. Mother recorded hundreds of birthdays like the birth of cousin Elmer in 1937:

> Apr. 13, 1937: Pa to Ireton for seed corn. String beans hoed and staked, tomato plants set. Mattie phoned, coming Sunday for coffee. Elmer James born by John and Gertie.

Beef and potatoes are the staples of dinner and supper. The menu is monotonous. Beef has been simmering in a pan of water on top of the stove ever since Mother took the bread out of the oven. Seven white loaves are set to cool under dish cloths on the oblong kitchen table. The oilcloth covering the table is thin in places and strains at each corner from the repeated scrape of plates and bowls, rolling pins, the dishpan and drainer, Crayolas, canning jars, and hot dish rags. The colorful print pattern of the oilcloth is faded.

Curtains are being blown in from the partly opened tops of two double windows behind the table. A semicircular metal lock is located between the top and bottom windows. Either window can be raised or lowered after opening this half-moon lock. A breeze comes in from either the top or the bottom. If the window sticks, I tug at the sash, trying to get it up. When raised, I count the dead flies on the sill between the window and the dented screen. At the screen doors hang coils of honey-gold flypaper, buzzing from the wings of insects beating out time, trying to escape a sticky death.

The big pan used every day to boil potatoes on the cookstove is dented from years of use, its cover not as tight fitting as Mother would like. Steam leaks out through unwanted vents. Cranky kids are underfoot, playing on the kitchen floor.

"Don't be a tattletale."

"But she took my doll and threw it off the ..."

"Run outdoors and play now ..."

My stormy look elicits a threat from Mother, "... unless you want to wipe dishes."

The doors down to the storm cellar are outside the house. Variously called the fruit cellar, or simply, the cellar, it is entered by lifting up two long, wooden doors that lie at an angle of thirty degrees to the ground. We are not supposed to play on these slanted doors, but Milly and I are sliding down them with our dolls. Chirpy and sunny, we are crooning to our dolls:

> Slide down my cellar door
> and we'll be jolly friends forevermore.

My Bonnie doll has china-blue eyes that open and close, stiff eye-lashes, real blonde hair, and a soft body. She's my one-and-only baby doll. Milly's Sharon is tall, brunette, and angular—a career girl going places. When we trade dolls, I go places. This afternoon Milly takes the lead, telling me how to play house with the dolls. We used to play on the storm-cellar doors with paper dolls, but not anymore. Last time the wind blew half of them away. Milly's dolly is doing funny things like losing its legs and standing on its head. She throw-slides it down the door, scaring me. We resume singing in a rock-a-bye-baby rhythm, "...rain barrel sliding off the cellar door..." But then, our voices grow catty and raucous.

> I'm sorry playmate.
> I cannot play with you.
> My dolly has the flu.
> Boohoo, boohoo, boohoo.

Suddenly the rhythm of our singsong teasing is interrupted by somebody running past yelling, "Don't play on those doors—they might fall in!" We re-trieve the dolls, shove them back into their shoebox beds, and run off to the grove to play "Seesaw, Marjory draw." The crude see-saw we ride up and down is a board placed over an old oil drum. To balance the teeter-totter, two little kids sit on one end of the board, while a bigger kid sits on the other end.

In the grove we make playhouses by sweeping twigs, leaves, and pebbles off the dirt floor with larger, flared twigs. Then we find the right-sized sticks to lay out straight walls, doors, and windows to make the rooms of our play-houses. Each kid's territory is staked out, each corner marked off by pound-ing in a stick with a stone. Baling twine is tied stick to stick or tree to tree. We make farmyards and sometimes, whole farms. Mud pies get baked in tin ovens, cut in pieces with sticks, and shared. I sweep out my playhouse every

42   morning and keep it neat and tidy. Chickens scratch up dirt floors. The
wind blows leaves down. Brothers kick down the sticks of our playhouses,
and there are fights.

In our wide and wonderful grove, we play out our dreams with treasures
salvaged from the rusting, stagnating junk pile that is, to big people, only a sinking pile of rotting, worn-out things, but is, to us, the stuff we play in, play with,
or play on, all summer long. Sharp-edged scraps of sheet metal jut out of the
junk pile. Rusted nails protrude from old boards. Mother commands, "You stay
out of the junk pile," then adds her familiar, "Run play now." Seeing our eager
faces and little bodies pulling away, unheeding, she changes her "Stay out," to
something we might do: "Wear your shoes. There are nails out there." At other
times when we are underfoot, she will approve of our explorations into the junk
pile. "Ja, it's all right to go in there. Just don't step on cut glass or bent-up nails
sticking out of old boards. Don't get splinters."

Her frequent "Ja" gave us permission to roam and play.

In the dump we search for playhouse furniture. A splintery two-by-
four resting on rusted-out, over-turned paint cans becomes a couch or kitchen
shelf. Sometimes we find a gallon can with streaks of barn-red paint that
once ran down its sides and is now dried. Its prized cover grooves into the
can and can be pounded tightly shut so we can keep private stuff that we
don't want others to see—or take. A gallon paint can is a rare find. We fight
over it. If one of those old paint cans has a wire handle and I win, I am in
seventh heaven. My small arms pull and pry to lift the can out of the junk
pile's jumbled up wire and matted debris. Now it is mine, all mine.

Needing containers for play-food on a kitchen shelf, we search for the
rusted-out tin cans left from store-bought food, but usually there are none. Mother
cans every August, re-using the same Mason and Ball glass jars with the lids that
have three parts to scrub: metal ring, red rubber ring, and flat lid. We are sure to
disappear into the grove during canning because washing jars, assembling rings
on lids, or snapping beans is a dreary, monotonous chore.

Inside the junk pile, we must avoid falling into jumbled-up baling wire,
or the coiled Vs of tired bedsprings, as we look for old wheels, gears, crankcases,
tires of any size, and old inner tubes. The prize is a big tractor tire, rarely found
because Mother uses it to contain her annual flower bed, protecting seed-

lings from chickens that are always flying up, settling down, and scratching them up. Once in a great while, we find a beat-up plough, disk, or other discarded farm implement with rain water settled into its shifting, covert cavities. Rainbows swirl through the oil that floats on stagnating puddles. Bugs emerge from larva on their clouded surfaces. Mosquitoes hatch. Ah! Bug heaven.

What we don't find in the dump, we must invent. To make stilts we sneak into the tool shed to borrow nails and hammers. I am still small enough to duck behind a larger tool or drum of oil in case Pa enters. Before taking the hammer, I stealthily reach up to try out the bigger of the two vises to see if it really pinches as I have been told. It does. I try out a razor blade laid on the tool bench. I see how quick, how deep, it cuts. The cut into the finger leaves a scar. Although going into the tool shed is fun, it is nothing like the adventure of exploring the junk pile.

Forgotten is winter: running out through the cold and snow to go to the toilet, living through the measles, mumps, impetigo, ringworm, seven-year-itch, and wearing long, scratchy underwear and snowsuits. Now we are gloriously free to run and play in the grove without shoes! Free to play house and to gather sticks fallen from the tall American elm trees in the grove. Free to find the seed-coin clusters that the money tree drops in August. The gold leaves shaped like glittering half-dollar coins that drop from cottonwood and poplar trees, and the real cotton that falls from the cottonwood. Free to spend our money and get to the store in town, we build roads using a dump truck and tractor, rusty from being left out too many times in the rain. Sticks and stones shore up our graded dirt road to town, and really-deep ditches border the road. Tunneled through the road, from ditch to ditch, goes a culvert made of an old pipe. We haul water in cans to make a creek flow through the culvert.

Tea time is recalled by Vicki Peterson:

> After we were all finished making our playhouses, we would sweep them out, make mud-pie cookies, and invite a neighbor over for tea. I would go to the house of Irene, or perhaps Milly, knock, and say, "Milly, would you like to come over for tea?"
>
> Milly would, of course, say, "Yes."
>
> Then we would sit in my living room, and I would say, "And

44   how are you today, Milly?"

        Milly would say, "Fine."

        "Would you like a cup of tea?"

        "Yes."

        Carefully, I would get my best chipped cup from the kitchen and pretend to pour tea into it. I would offer her a mud-pie cookie.

        "Very good," she would say, pretending to eat it. We would sit for a few minutes.

        "Well, thank you for the visit." And she would be gone.[8]

We learned how to make playhouses in the grove from the older siblings, the same way we learned almost everything. The big kids soon grew up and recalled, with nostalgia, playing in the grove:

Childhood's Passing

It was Spring
    And every Spring we made a playhouse
        Rooms spaced off with binder twine
            strung between trees.
Maple stumps becoming chairs and tables
    and dressers
Gunny sacks—smelling of ground corn—
    covering rusty bedsprings
A clouded mirror—one corner cracked—
    hanging from a branch.
School drawings (dinner-pailed home)
    dangling from twine walls.
All was ready to play house
But me
This Spring the old familiar excitement
    was missing [9]

Three kinds of swings hang from the big branches of the tall trees in the grove: board, tire, and sack swings. The best kind of swing is the gunny-

---

[8] Vicki Kooi Peterson to author, letter dated December, 1999.

[9] Gladys Gritter, "Childhood's Passing," *Pen Queens 1979-1980.*

sack stuffed with hay, tied to the end of a long rope. After we each have had a few turns swinging back and forth on the sack swing, it becomes too tame so a new kind of swing is discussed. To make this swing, we need to borrow sawhorses from the tool shed. Days of figuring and planning are spent on how to drag the sawhorses from the tool shed, across the yard, and into the grove without getting caught. When we accomplish this feat, a sawhorse is placed at either end of the sack swing's longest arc, measured by the distance and height we are able to pull the sack swing. Now one of us stands on a sawhorse, winds our legs around the sack, hangs onto the rope, and pushes off with enough force to swing through the air all the way to the other sawhorse, land on it, and stand up on it. I swing nearly as far as the distant sawhorse, but then, instead of landing on top of it, my legs hit it and get bruised. Once, I made it all the way to the top of the sawhorse and then fell off.

Soon we tire of this kind of swing. The bigger kids agree with the littler kids. "Way too easy, no fun." A new idea is thought up—an elevator to get up on top of a high, large tree limb. "Let's fill a gunnysack half full of rocks, then tie it to a rope long enough to reach all the way up to the branch, around it, and fall back to the ground. Then we'll tie another gunnysack filled with straw to the other end. Since the sack of straw is lighter than the sack of rocks, the sack of straw will always fly up to the branch. In turn, each one of us can fly up to the high branch while our legs and body are wrapped around the straw sack, and our hands hang onto the rope."

Finding a long-enough rope is not easy. Then we discover we will need to anchor a pulley on top of the branch to keep the rope from sliding around and also to keep the straw sack—and us—from hitting the trunk of the tree. Since we have to borrow the pulley from the hayloft of the barn when Pa or an older brother is not looking, this takes a few days. After the smartest kid figures out how to borrow the pulley, a smaller kid is sent to do it—me. "They won't see you so easy, since you're little, and besides, no one will suspect you could think of what to do with a pulley. You ain't that smart."

The biggest kid climbs the tree with the rope to get it over the branch. We tie the sack of straw to one end of the rope and the sack of rocks to the other end. There is, of course, lots of talking and some fighting about this plan, but after awhile we agree. "If this works, we can all take the elevator up and make a play house in the big tree. The weight of the sack of rocks falling to the ground will carry us, one at a time, up into the tree." The rope is pulled through the borrowed pulley positioned on top of the big branch. Then the oldest and biggest must climb the tree and wrap his legs around the straw sack to let his weight pull the sack of rocks up to the limb. Then, each little kid can take a turn, fast-riding the straw-sack elevator straight up to the top of the big branch, grabbing onto the branch, and straddling it.

The first elevator ride is big excitement. Picked to be first is the oldest of the four little kids. We reason that the sack of rocks won't pull her up too fast because she is pretty big. She winds her legs around the sack of straw and hangs on. Before we realize what's happening, she is zooming up toward the branch. Then she loses hold of the rope and falls. At the same time, the sack of rocks comes crashing down to land on her with a thick thud. She just lies there—not even a whimper.

"Get those rocks off'n her quick!" yells the oldest kid, who is dangling from the branch above. We do, and fast, but she just lies there. Any kid who doesn't yell is clearly an emergency. We run for help. Her sprained ankle turns purple and is swollen. For a week or two she can't walk, then she limps.[10] Obviously something heavy fell on her, but no kid will tell what happened. "Cross my heart and hope to die, I didn't do it." On orders from Pa, we are made to dismantle the sack-of-rocks elevator and return the borrowed sawhorses and pulley. From then on the swings in the grove are all the tame kinds of swings made with the usual sack of straw, old tire, or board.

[10] Letter from Milly Kooi to author dated June 23, 2002: "I remember the sack of stones in the tree that sprained my ankle. It hurt a lot until Mother put some liniment on it. Then it seemed to heal."

Yard and groves seen from house with fence down
from snowdrifts, 1946.

5

Eyes in the Cellar

Pa plants potatoes in the field behind the barn each spring. We little kids help by pushing the quartered potatoes deep into the moist soil at a certain depth, at certain intervals. Then our bare feet tamp down the dirt, stamping up and down, over and over. Soil squishes up between our bare toes and feels so cool and gooey-good. The eyes of the potatoes send down roots to make new roots and more tubers. Mother mashes potatoes for noon dinner, and for supper, she uses the leftovers or else fries potatoes with onions. Potato peelings and the occasional sour potato found in the potato bin go into the slop bucket. I am not big enough to carry the bucket outside to the pigpen. Anyway, Mother would not want a little kid to get anywhere near the sow while she is suckling her twelve little pigs and is meaner than usual. Slopping the hogs is a chore given to a big brother or sister who can lift a five-gallon bucket of slop high enough to clear the edge of the slop barrel.

> If the boy was not stubborn, he began to fill the bucket half full so he could pull it out of the barrel without slopping himself. But even then, slopping the hogs required art as well as strength. What a boy had to do was tiptoe to the slop barrel, lay the lid off the barrel without making a sound, and get the slop in the trough before being seen or heard by the hogs. For, once the hogs heard the slightest noise associated with feeding, they thundered in and stood in the feeding trough where the slop was supposed to be poured. Now the boy was faced with a sea of pig faces through which he must pour the slop. If Pa wasn't looking, a boy might, on occasion, pour one bucket of slop over the heads of the hogs just to teach them a lesson, but this never taught them a thing."[11]

Every day someone gathers eggs and carries in the milk. Someone also must fetch potatoes from the potato bin at the back of the storm cellar under

[11] Mike Vanden Bosch, ed., *A Pocket of Civility, A History of Sioux Center* (Sioux Falls, South Dakota: Modern Press, Inc., 1976), pages 62-63.

the house. The potatoes dug up last fall are heaped up here, bound by two-by-four boards on one side and cellar walls on the other three sides. In the fall, potatoes are piled high against the walls. Every year every potato is used. Green potatoes or sprouting ones are tossed aside into one corner of the bin, saved for planting in the spring. Then, potato eyes will watch hairy roots go down into the black earth. Go how far? When I pull up a carrot, the fine endings of its tiniest hairs disappear. Why can't I see where the root hairs end and the earth begins? I wonder where Mother will go when she is old and looks like the sister she loves so much who is thin, wrinkled, and shrinking. Who grew Mother? Where was she before she got here? Carrot seeds come from a flat envelope with a picture of orange carrots on it, but there is no picture of Mother when she was only a seed. After planting carrot seeds, Mother spears the empty envelope onto the stake that marks the end of the row. Twine guards each row of seeds before the seeds sprout out of the ground. Every spring the garden has rows and rows of twine tied to stakes speared with seed packets. Once, I pulled off all the packets and brought them to Mother to show her the bright pictures before they got rained on, faded, and dirty. She looked mad. "Ach heiden, you must leave those there so I can tell what was planted in each row before sprouts push through and grow to reach the twine."

"But, Mother, I will put them all back. I just wanted to show you the pretty pictures."

"You must leave those there," she repeated. Then the anger drained from her face, she smiled, and her face softened.

"Ach heiden, kleine kinder, ach, so small yet."

A month later Mother is thinning a row of carrots when she sees me pull up a whole bunch, rub the dirt off the largest of the tiny carrots onto my dress, and start to eat.

"Wait until they get bigger. Then they will taste sweet."

Mother sends me to the potato bin to get potatoes for dinner. I hate this job, but I must do it. Trap doors painted white open to the storm cellar under the house. If they are padlocked, someone older unlocks them, helps lift them up and then folds them back on their hinges.

During an afternoon thunder storm, lightning shows up the backside of something indistinct, white and flat. The storm cellar stays covered up, hidden way down deep and far below, where other things get covered up. Mother warns us to "keep quiet about that." In the grove, the other kids say—I must remember not to say kids. Kids are baby goats, we are children, Mother said so—"Better not tell. Don't be a tattletale." What comes at night from corners that I can't see into? In the dark I might lose something important, seen only in flashes of lightning, something important cracked opened only by a creaky door too big and heavy, by cellar doors unhinged, lying in wait.

Looking into the hole, I peer down through the darkness at crude steps too bumpy and narrow, too close to the door at the bottom of the stairs. Wet cement has been slapped together to fashion uneven steps so steep that I must lower one foot at a time, my hands reluctantly letting go of the step above as I back down. Feeling my way down, I go slowly, imagining what's below. When I reach the bottom step, I hold onto the step above and look up, afraid to turn around and look at the door leading into the cellar. In the opening at the top of the stairs, Milly's face is the only sun I see. "Sissy, sissy, something'll git cha down there."

The door at the bottom is almost too heavy for me to push open into the dusty air. The dirt smells like fungus, something strange growing down here. I go slowly over the uneven dirt floor, feeling my way into the darkened cellar. Unseen in the dusky haze are cobwebs that catch in my hair. I jump away. Hurry past dark corners, past a small window caked with grime and nailed shut. I follow stray rays of sunlight glancing off walls made of dirt and peer into dark corners, hurry past cast-off broken bushel baskets. The dirt smells strange. Something coming from far away stops me cold. I am climbing the cold stairs to bed. Under the bed is a white-enameled potty with a handle like the ear of a cup and a cover with a handle on top of it. Mother warns, "If you use the potty, be sure to replace the cover." Then adds, "And be sure to say your prayers." We are taught to kneel by the side of the bed, fold hands, close eyes, and say "Now I lay me down to sleep. I pray thee Lord my soul to keep. If I should die before I wake, I pray thee Lord my soul to take." We carry hot-water bottles upstairs to the unheated bedrooms. Three in a bed, we warm each other. Soon I am sleeping and dreaming.

Shifting, I hear rattled keys in a bright, fluorescent light school-room. I don't like the harsh order and the commanding tall windows in tall walls. A blackboard with chalk screeching across is wailing out tiredness and fears. "Hear, now, Miss___." Here, where I am tested, right now my belly knotted into chicken chow mein. White paint is peeling off the schoolhouse, its harsh book of doctrine, Question School, the white chalk is complaining, "not amountin' to anything worth..." Hear... Here now is a blank white, rolled-up Daylite screen: an undescended map of the world leading back to corners, the dirt earth, uneven coal, and cold orders screeching urgency. Here, where I am tested right now.

I hurry through the dark, past mice ready to attack, scared to death of something. I have dragged my sister Milly with me down into the storm cellar because I'm scared. Beyond this empty hole is a broken-down furnace with the coal bin, a black shovel stuck in lumps of coal. I want to see the diagonal rays of sunlight bouncing off the lumps of shiny coal, but Milly says, "Don't go in there. Coal's dirty." Anyway, there is hardly any coal left in the bin. The furnace has never worked. Near us on the floor is a large gray pickle crock covered with a board. The crock always has sour pickles. Only sweet pickles tempt me, but Milly wants to try one. The long dill weeds in the crock branch out like miniature trees with dill lace fanning out from stalks to twigs. The scum on top is ugly, its mottled grey not the soft gray of storm clouds that hover above the grove. I feel guilty even looking into the crock, remembering Mother's, "Leave that board on while the pickles are curing; they're not ready yet." The pickle Milly holds up drips into the crock as she takes a tentative bite and holds it out to me.

"Here, try it. It won't kill ya."

I draw back but she urges, "Go on."

The smell of vinegar turns my stomach. I turn away saying, "Mother puts lye in there."

"Naw she doesn't, silly. She puts lye in lard to make soap." Milly runs to the creaky door left open a crack. "Scaredy cat, scaredy cat, nothing's gonna get you down here." I beg her to stay. She taunts me. The damp dirt underfoot is studded with sharp stones that hurt the soles of my feet. I must cross the middle room and go to the far-right and into the next room to get the potatoes. Taking in the dank smell, my heart races to get through, gather the potatoes for Mother, and get out. I trip on the uneven dirt, lurch forward, trip again, get red-faced, and go faster. Past spiders and mice with eyes that dart forward—mice ready to attack bare feet, I race, scared to death that something will reach out and snatch me. I want to escape. Milly is threatening to go up and leave me trapped in this hole under the house. I beg her to stay. Milly drags behind, wanting to go up and out. She threatens to let the cellar doors slam down and trap me in this dark hole. Behind me, I hear her climbing the stairs, and I yell over my shoulder, "Don't you dare!"

As I enter the potato bin, furry bodies scurry away behind the shelves of bluish Mason jars filled with peaches, pears, beets, beans, apple butter, jams, and a great many jars of tomatoes. In June, yellow blossoms pop up every day on tomato plants whose branching arms, hands, palms, and fingers lift outside the twine that keep the plants upright. I pluck a couple of blossoms and carry them to Mother. Wistfully, I think about last July's spurt of red juice from a warm tomato, the juice running down my chin, the kitchen windowsills decorated with lines of anemic tomatoes, their still-green blossom ends ripening in the sun. Mother chides me, "Don't pick those blossoms or we won't have any tomatoes. Now, go run and play."

Eyeing the jars of ghostly tomatoes swimming in their hairy fluid like tadpoles in the muddy creek, I recall how awful those canned tomatoes taste in the winter. I look up at the jars of pale tomatoes and count how many more quarts are left to eat. From the captured tomatoes, fiber threads escape into shadows unfolding, refolding, and reforming themselves into strange images caught in shifting light. I feel guilty knowing I shouldn't have sneaked that salt shaker off the table and out to the garden yesterday. But I love to run out to the tomato vines, pick the ripest tomato, sprinkle each bite with salt, and eat it sitting under the grape arbor where nobody can see me. I've tried eating ripe tomatoes without salt but don't like them that way. Once I'm outdoors, I forget that the salt shaker is supposed to go back on the kitchen table.

At supper last night, Mother said, "More and more salt shakers are disappearing. Now you children *know* you shouldn't take those salt shakers outside. Pretty soon we won't have any salt shakers at all to put out on the table." Right after supper I ran outside to search for the salt shakers I left in the grove, under the porch or grape arbor. This morning I did find one, its metal cover rusted shut, its thick bubble glass caked with dirt. Shyly I ran into the house to give it to Mother. In her gentle, patient voice, she held onto the weight of each word, "So, well, now, just don't do that anymore."

Something powerful lives down here in this far corner of the cellar. In this cool bin of roots and jars, something is hidden, way deep down. "Better not tell." Only Mother's words keep me here. "Get them big enough. Enough for supper. None with green sprouts. Green sprouts or eyes we don't eat. Poison. Go now and come right back. Don't stay down there and play."

"Oh I won't, no I won't, I'll be right back."

I pile potatoes into the skirt of my dress, rolling up the sides to hold them in. Still, some keep rolling out. Choosing smaller ones, I keep at it until I think I have enough for supper. The dress gets dirtier. I hate the soiled smell beneath my bare feet—hate the dirt that potatoes leave on my dress. Just then something darts from behind. I imagine hands coming around to hold my eyes closed. Shaking free, I run breathless to the steps and struggle up, trying to keep the potatoes from falling out of my skirt, and my knees from scraping on the cement of each steep step. Once, I nearly trip and fall backwards. In the kitchen, Mother holds a pan under my skirt and notices how eager I am to let the potatoes roll down into it. She gives me a big kiss, and I run outside to play, the screen door banging behind. At the supper table, Pa's sky-blue eyes pierce the air between us.

"That's just a story. Don't 'mount to a hill 'a beans."

"What doesn't 'mount to a hill 'a beans?"

That something behind me, those hands coming up, imagining that.

"Mind you, you better keep quiet about that."

Threads from the fabric of childhood slowly unravel like the boldly patterned flour sacks that reform themselves under the needle of the Singer sewing machine to become bloomers, house dresses, skirts, shirts. Sewn together on the bias are slanted memories, dreams, and nightmares. I hate scratchy bloomers and guilt, its crazy quilt whirling around in the dark like a spider web broken, swinging, entangling bare arms and legs.

I go outside to wander around in the grove. Lightning streaks through the din and then through potato eyes into swirling clouds. On top of the house a lightning rod points to a heaven full of fluffy clouds that look like mashed potatoes. Clouds scatter, evanescing, and then coalescing to join the heavenly hosts going somewhere, leaving, like people do. Clouds grow, like the fluffy white potatoes, mounding higher and higher in the pan before they disappear into our mouths. Mother mashes potatoes in the battered pan on the black cookstove. Sweat stands up on her forehead. Her apron is greasy; its patch pocket bulges with the ever-present hanky for wiping our snotty noses. Glenny is standing on the round wooden kitchen stool next to Mother. From this elevation he can watch Mother's strong arm whip the potato masher around and around. Mounds of white potatoes grow higher and become fluffy. I stand on tippy toes next to Glenny to watch Mother and see the masher's double steel S's whipping the potatoes. Mother lifts the pan above a chipped china bowl and guides the potatoes down into it, sharply bangs the metal masher on the side of the pan to loosen the last bits of creamy potato and then hands the masher to me to lick off the last bits. She takes a big spoon and wearily scraps from the pan the last streaks of white.

All of us sit down to eat around the long wooden table. Flies buzz, some stuck, some struggling on a new strip of sticky flypaper just inside the screen door. Pa mumbles a long blessing. He stops. Everyone waits, hungry, tensed to attack the food. At my turn in line, I pray as fast as I can. Hands of the bigger kids reach for the bowls of beef, peas, mashed potatoes, and gravy. Bread and butter go around.

"Pass the salt and pepper down."

Mother lifts the white pitcher of milk above my glass and pours it full, then passes the pitcher to Pa. Everything gets passed in the same direction around the table. Everyone eats all the food on their plates and drinks all the milk out of their glasses. No one talks. It is twelve-thirty on the sixteenth of June, 1944.

56

Gladys, Mother, Bernice with Glenn
above storm cellar doors, 1944.

6

Tornado Warning

In the grove, we look up from our play to see billowing black clouds rear up from the horizon, gradually shutting out the sunlight. Their pressured heads are fomenting and colliding, then rapidly covering the entire sky. The afternoon air grows heavy. The sun stops shining. This rare darkness is strange. This is not the way thunder storms usually start. We stare in wonder at this sudden change. As we grow quiet, we hear an unfamiliar kind of clucking coming from chickens scratching around inside their hurricane fence. Dead calm grips the branches of the trees. The air feels suspended, as pressured and heavy-lidded as the large canner on the hot iron cookstove each August. Mother notices us playing dominoes on the floor at the end of the stove and commands, "Not here. Go play someplace else."

In the grove, nothing moves. We stand still and look up. Startled by something invisible, chickens begin to fly up into the trees in a wild flurry of beating wings, cackling in nervous voices. The rooster screeches, definitely not his usual cock-a-doodle-do announcement of impending dawn. He struts another high-pitched scream. Huge clouds are roiling into each other, eating up the darkening sky. Kittens race after cats, crossing the yard to get under the front porch. They whine in the damp dark underneath. In the barn, horses buck and pitch against the sides of their stalls. The sound of their high-pitched neighs shrills the dense air and is awful to hear. These things never happen in the middle of the afternoon. We stand still, intent, every sense tuned. The sky feels like a black hole descending into the devouring mouth of earth.

Suddenly, a great wind lifts the branches of the trees and the whole grove of trees bends, flowing away like long hair streaming out behind a woman racing away. Everything around our feet is being swept away, everything flattened. Fear catches hold, but then, just as suddenly as it began, the wind stops, and a second eerie silence settles over the farm. Even the chickens are still in the dead silence that holds us in the eye of the storm. Then the quiet is broken by an even greater wind that keeps us from running toward the house and Mother's urgent voice.

58   "Quick! Hurry! Get those little kids inside!"

My dress is whipping around my legs and flying up as I try to move toward the house, but first I must get past the fence that surrounds the house. On top of the gate in the fence are two scrolls of iron shaped like the bass clef in the *Psalter Hymnal.* As the gate whips back and forth, these steel clefs ram heads. Fast walking is the best I can do as I struggle against the wind, knowing that I must get to the house as quickly as possible. The steel gate swings wildly on its hinges, screeching a warning whine. If lightning jumps the space between the two metal posts when I race through the gate, I will be electrocuted, but I must either get out of the wind or be blown away.

Patient, mild-mannered Mother is flying out the screen door she never bangs, the screen door she is forever telling us not to bang, yelling at the big boys. "Get those chickens down out of the trees right away into the coops!"

Everything is chaotic—running, yelling, "Help! Help!"; braying cows, nervous chickens, men in the fields rushing home. Never mind Elmer now; I must try to get myself through the banging gate, through the swinging screen door, and into the house.

Huge drops splat, thunder claps, lightning streaks. A great wind like no other sweeps down from the evil-eyed sky. A large black funnel twists and turns like the long snaking tail of a kite that has broken away. Larger drops begin to pelt the smooth skin of dry earth like bullets shattering window panes. Lightning cracks open the sky—but before the ensuing clap of thunder, I make it through the gate. I'm past the pump faster than you can say, "Jack Sprat could eat no fat," up the steps and into the house lickety-split one second before it starts pouring.

Inside and out, everything shakes, and yet, the chaotic disorder seems to possess an unseemly kind of order: black clouds like frenzied ballet dancers cover the sky. It is only four o'clock and nearly as dark as night. Mother has come up the steps, through the wash porch, and has crossed the kitchen and gone into the bedroom to get the baby out of the crib. Now she is sitting close to the outside door with him in her arms, ready to go to the storm cellar. Screens flapping outside the windows and doors are being closed and hooked. Inside doors and windows are closed and locked. Everyone is beginning to gather around the wooden table in the kitchen where we gather to eat. Someone says, "Don't touch the phone. If the lightning rod on top of the house doesn't hold, lighting could come down the wires."

There is no time to see if the floor radio works. One of the big people takes the kerosene lantern down from where it hangs on a nail high above the stove. The cap on the tank is unscrewed and a can of kerosene taken down from a high shelf. Kerosene is poured through a funnel into the tank, and the mantle and wick are adjusted. Matches are fetched. Torrents of rain slash the house like Pa lashing his razor against the leather razor strap in sure, swift strokes. A great wind shakes and batters every door and window—but now we are battened down, quiet, listening to the fury of the storm. There is nothing to do but wait.

The older ones start to talk about what we'll do, "If." Someone tells me not to be scared and holds me on her lap. I squirm off. The lights go out. Across my mind flashes the image of Mother running, feverish with fear, banging out the screen door. The heavy unknown looms. In the dark, Mother removes the glass chimney from the kerosene lantern in the middle of the table and lights the wick, lowering the orange tongue that shoots up until she has a short blue flame. She replaces the chimney and adjusts the wick. Gray smoke clouds the glass. She turns the screw that raises and lowers the wick. Pale light flickers. Shadows crawl around the room. Another lantern is fetched. Kerosene lanterns lit, we wait.

"How will we know when to go down into the storm cellar?"

"We'll wait a little while." Everyone is quiet, listening, waiting. I want to go down below and be safe.

"Wait," says the taciturn silence of Pa.

"Wait," says Mother's stolid, patient look.

The big kids start to talk about what might happen, then become tight-lipped in an effort to stop the fear they see in the eyes of the little kids. An eerie glow comes from the lanterns' twin mantles hissing in the middle of the table.

"What if we have to live down there? What will we eat? Will God watch out for us?"

Shadows creep around the room. Things come out of the dark: eyes in hidden, furry bodies, eyes in the storm cellar, eyes in corners we can't see into. The shadow of death dances through slanting sunlight—one image running upstairs, while its shadow cautiously ventures down steep cellar steps.

Mother's patient tone is not so much a comfort as a protest. "Ach heiden, kinderen, but there's nothing down there."

There is nothing to do but wait.

7

Eyes of the Tornado

The next morning the phone lines are tied up. Some phone lines went down when storm winds blew over telephone poles. The party line is busy: farm wives are talking on the party line we share with five, six, or seven neighboring farms. When Mother finally does get through to an aunt who is not already talking on the phone, she listens intently, nearly in tears. The tornado hit near Lebanon. The farms in this part of Sioux County are where Pa's six brothers and sisters, and all of Mother's brothers and sisters live, except for Uncle Sam and Aunt Carolina and their twelve children, who live in South Dakota. We know all our many cousins pretty well and are worried about them. What finally does come through the party line is that no relatives died in the tornado and only three of their farms were badly hit. Thank the Lord, our old farm was not sucked up into the eye of the tornado that swooped down to take one farm but left another right beside it untouched. The sigh of relief that rises in the air as Mother hangs the earpiece of the wall phone back on its hook is like a stream of steam escaping from the spout of the heavy hot teakettle on the cookstove.

Pa comes in from the fields and says the tornado damage to our farm is not much more than that from a severe wind storm. As soon as the morning chores are done, we get into the gray Chevrolet and drive the twenty miles, at thirty miles per hour, over graded dirt roads to see what the tornado did. The trip is an event, coming as it does in summer when the only trips away from the farm are to Hospers for church or to town for supplies; plus on a Saturday, which is always a day at home preparing for the Lord's Day. Only absolutely necessary work is done on Sunday, chores like feeding livestock and milking cows. Saturday chores include bathing, washing hair, and shining Sunday shoes. Food is made ahead—picked, cleaned, and prepared. Peeled potatoes will wait overnight in a covered pan of cold water on the end of the cookstove; peas are shelled or green beans strung. A cake is baked and frosted, and pudding or Jell-O made.

62   Our little faces press against the front seat, eyes peering over the seat to see out the windshield. Noses press against the back-seat windows. We go the ten miles to Sioux Center, then onward west, ten more miles to see the Kooi farms surrounding Lebanon. Nearly there, we see that the tornado acted like a giant eggbeater gone berserk, spewing out stuff all over the place, messing up the tidy landscape with its neat squares of corn and waving grasses that yield oats, barley, timothy, and alfalfa. As we turn off the dirt road into Uncle Adrian's and Aunt Jennie's farmyard, we see that everything is a twisted wreck. Even their driveways no longer lead to their tool shed, barn, chicken coop, silo, hog house and farmhouse.

From the safety of several feet away from their wrecked house, I ask Mother, "Where did they sit, down there, in the cellar?" And then, "How long did they have to stay down there?" Following Mother around, I keep asking questions. "Did they have a kerosene lantern down there?" Trying to put me off, she keeps looking around and talking with the adults, but I hang on. I feel relieved when I overhear that the five cousins I like so much have survived: full-bosomed, soft Marie; lean, dark Greta; and Aunt Jennie's three small boys with their freckled faces, apple cheeks, sky-blue eyes, and thick shocks of hair.

"Did they have anything to eat? How did they know when to come up?"

Finally she relents. Her somberly soft voice reveals some of the terror and incredulity they must have felt while waiting for that awful noise to die down so that one of them could push up the cellar door a crack to see what had happened. Mother's answers are short and nearly inaudible. Can't she see my heart's wild thumping, the lump pumping my ribs up and down?

"Where did they go?"

Now her voice rises, and I smell the scent of weariness and sense her exasperation held in check by sheer willpower. She gestures toward the homeplace, the farm across the section. "Of course. Right away they went to their folks. *You know*—just over there." I see that it was a dumb question, the last one I dare ask, I know that relatives always take care of each other. Except for the people at church and a few neighbors, relatives are the only people we know. On Sundays they come visiting, and we go visit them. Our cousins are like brothers and sisters, the uncles and aunts like parents. All have Dutch backgrounds and are Christian Reformed and God-fearing. They are as fundamental as the soil, rain, and air; as sure as the lightning firing up the clouds, the roar of God's thunder, His rainbow promise. They are the earth itself, the only world I know. Pa seems to be as fond of his youngest sister, Jennie Marie, as their father, Remko Kooi, was of her, his youngest child. She married Adrian Haverhals, and they had five children. When the tornado hit their farm, she was six months pregnant. Aunt Jennie tells about that time in her life:

That tornado came down on our farm, 3/4 mile north of the original Remko Kooi homeplace. We were the first place hit in Sioux County, Iowa, at 6:30 p.m. on Friday, June 16, 1944. We had no tornado warnings then and didn't know the tornado had struck some 30 miles west in South Dakota at 4:30 p.m. Since the weather was threatening, we had our five children go down into the basement into a partial storm cave. When a strong surface wind came from the southwest and we saw a whirling cloud formation directly above us, Adrian and I joined them in the cave through the inside floor door in our wash room. Wind suction kept the door banging up and down. The noise was tremendous. When it quieted, Adrian went up. Our new, six-feet-thick, cement silo was a complete mass of rubble, the pin point of the twister probably came down directly on it. There was damage to all the buildings as well as the house.

Adrian quickly loosened the cows still standing in the stanchions—even though the barn around them was gone—where Marie, age twelve, had been milking. Soon the storm returned, whirling around back and forth, and Adrian was back down in the cave. The second time was scarier, although shorter. The suction of the air pressure in our ears was like a very noisy locomotive sound. When we first emerged from the cellar and surveyed the damage, we saw that only the shell of our house remained; the windows were all sucked out. The boys' felt hats, worn for church, were lying in the frame of a window. The roof had been blown off the higher part of our house. Winds had wrought havoc inside. Most of the damage was in the upper story. The kitchen remained untouched inside. Small articles on the table were unmoved. Doors had blown shut. Living rooms and bedrooms were a rubble, and the linoleum was gone— torn in shatters.

All buildings were gone except a large corncrib. It became apparent that the cribs had been lifted by the wind, then set down again, because of the articles blown between the foundations and the cribs. Corn stored in there may have saved it. We were so thankful for safe children: the girls twelve and nine, the boys five and seven, our third son just two, and the fourth unborn. Rains followed the winds, pasting down dirt and debris on floors and furniture.

Going upstairs to survey the children's bedrooms, we saw our neighbors, one-and-a-half miles northwest, down in our driveway. They had watched the storm, had seen the funnel come down on us, and came as soon as the wind stopped and the funnel rose. We threw blankets and items from one open closet down to them. They took care of what they could. I had been crocheting a tablecloth, which was three-fourths done and lying on a table in the sitting room. A brother-in-law found it attached to a yard fence in a cattle lot, not damaged but black with ground-in dirt. For several weeks the washing machine ran with the blackened, tattered clothing that had been picked up. All the clothes in one closet in an upstairs bedroom were blown out of the roof, another closet's roof was off, but the blankets and clothing remained, and the closet under the staircase stood with its door closed and everything intact.

Our four oldest spent Friday night at Grandma Haverhals, while two-year-old Art and I went to in-laws, Anne and J. Wiechers. On Saturday morning they took Art and me back, on roads that had been cleared of trees and wires on Friday night. It was just a mile to get there. We saw animals injured with metal embedded by the storm's fury. Rains in the night had further damaged the oak floors in the newer part of our house. That Saturday morning the mailman from Hawarden had come, so Marie and I sat on a bed in an upstairs bedroom (although the bedding was gone), looking at the mail. As we sat there looking at a letter that had come from Uncle Ben, a stream of sightseers came walking through, right past us, talking about what the storm had done to the house, even about "these people who live here," just as though we were not there! They went through all the rooms, up and down, crunching debris, broken glass, etc. into the floors and steps. Meanwhile, on the road below, cars continually passed by. Since we lived on a corner with two driveways, some cars even risked driving onto our farm right over our yard.

On Saturday afternoon, Greta, age nine, helped me. I moved debris on floors and steps with a makeshift kind of rod, while she picked up what we saw of any value: jewelry, keys, anything. People walking over the debris had not helped. I remember your folks coming and your father giving us a gift to help us through.

Everyone helped with cleanup, etc. By evening the State Guard had posted men at each farm hit by the tornado. Two men with bayonets stood at each driveway. No more traffic came through our house and yard.[12]

On Sunday evening, a special church service was held in the Sioux Center Christian Reformed Church for tornado victims and out of gratitude for lives saved. I went. Clothing for children was donated by the box full. The next day the neighbors and a crew of men had moved our remaining belongings (all caked with a hard crust of dirt) to an empty home one-and-a-half miles away on a vacant farm on the hill north of Aunt Bertha's. So, when my girls and I returned in the afternoon, we found an empty house.

Much help was given to us throughout the summer by others. Groups came from nearby towns to pick up debris in fields. The June corn had been taken away by the suction of the wind during the tornado, and in the south field even the loose soil was gone. Huge piles of debris were burned. I had many mouths to feed during June and July—carpenters, etc. And then, on August 19, Lawrence was born, and we continued to ride back and forth from the vacant farm to our own farm, the kids and nieces helping me with the cleanup. Now we worked with baby Larry in a basket. Art was two. Getting settled into our "new" house took time, cleaning furniture and sorting all the hastily boxed possessions, and washing clothes. I had plenty to do. The oak floors had become warped from being wet for some time, so, as our damaged house was rebuilt, we updated rooms. For four months we lived on that vacant farm a mile and a half away from our own farm. We moved back onto our own farm and into a partially repaired home in October, when baby Lawrence was two months old.

The tornado had zigzagged up and down, and side twisters came off the main one to hit adjacent places. No towns were hit as it veered east some twenty miles. The path it took after the first strike at 6:30 could be seen by all the articles that blew from the house and later were found to the northwest, up to a mile. The tornado went one mile south, just missed the original Kooi farm

[12] "Governor Sends State Guard," *Sioux Center News*, June 22, 1944: "Governor Hickenlooper sent out the State Guard Saturday afternoon to guard property and help regulate the heavy traffic of sightseers. Thousands of cars moved slowly through the area Sunday."

66   3/4 mile south, completely took the farm 1/4 mile south of there,
across Dry Creek, then veered east toward Lebanon, taking the
farm 1/4 mile west of Lebanon. The church was totally wrecked.
The grocery store was gone, another two to three homes hit, and
there was damage to Uncle George's farm.[13]

When the tornado hit the Haverhals farm the second time, it did
even worse and more powerful damage to the farms to the east. Some
twenty farms were damaged totally or partly. Over 2000 farm animals were
dead or had to be destroyed because they had been injured. No persons
were hurt, although a miracle occurred near Sioux Center when a baby
was pulled from its mother's arms and blown quite a distance.

Baby Pulled from Mother's Arms
Their house was swept away so they had no protection from debris piling on top of them in such quantities they could see nothing. The suction of the wind became so strong that Mrs.
Heusinkveld could no longer hold onto the baby, and she dropped
him. He fell on his face, and before the frantic parents could find
him, he was completely covered with debris flying in from all
directions. After the worst force of the wind was spent, they found
only a tiny piece of blanket showing from a pile of trash. Mr.
Heusinkveld extracted the unconscious baby, certain he was dead.
While shaking him and trying to revive him, the baby began to
cry. Once he got some air into his lungs he was OK—bruised but
OK. Their car had disappeared; all that could be found was a door
hanging in a tree and the motor in a ditch. The entire farm was
swept clean of trees, buildings and equipment.[14]

After visiting the damaged farm of Uncle Adrian and Aunt Jennie,
we pile into the car and drive along, all eyes. A large evergreen and a
cottonwood are uprooted. Another cottonwood has fallen to make a natu-

[13] Letter dated May 18, 1992, from Aunt Jennie Haverhals to author, additional letters
over several years, and oral history in 1995. Aunt Jennie's description of the path the
tornado took was corroborated by the *Sioux Center News* on June 22, 1944.

[14] Story in *Sioux Center News*, June 22, 1944.

ral bridge over the road just north of Peace Lutheran Church, and cars are passing under the tree without difficulty. The farm of newly-wed cousins, Siebert and Fannie Haverhals, is wiped out. When the tornado hit, Fannie had been sick in bed. She got to the cellar just in time. The only furniture they have left is the rocking chair that Siebert carried to the cellar for her.

Not since May 3, 1895, had a major cyclone hit the Sioux Center area. That cyclone moved in a mile-wide swath, with funnels touching down over 30 miles, killing 75 and injuring 47. Livestock loss was considerable, as was the damage to schools and farms. From that time on, the people in the Sioux Center area began to dig storm caves for shelter.[15]

As recently as the spring of 1944, some of the storm cellars near Lebanon farmhouses were dug out and hastily covered with makeshift plank doors. This was the case at the Haverhals farm, but at least Siebert and Fannie both got out of the house and into the cellar. We walk around the door, laid flat above a hole in the ground, while glancing over our shoulders toward the wrecked house. Wanting to see where they hid from the storm, I beg Mother to lift up the door. She protests. "Ach heiden, kinderen, but there's nothing down there." To stop my whining, she tells someone older to lift up the door. She is right—there is nothing down there but a dark hole. The steps hacked unevenly into the black dirt are now nearly covered up. I hear an impatient voice behind me. "Well, are you gonna go down there, or what?" I cling to the skirt of Mother's thin cotton dress, glance down at her black shoes, and turn away. The eye of the tornado swooped down, picked up this farmhouse, sucked the air out, whirled it around inside its black funnel, and then flung it away. I do not go down into the black-eyed hole.

As the tornado pursued its snake-like course, it took Uncle George's farm buildings just west of the Lebanon store, leaving only their house, then striking the Lebanon Store itself, removing the roof and all four walls, and churning all the supplies in a heap on the floor. When we stop and get out of the car, Aunt Grada is nervous, and Uncle George's face doesn't

15 Mike Vanden Bosch, *Pocket of Civility, A History of Sioux Center* (Sioux Falls, South Dakota: Modern Press, Inc., 1976), pages 11, 92, 95.

break into its usual quick smile. The folks do not stay very long. Nearby, the parsonage for the Lebanon Christian Reformed Church is half blown away. The Reverend Reinsma said that it looked as if dirt had been shoveled in by the carload. The church itself is leveled by the storm and the new $2,500 pipe organ is a twisted pile of pipes.

This church is where eleven of us were baptized. In the cemetery behind the church stand the gravestones of one brother and our grandparents. Easily visible from here is the original Kooi farm where Pa and his nine siblings were born. As we drive home, we see that every kind of household and farm implement is scattered helter-skelter over acres and acres of farm land. Parts of buildings are flung over several acres. Things are twisted into grotesque shapes.

Sioux Center businessmen had formed The Civic Club in 1935 to promote the town. When the 1944 tornado hit, they organized to help clean up the damage. Each Tuesday local businesses closed, except for those needed, and work crews went out to clean up debris strewn over fields in a wide area—west as far as ten miles from Sioux Center and east as far as Newkirk. These volunteers made it possible for field work to proceed. The same plan was carried out at Hawarden, Rock Valley, and Orange City. For many evenings the crews returned to hundreds of fields, buildings, dwellings, and the store and church in Lebanon. Churches also responded with help: a joint prayer service was held on Sunday night and a collection taken up for the distressed families.[16]

For months after the tornado, people find pieces of plates, battered pans, even a twisted sewing machine sticking out between rows of flattened corn stalks.

On the ride back home to our farm this Saturday, we come to the mailbox corner and see the red flag is still up, the letter with the three cent stamp is still in the box, and the *Sioux City Journal* isn't there. It would have had to come on the train through Sioux Center and then on to Sheldon

---

[16] Henry S. Lucas, *Netherlanders in America: Dutch Immigration to the United States and Canada, 1789-1950* (Ann Arbor, Michigan: University of Michigan Publications, 1955), page 341.

before it would be delivered into our mailbox. On Monday, though, the mailman does make it around trees fallen across roads and through low spots flooded from sloughs backed up by swollen creeks. The newspaper, however, doesn't tell us much more than we already know. The paper speculates about the dollar amount of the damage, but that doesn't interest little kids. We want pictures, first-hand reports, graphic details, and *Believe-it-or-not-by-Ripley* stuff. Later on, when a photo showing a lone straw driven clear through a tree trunk appears in a national magazine, we gaze and gawk, study details, and exclaim with awe, "Isn't that something?"

Usually, someone older gets to see the daily paper first. We younger children jockey for position, fighting to see, grabbing the paper. "Hey, lemme see that again. Look! It says here, 'Straw was found forced into trees and wood driven into wire fences.'" Someone older reads while we younger ones study the pictures. "Look! It says, 'A car lay on its top, horn blowing in the stillness following the storm. Three families survived by taking refuge in a storm cave. The noise was like that of a train rolling overhead. Outside the cave, every tree was a twisted, splintered wreck, stripped, torn or uprooted.'"

"Wow, like a train roaring through, whistling. Imagine—nails driven clean through boards! Wish we could see that. Do you think it's true?" And, when we read about the baby swept away: "What a thing to happen! House, baby, car just simply gone—an entire farm swept clean of trees, buildings and farm machinery." Stunned, we look, read again, and again exclaim, "What a thing to happen!"

Soon, electric lines are back up, singing in the sunlight, humming with rows of blackbirds perched on the two wires. Hearing the vibrations, I remember Pa's merry sing-songing at twilight after supper last week.

> Four and twenty blackbirds all in a row.
> When the pie was opened,
> the birds began to sing.
> Now wasn't that a jolly song to sing....

Soon, the farm is picked up, repaired, and back to normal. Clarence comes home from the Army Air Force on furlough for a few days. He drives off to see Siebert and Fannie Haverhals' farm, which was Uncle Case's farm before that, and reports, "It is, indeed, leveled. The family took refuge in the storm cellar and emerged unscathed. Seibert, however, according to reports, was crying like a baby." The June 22, 1944, *Sioux Center News* reports the servicemen home on leave and their activities:

> The Henry Sandbulte family of fourteen survived in a small cave but had difficulty breathing. One of the children, Private Bernard Sandbulte, home on furlough, found his training standing him in good stead when he showed them how to keep their jaws moving and their mouths open to keep from choking from lack of oxygen in the crowded cave. Their farm gone, they rented the former residence of Ben Kooi in Carmel. Members of the Carmel Church went out to the Henry Sandbulte farm all day Monday to help the family clean up the place.

Instead of running off to play on Sundays after morning and afternoon church services, and after Sunday School is over, we kids hang around the edges of the knots of farmers, farmwives, and youth who gather to talk. Bit by bit we learn more. Fat cattle were so badly bruised from flying cement and debris that they were nearly worthless. From Pa's long prayer after meals, it is apparent that God's great mercy has spared us. Still, I wonder if the wrath of some evil eye descended that day, if a large person living in the sky takes some people away and leaves others. In Sunday School we sing rhymed verses, our hands and arms moving up and down in rhythm with the other children:

> Climb, climb, up Sunshine Mountain
> Heavenly breezes blow
> Climb, climb, up Sunshine Mountain
> Faces all aglow

Singing, we together become, "Daniel in the Lion's Den." Emphatically, we tell "Old Pharaoh" by way of "Moses way down in Egypt's land," to "Let my people go." The songs seem to be saying: Do not question God. He is a Capital Letter. He knows. He is orderly. He lives far above black tornadoes that suck up earth, ruin farms and take crops. At bedtime, Mother leans down to kiss me and says, "Now be sure you kneel down and say your prayer before you get into bed."

Emphatically, "I will, I will."

Upstairs, I fall to my knees and let my closed eyes fall forward to come to rest between my folded hands on the chenille bedspread. "Now I lay me down to sleep. I pray thee Lord my soul to keep. If I should die before I wake, I pray thee Lord my soul to take." As I fall asleep, Mother and Pa become jumbled into, "Lord my soul, keeping, dying, taking night." Clinging to the light, I listen intently to a flute being played by someone older. The sweet notes of birds in trees are growing, floating high above me far into the distance. More than usual, after the tornado I absorb what is happening, attempting to pick up clues.

Our playhouses in the grove are no more. Pounding in newly-found sticks with stones, we find frayed lengths of twine to connect stick to stick, making fences and walls. We go about the busyness of little-kids' play, gathering the bits and pieces that reconnect us to the world we knew before the storm, taunting, teasing, "Copycat! Copycat!" We are easily irritated by another little kid's questions, "Figure it out for yourself, dummy."

"Now, you little kids stay out of the away, you hear?" Warnings echo the tensions in the unsettled air. Like rag dolls inflated with air, we have become sponge replicas of make-believe grownups. We are entirely bound by the sticks and stones of childhood bones, the swaying of trees into afternoon thunder storms. The late twilights of June that let us play outdoors past nine.

Upstairs, we unhook the flimsy window screen between us and the porch on the roof. Mattresses are dragged out onto the black tar roof over the front porch running the length of the house. We tiptoe to the internal replay of Mother's "Don't do that. You could fall through the roof." Aware that she or Pa might hear us, our guilt makes us grow even more quiet, more careful. Afraid to sleep out here, I squeeze my eyes tightly shut and pretend nothing bad will happen. Surprised when nothing does, I take quick peeks at the stars and see twinkling pins poking through the black velvet canopy. The Milky Way seems to rock and sway, like the swaying warm milk in the bucket carried from the barn to the house each night just before supper. Pretty soon the mosquitoes go away. Fireflies come out and prick holes in my hazy thoughts.

Stars turn around and fall into the ground. Bright colors explode like the lights of a Ferris wheel going around, turning the sky into a bowl of navy blue pricked by brilliant green dots popping out. I relive the taste of freshly-popped popcorn that big brother Stan popped for us last night. He is holding the black corn popper by its long metal handle, and pushing it back and forth, over and over, across the hot top of the black cookstove. Yellow kernels of corn pop, a few at first, then more, then an explosion. Stray kernels escape the popper and explode off the black stovetop. "You little kids stand back from the stove." We wait. Stan lifts the corn popper from the stove, pulls back the lid, and lets the popcorn fall into the battered dishpan on the table. As he shakes salt onto the popcorn, he warns, "Wait." We wait. Then we grab. "Wait while I get the salt mixed in." We wait again, then five sets of hands grab the popcorn. Soon, nothing is left in the bottom of the pan but old maids.

Organ pipes jut from destroyed Lebanon Christian Reformed Church,
June 16, 1944.

Fred and Ida Kooi dressed for Hospers Christian Reformed Church, 1944.

8

Death in an Iowa Farmhouse

Eleven of the twelve of us were born in the bedroom of the house on our farm near Lebanon. One baby brother died there and was laid out in the parlor where the funeral was held. When we moved to the farm near Hospers in 1939, Uncle John, Aunt Gertie, and their six children moved onto the Lebanon farm. My two oldest sisters, Gladys and Bernice, and Ray, my oldest brother, recall the baby's death and burial, each sibling viewing the event from a different perspective, embellishing each other's accounts.

Gladys recalls that "I am ten and a half when my baby brother, Elmer George, is born prematurely at home in the coldest month of an Iowa winter. He weighs four pounds and looks white and thin and blue. After I get home from school, I help Mother care for him, gently rocking the wicker buggy when he cries, keeping the hot water bottle by his feet filled and warm. He is too weak to nurse and doesn't grow, so Mother makes a gruel of oatmeal and milk strained through cheesecloth. We feed this to him, patiently urging a few drops into his mouth with an eye dropper, hoping he will swallow. Early one Saturday morning, Mother says to me, 'Sis, I don't think the baby is breathing. Would you check him?' I listen, and he is so quiet and still. His little bony chest is not moving at all. Mother suggests that we get a feather and hold it by the baby's nose, but we don't. She says, 'Take the hot water bottle away from his feet.' And after ten minutes or so, 'Now see if they are cold.' They are. How stunned and sad my Mother looks. Pa is called in from the barn."[17]

"Death in an Iowa Farm House" is the title of Bernice's story. "The baby dies before dawn two days before Christmas. Everything is muted today. No sun, no wind, none of the normal family sounds of a father, mother, and seven children. No baby cries. I am seven years old. I have not seen death before. Pa and Mama make decisions in quiet, sad voices. Grandma, aunts,

---

[17] Gladys I. Gritter, "My Memories," nd.

uncles, and neighbors are called. But no doctor, no mortuary. Pa goes to town and returns with a small white coffin inscribed: OUR DARLING BABY. Aunt Mattie comes, bathes and dresses the tiny baby, and places him in the white coffin which is placed on the oval oak table in the bay window, facing south. No sun today, though. At noon they come, the Dominie, Grandma, uncles, aunts, neighbors. All are farmers except the Dominie. All are dressed in dark suits and Sunday dresses. We sit in a circle in the living room. As always, the oval oak table in the bay window is the focus of the room. Today the white coffin rests there. The Dominie speaks, 'The Lord giveth. The Lord taketh away. Blessed be the Name of the Lord.'

"Uncle Watse sits in the back seat of Pa's car. On his lap is the baby in the white coffin. He places strong hands around it as we begin the slow journey to the graveyard. The baby has never been outside our house. He was born too early, born in the bedroom where he died. He had only twenty days of life."

Tears are in his eyes when Ray recalls the little white coffin sitting on the oval oak table in the bay window before it was carried to the graveyard behind the church. "On the road leading to church, cars of uncles and aunts get stuck in a low place in the muddy road. The men get a team of horses harnessed to heavy chains to pull the cars through this wet and muddy slough. Through it all, Uncle Watse calmly sits in the back seat holding the little white coffin."

Bernice's memory of the event continues: "The white clapboard church stands on a hill. Behind it is the graveyard. This is land my Grandpa donated to the community. His farm and his children's farms surround the church and grave-yard. Grandpa is buried here. We stand at the grave, dug this morning out of the half-frozen dirt. The white coffin looks strange and clean against the black earth of Iowa. It is cold. Mama tried so hard to keep the baby warm. Sixty years later, seven hundred miles from this place, the oval oak table that once held the baby in the white coffin, stands in my mountain cabin. Sixty years later, I stand again in the Iowa graveyard. It is hardly changed. The large dignified stones are for Grandpa and Grandma. The small stone is for my brother:

ELMER KOOI
1933

"The oak table began its life as a library table, but later the round pillars were shortened to make it a coffee table. A torn and yellowed label beneath the table declares in bold letters that it is a product of a small company in Clinton, Iowa, which manufactured Hawkeye tables, illustrated by a drawing of the Hawkeye eagle, official bird of Iowa. The simple table is what Iowa was—and is—all about. Built of sturdy oak, built to last, it reflects the simplicity and ruggedness of rural life. No elegant, fine-grained wood, delicate spindles, or fine details—just a durable, functional table, the bold striations of oak a comforting presence in the often harsh life of a farm family. My parents purchased the table when they were married in 1921. It always stood in the bay window of the living room, which looked out over a tumble of yellow roses. I loved the fragrance and beauty of those banks of roses. Irreverently though, we would tear the soft petals off, stuff them in our mouths, then blow hard to scatter the petals to the winds. There were two large lilac bushes in the front yard, and we climbed in the one nearest the house. And there were wild flowers. Pink roses and violets could be found in the spring in the ditches on the way to the little country school.

"Covered with one of Mama's crocheted cloths, I thought the table in the bay window was the most charming area in our house. It often served as a place to bathe babies and also was a place for books, puzzles, and games. Underneath remain the pencil scribblings of the children who played there. Tears fell on this table in 1933 when it was the resting place for the small coffin. I was a sad, scared, seven-year-old looking at the coffin and beyond, through the bay window, out into that cold gray day.

"When we moved to the big square house on a larger farm, the table went with us. A humble table really, oak was then considered rather plebeian and old-fashioned, not having the status of walnut, cherry, or mahogany. After we moved to Denver, it was banished to the basement and covered with several coats of paint. I was a young, married mother when I asked my mother if I could have the table. She gladly gave it to me. With a great deal of care and effort, I removed the coats of paint until, once again, the bold, rugged grain of oak began to appear. Many hours of restoring it followed, until finally it was rejuvenated into the golden oak table of my childhood. Again

78 it glowed with life, again children, then grandchildren, played checkers, put puzzles together—and left marks. The oak table has now absorbed the laughter and tears of four generations. It is a place for a cup of coffee, for books and magazines, stories, and always, a place in my heart."[18]

Old oak table in use since 1921.

[18] Bernice Kooi Afman, "Death in an Iowa Farmhouse," and "Oak Table," 1995.

9

Clotheslines

At twilight last night, I wandered down the hills toward the town of Eilat, taking in the view. A gunmetal-gray fleet of toy ships seemed to be moving into the harbor. The air was still, the ships were anchored, and a white moon moved across the sky to join the lowering sun hanging red in the mountains of Jordan. The sea became a long pink tongue lapping at the shores of four countries as each country turned on its lights. The first star of evening twinkled. The rocky slopes turned into hills smoothed off by earthmovers, then into the upper part of neon-lit Eilat. I walked past a recessed school yard and into a quadrangle of scruffy grass below our apartment building. In the fading daylight, I joined some kids who had come out of their apartments to play soccer.

Only a few cars are parked outside the buildings because most of us walk, take public transport or the cheap, ever-present taxis. The drab buildings reflect the landscape—the monotonous dun of sand from the Negev Desert that creeps into every crevice. Mountain rock crumbles into waves of sand that blow into Eilat from the desert, as do the ripples of sandy shore that move up from the Gulf of Aqaba and into town.

This afternoon I am doing laundry on our small balcony high above the quadrangle. Buffeted by a swift wind coming off the Negev Desert, I stand next to cooing pigeons. While I pin wet garments to cold clotheslines with plastic clothespins, I watch the antics of the children playing far below with bits and pieces—scraps of this and that left out next to the bomb shelter underneath the building. One of the clothespins slips and falls to the ground down below, another falls, then another. The shouts of children pull me down the five flights of stairs. To retrieve the fallen clothespins is only an excuse. I clutch my camera, eager to capture the progress of the children making a train from boxes. Their playing and excited Hebrew chatter is a language that is disarmingly open. As I trudge back up the flights of steps, the lines of a poem begin to weave back and forth in my head. At each turn, each higher

80   landing gives more glimpses of shadowy children.

Clothespin Dolls

Five stories below clotheslines
in Israel, doll-sized children
fashion dreams from scraps.
Abandoned plastic boxes
used to carry groceries home
become box cars in a train.
A rope is tied around the waist
of a boy-engine. Boy-travelers
jostle for space in the coach.
Freight cars are piled high
with cracked-off chunks of sidewalk,
loaded just so, to balance the ride.
Pulled and pushed, the train grunts
and screeches over desert sand.
Connections break. Shouts of glee and
bits of wasted wire get twisted into use.

In Iowa on the farm
we often made our toys.
Corncobs from the bushel basket
of tinder drying near the iron stove
laid end to end on the cold linoleum
became roads to town, tractors
in cornfields, and playhouses.
From the Singer sewing machine,
scraps of cloth fell to become
fashions for clothespin dolls—
boys in overalls, girls in dresses,
mothers in aprons, papas in straw hats
fashioned from real straw.
String hair got combed
with ragged fingernails. Blue Crayola
eyes and red lips—blurred dots, bits from
the tinder bin twisted into connection.[19]

[19] Irene Chadwick, "Clothespin Dolls," *Dawn Pearl* (Modesto, California: Ietje Kooi Press, 1994), pp. 8, 9.

Washday on the farm comes every Monday. Set into the scruffy lawn in the side yard next to the house are two tall poles in the shape of T's leaning inward from the heavy weight of wet clothes pinned onto four long wires. The poles tilt at a rakish angle toward each other. A few clothespins remain pinned to the ends of the clotheslines. Made of wood, their two sides are shaped like two legs that hold clothes onto the clothesline. The long, lean wooden pin has a head, body, and two legs. In stiff winds the heads dance, and the legs pull up from the wire. In winter, the wet clothes freeze stiff to stretch the wires taut.

In summer, we play the game, Fox and Geese, under the lines of drying clothes. My hands grab a slick metal pole to steady my body, swinging around it as my eyes keep following the fox chasing us: the geese. Whirling around the pole one way, then the other way, I use the momentum of my spinning body to carry myself away from each pursuer. Feeling light as a kite, my body catches the wind and speeds away to the grove. "No fair! No fair!" shouts Elmer, "Ya gotta stay under the clothesline!"

Racing back to the far pole, I whirl around it faster and faster until my hands slip off. Squealing, I whip off my center of gravity, off the pole, and into the nirvana of escape from a would-be captor. Pure delight floods my senses. Shrieks rise. My skirt billows higher and becomes a rising balloon. In a flash I see all three pursuers, one ready to get me. Racing away breathless, frantic, now I can't avoid him. Tagged, I'm "It": the fox chasing the geese.

In Israel, the children stop their play to watch the passing parade of grownups. They mimic their mannerisms, their walk and talk, and laugh at stodgy elders. Clowning around, they suddenly tire of the pedestrian parade and turn back to their box cars. In dead earnest, they begin to patch, repair, strengthen, extend, and connect the boxes. Dirty sand whips off the barren hillsides and flatlands to form little whirlpools in the streets of Eilat. The omnipresent sand grinds along underneath their feet and into my train of thought. Fine dirt whirls up. I stand hushed, reverently watching the gray dust on the Iowa farmyard whipping into a thin spiral, then slowly settling down. The sun shifts, then sifts through the dust as light pours through a whirling mist. Mother turns the handle of the flour sifter around and around. Light passes through the fine white flour sifting down into the big yellow mixing bowl.

Hayseeds

Haying on the Iowa farm in August—
Faces busted out in ladders of laughter
Hay tumbling out of the hayloft pell mell

Flying from the pitchforks of big brothers
And landing on five little kids playing
Finding straws to suck up summer's nectar

Real but elusive, quick as imagination
Playing, the wind is playing games—
Gusts pick up dust rabble and hay

Whip them into a circle just above the earth
And set them down again in seconds.
Whirlpools evaporate into the thin blue air

Like ghosts, we whisper, just like ghosts!
The wind singsongs, scores waves of
Whirlwind and birdsong against our ear drums

Hayseeds, we are backward, barefoot all summer long—
Laughing lines and rhythms racing after the wind
Eyes running, noses sniffling, knees skinned [20]

The grinding of shifting gears interrupts our reveries. A tractor enters the farmyard and lumbers along over bumpy ruts. Someone not much older than we are grumbles, "You kids get to play while we have to work." We scatter. Best to avoid work as long as possible. I drag myself up the stairs, past dimly-lit corners in the hallway to the bedroom door, past the dark under the bed and behind the closet door. Shadows reach out. Is there a bogeyman hiding in the attic?

In Israel, an ample mama leans out of an upper-story window. The wide windowsill supports her arms and breasts. She shouts at her son playing below, "Come in and finish your work." She waits, commands, "Now." From the wreckage of broken toys and the castoffs from passing pedestrians, the

---

[20] Poem by author.

boy loudly protests, "But mama, play is little kids' work."

A line of clothes rises in the wind, all together, like a regiment of soldiers marching off into the distance, down a street in Sheldon, Iowa, during the Fourth of July parade. Guns over shoulders, arms moving forward, back again, forward, over and over. The noisy strut of sheets whipping back and forth becomes the rhythmic grunt of a giant ship surging back and forth against ocean waves. Flying clothes almost jerk free, trying to run away, tethered, crowding the line, bumping along, jumping up, rocking, then rolling. The wind dies down and the clothes fall slack, unteased by the breeze. Hollow, they stop breathing until inflated again by air, they grow fat. The sun beats down to kiss the wet lips of laundry, to dry the skin of everyday.

Elmer, Glenny, Milly, and I are playing Hide 'n Seek under the clotheslines. The wind ties cotton and flannel arms and legs into knots. Union suits fly and their seat-flaps open. Lines sag, then buck and snap under the pull of kids, one grabbing a leg, another, an arm or waist, using it to counterbalance his body weight or straining to hide. We evade snapping apron strings and metal buttons on cuffs as we race through, under, or around airborne bodies. We fling aside arms and legs and hide inside the billowing skirts of housedresses or pants full of hips.

"First one out is a nincompoop!"

"Gotcha!"

Looking out the kitchen window, Gladys yells, "You kids go play some place else!" Even if we actually do hear her, we can always say that her voice was drowned out by the noise of swooning bodies, snapping sheets and buttons hitting metal poles. Whooping it up, we race faster around lines of wash pinned down against the grasping air. Shouting, darting, hiding inside a pillowcase grown fat, our yells barely rise above the voices of the wind.

"Who's 'It'?"

Rising up to hide us are ghosts flapping against the metal poles, jerking away from the wires, twisting, releasing and reforming into weird shapes. Overalls rise up. Dresses and undershirts sport bosoms; arms embrace wires and play their own kind of game. Empty bushel baskets skitter against the poles. They were used this morning to carry out the heavy, wet clothes, and will be used again in the late afternoon when a hired girl or an older sister

84   takes down the dry clothes. By then, we little kids have left, unless some-one snags one of us to stand still long enough to fold sheets. If I am snagged, I must hold two corners while the girl holds the other two corners and pulls the sheet taut, folding once, folding twice, and folding once again. As she takes down each garment, she examines it. Some will go into the mending basket and some into the ironing basket to sit inside the screen door of the washroom until the day designated for ironing, mending, darning socks, and sewing on buttons. Before sunset, bushel baskets of neatly folded towels, sheets, dresses, bloomers, and matched socks rolled into balls, will be carried inside.

Twilit Red Sea with towns of Aqaba, Jordan, and Eilat, Israel, on Gulf of Aqaba, August, 1989.

Israeli children creating train from boxes, Eilat, Israel, 1989.

Part II

DUTCH ANCESTORS

10

Family Lines

Moving air puffs up the clothes on the clotheslines. When the wind dies down, the clothes hang lifeless. When the air went out of ancestors they died too. Is this the same air that breathed life into Adam and Eve and into our family lines?

After we finish eating and Pa reads a chapter of the Bible, he places a long red ribbon at the page where he closes it, so that he can find the next chapter to be read after the next meal. The Bible is placed on the windowsill before he says his final, long prayer. Then we fidgety, little kids finish with, "Lord, we thank you for this food. For Jesus' sake, Amen." Pa's prayer before each meal is shorter, no doubt necessitated by hunger. When Pa finishes reading the Book of Revelations, he starts over at the Book of Genesis. "In the beginning God created the heaven and the earth. And the earth was without form, and void; and the spirit of God was hovering over the face of the waters. Then God said, 'Let there be light,' and there was light" (*Genesis 1:1-3*). That first chapter holds such mystery. I raptly listen to the line of days and how the Spirit of God moved to create the moon, stars, fishes, and beasts. How He breathed life into Adam and Eve.

Are family lines like Mother's string beans tied pole to pole with baling twine? Do we have string-linked roots keeping us in place? Like spiders spinning angel strands from leaf to leaf, will we bounce beyond the Milky Way? Does some invisible puppet-God pull strings, tying spines to roots? Do we come from seeds or from roots in the ground?

Rising from a crevice in a rock, a seed ascends to the sunlight by reaching for a drop of dew. Emerging from the seed is a microscopic hair of life that crumbles rock into sand and decomposes sand into soil. The soil supports the hair, whose breath is long and steady, biding its time. Without darkness, nothing comes to light. Maybe ancestors rise from the earth, their string-linked roots keeping them in place, reminding them of their place in the world.

88 "Dust to dust," says the preacher. Do we come from dust?

By age six I can almost recite all Ten Commandments by heart. We hear them at church services in Hospers every Sunday. During the service, the commandments come before The Apostles Creed and the long sermon. "Honor thy father and thy mother that thy days may be long upon the land which the Lord thy God giveth thee." I'm not sure if this commandment to obey Pa and Mother is the fifth or the sixth Commandment, but the days seem long enough. The minister drones on. "Thou shalt not kill." That's clear, but the next commandment isn't. "Thou shalt not commit adultery." Well, that's something to do with adults, so I'm not interested. At catechism class on Wednesday I will have to recite all Ten Commandments by heart, plus one Bible verse. The shortest one is easy to remember. "Jesus wept." Not easy to remember is where it's found, maybe at John 11:35—not at John 3:16; that's where the most important verse in the Bible is found: "For God so loved the world that He gave His only begotten Son, that whosoever believeth in Him should not perish but have everlasting life." That's easy, John 3:16 I could recite in my sleep, even while day dreaming; easy because it flows in rhythm. But it is no good to learn Bible verses for catechism unless I can recite book, chapter, and verse right afterwards and in the right order. Until I get it right, I'll be made to stand up and try again.

Where do we come from? Were we "begat" like God's "only begotten" son? Pa reads from the Old Testament. "Abraham begat Isaac and Isaac begat Jacob and Esau. Now it came to pass that ..." Pa goes on and on, reading a whole chapter of begats. From I Chronicles he reads the genealogies of the twelve sons of Jacob (Chapters 1-9) who became the twelve tribes of Israel. The language of the King James version of the Bible is a glimpse into another world—often a grim fairy-tale world. Before I am old enough to know the meaning of a three-syllable word, such as poetry, I memorize Psalm 23, Bible verses, and the Lord's Prayer. I can follow the rhythm and feelings of a Bible story: the scorching hate, the longing and desperation, frail beauty, betrayals, and conquests. Jacob's eighth son was Benjamin, his favorite son after he was told that his first favorite son, Joseph, had died. Benjamin became Jacob's right-hand son. His brothers tried to trade him in their dealings with the pharaoh in Egypt, but Jacob did not want to risk losing another favorite son.

The adventures of the brothers got pretty hairy, especially what they did to Joseph and his coat of many colors. But then, Pa would come to chapters of "begats" again.

Like the buzzing flies at the screen door in the July heat, the "begats" went on and on. Pa, himself, would get tired of the "begats," stumble over tricky pronunciations of Hebrew names and skip certain chapters. What the long litanies of "begats" revealed was that the "Tree of Jesse" and the "Line of David" came from Adam and led to the most important guy—Jesus. "And it came to pass" that my attention would wander, but then, gradually, each name took on some pointed meaning, and assumed the cloak of a story. Joseph became his Coat of Many Colors. Daring Daniel emerged unharmed from the lion's den, and Jonah came out of the belly of the whale after being swallowed.

Pa's sing-song voice blends lyrical beauty into the hard, work-a-day routines of farm life. He sounds like David singing psalms to Bathsheba while plucking the strings of his harp. Dependable, orderly, three times a day every day, we sit around the kitchen table to eat and hear that God is in His heaven and all is right with the world. Once, when God appears to Moses in a burning bush, God tells him who He is: "I am who I am" (*Exodus 3:14*). We too, are who we are and come from a long line of names. We are begotten, marked by God. "As far as I know," says Pa, "all of you are named after somebody, and that name means something too."

A name tells who someone is—where she comes from, her country and language, what culture and values she has been exposed to. A name places a person in a time period in the stream of history. For many generations our Dutch ancestors passed on their names according to a tradition that dictated which names went to whom and in what order. Additionally, a name might indicate the person's occupation, the place he or she lived, or something thought to be important about that person or place. The continuing line of a name in this way reveals hidden or forgotten family history. As a small child I would overhear Pa say to Mother, "Ja, on the way there, I will stop to see Aunt Grace by Ireton." Or it might be Uncle Syne by Hawarden, or Uncle Gerrit and Aunt Bertha by Lebanon. Naturally, name and place became a permanent association. In Holland, the common "van" preceding a Dutch surname means "by" or "from," and "der/de" means "the." My niece, Barbara Afman Houwer,

90   reports that:

> An elderly Dutch woman who grew up in Holland told me the fol-
> lowing about the name, "Kooi." Some people in Holland who have
> the profession of trapping, killing, and selling wild ducks are called
> "kooikers." They set up a trap or cage (kooi) at the edge of a pond or
> wetland area. Then they lure the ducks down with decoys (de-from,
> coy-cage), and herd them into the trap, or kooi. Someone named
> "vander Kooi" could be found van der kooi or "by the cage."

More about our name comes from sister Gladys:

> Many generations ago, the folks in the Netherlands were simply called
> Peter or John with no last names. It got to be pretty confusing. "That's
> John, you know, son of Henry and Henry's Dad was Cornelius—
> they were those birdcage people in Harlem." So finally, the authori-
> ties went from door to door and asked every one to choose a last
> name. Most often people chose a name related to their work, and
> since families stayed with the same business for generations, this was
> a very satisfactory thing to do. Onc family chose the name Van der
> Kooi, which literally means "from the bird cage" in Dutch, and, as
> with many Dutch names, eventually the "van der" was dropped. In
> our case, it now is simply Kooi.[21]

In an attempt to locate family lines and clarify the meanings of names,
I went to genealogies, archival records, graveyards, and recorded oral history
in places where family members now live or once lived. Doubts assailed me: If
I get it only half right, is it worth anything? "Get it right or forget it," Pa used
to say on the farm. His intimidating tone no doubt was influenced by his
Pa and brothers and those who went before them. Pa retorted to what he
considered just a story, "C'mon now, that can't be so."

Uncertainties prompt escape. Outside the room where I write is a bird
bath. Each day I fill the white basin with water. Red-headed finch congregate
on the rim. One dives in, another flies off, two fight, five gather to talk,

---

[21] Gladys Kooi Gritter, "Our Family Register" (1981). This 'Ancestral Book' contains Kooi and Sybesma history, much of it is oral. "Because our lines back tell
each of us much about ourselves, they also have a base line forward into the
future unknown to all but God. What the years hold for those who call us ancestors is in the hands of our almighty and loving God."

two to drink. A female chases off a male. They all leave but one. She bathes, splashing water out onto the surrounding soil where a group of birds congregate in the shower, chatter, bicker, then fly away. I, too, must fly away, go across an ocean, go back to the source waters of ancestors and then forward to the emerging tributaries of descendants. Before leaving, I ask my oldest sister, Gladys, for names of relatives in Friesland.

> At birth all we are is what all those before us have been. If our birth name were to accurately reflect this heritage, we would be given all the names of our ancestors. A boy would get his father's, grandfather's, great grandfather's names, plus all the names known before that. A girl would get the names from her mother's side. A boy would get many more first names. Ray would have gotten Fred, Remko, Pieter, Klaas, Benart, and more. But a girl would additionally carry many last names. I would have gotten Kooi, Sybesma, Kroeze, Kastein, TenBrink, and more. What a moniker that would be to spill out, to explain, much less to spell each time. Although too cumbersome for everyday use, such a practice would name our place in the stream of history.[22]

More than the accumulated names of ancestors or an identity on a passport, a name is a wellspring, a source that gives strength, establishing the way stations a person comes from, goes through, and is going to. "Irene" comes from the Greek "Eirene," personifying the goddess of peace, depicted carrying an olive branch. "Margaret" comes from Aunt Mattie, Mother's older sister, who brought small Ietje from Friesland to a new place: Iowa. From Mother's Friesian surname, "Sybesma," comes the courage to resist alien oppression. From my father's name, "Kooi," comes flight from the birdcage of being an isolated housewife. From my husband's name, "Chadwick," I draw on Scotch-German-English forbearance, and the kind of charity that starts at home and travels abroad.

To find family lines requires travel back to the graves of ancestors in Friesland to search for our roots. What I find are puzzle pieces from ancestral lands in Europe. From the Mediterranean basin comes the origin of the Christian Reformed Church, where baptismal waters map the past and predict

---

[22] Gladys Gritter, Journal No. 1, *Kooi Name*, pp. 6-80.

the future. In Israel, the 1989 Intifada evolved into images from the Iowa farm, somersaulting back into the shadows of World War II and Mother.

Cage

To unravel the fabric of Mother
I must let her pulsing heart
beat against its damaged rib cage,

the bird escape its kooiker.
Pulling her heart strings
through the body of Iowa

I must unravel each nerve
sting by sting. Let out
the breath of her finer spirit [23]

In twelfth century England, only the nobles perpetuated their family names, or "sir names." This surname was the family name or last name. Our Dutch ancestors perpetuated only their given names—also known as their first, Christian, or birth name. And so, several generations of one family might all have the same given names. This appears to be the case with Mother's side of the family until Napoleon conquered Holland and decreed that everyone had to take a surname.

During the French Revolution, Napoleon regarded Holland as a natural part of France, since it was made by the silt and ooze brought down from the rivers of France and Germany. He entered Holland and established a naval base, den Helder, on the North Sea. Some historians say that this invasion was good for the Dutch in that it brought with it the ideals of the French Revolution: freedom, equality, and brotherhood. Its impact has been compared with that of the Renaissance and the Reformation. In any event, the taking of surnames was mandated during French domination of Holland (1795–1814), but not enacted without struggle—especially in the province of Friesland.[24]

[23] Poem by author.

[24] Sacheverell Sitwell, *The Netherlands* (New York: Hastings House Publishers, 1974).

Napoleon wanted to centralize Holland's government, make provincialism disappear, and conscript new recruits for his conquest of the world. So, he made laws for the registration of deaths, births, and marriages. A first step was to order a census taken. The Fries are a proud people and they were reluctant to follow Napoleon's order, so Napoleon marched into Holland in 1805 and insisted that all Dutchmen adopt a surname. Historically, the Friesians are known to be an independent-minded people, even cussedly stubborn. Stolidly, vigilantly, they went about their business in an orderly manner, repeatedly ignoring Napoleon's order.

When he returned to Holland in 1806, he installed his brother, Louis Bonaparte, as "Napoleon I, King of Holland." The new king, however, immediately fell in love with the country and remained faithful to it until his death. He converted Amsterdam's Town Hall into a palace, renovated the Het Loo Palace in Apeldoorn, conferred the status of city on The Hague, and formed the Royal Institute of Arts. He also had an adverse effect on the country during the course of his reign. He closed down or suppressed the universities of Franeker and Hardewyk and reduced the universities at Amsterdam and Utrecht to secondary schools. In 1806 an economic depression was in full swing, so King Napoleon tried to reduce the prices of food but had little success. Furthermore, since his brother, the Emperor Napoleon, continued to see Holland as cannon fodder for the French Army, he urged conscription for all males above the age of twenty (one-fifth of the population). Although the King of Holland did his best to change the manners, habits, and customs of the Dutch people, he met with resistance, and in 1810, Emperor Napoleon forced his brother, Napoleon I, King of Holland, to return to France.

Now, Emperor Napoleon added the Netherlands to the French Empire and the Code of Napoleon replaced the ancient law of the land. Serendipity helped me find Napoleon's Decree on taking fixed Christian names when I was in Holland in 1995. I was with my daughter, Nanette Chadwick-Furman, of Israel, to care for her two-year-old son, Benjamin Chad Furman, while she attended marine biology meetings. Early one morning, Nanette and I loaded Ben and his equipment and stroller into a car for the drive from Heerhugoward to the Leeuwenhorst Congres Centrum in Noordwijkerhout. Here we left Nanette to spend the day at meetings. Then, with breakfast in Ben, he and I started out for Rotterdam. Several times I got lost in beautiful places where people smiled, Ben slept in his car seat, and I got tangled in dialogues leading elsewhere. When we finally found the docks and the Euromast tower, we went straight for ice cream in the adjoining park.

Reports indicate that all of Europe can be seen from atop the Euromast, but it was cloudy and anyway, we were there to look down at the docks where eight-year-old Ietje left the old world for the new. When we were ready to ride the elevator down from the top of the tower, we had a long wait. I was finally down to the last of the candy in my bag of tricks to keep Ben happy. A young couple was also waiting for the elevator and we began talking. After awhile we considered carrying Ben down the steps, but Ben's stroller was overloaded with baby stuff, and it looked like it might be a bit difficult to maneuver both him and his equipment down the narrow, spiral staircase. As they played with Ben and we began to get better acquainted, it turned out that the young woman, Karin Zuiderhoek, was an archivist based in Groningen and Leewarden, interested in documenting family history, and she said she would send a copy of the "Napoleon Decree on taking fixed Christian names."[25] The decree she sent to me was signed in both French and Dutch on August 18, 1811. Napoleon ordered everyone to take a surname. Births were required to be registered within two days of a child's birth, and a surname was required. Civil registration was instituted in the various provinces of the Netherlands. A census was ordered.

Again, these proud people, who spoke their separate language and remained separate in more ways than merely by geographic isolation, found a way to confuse and delay Napoleon. The third time Napoleon marched into Friesland and found that there was no census and no surnames, he promised, "When I return, you will have surnames or off with your heads, you infidels!"

---

[25] Louis Bonaparte, *Louis Bonaparte En Hollande D'pres Ses Lettres, 1806-1810,* Avec Un Portrait En Heliogravure, Andre Duboscq, Emile-Paul, Editeur (Paris, 1911). Three hundred letters written by the King of Holland about the war, royal house, family, etc. in French and Dutch. Decree is on p. 20, Art. 1-8, Signé Napoléon.

On December 12, 1811, the surname, Sybesma, was adopted by the Sybe and Sybes among Mother's ancestors. The suffix, "sma," means "son of," and Sybe means "Sam," so Sybesma literally means "Son of Sam." Each generation was now: Sam, Son of Sam (Sybesma), instead of only Sam (Sybe). Once again the Code of Napoleon was circumvented!

Mother's birth name, Ietje Sybesma, translated into English, is "Ida, Son of Sam." This explains the note on the last page of my 1994 book of poems, *Dawn Pearl*: Forthcoming from the Ietje Kooi Press is *MOTHER: SON OF SAM* by the Four Kooi Sisters. "Son of Sam" strikes a sinister chord in the memory of many people because he was the much-publicized serial killer, David Berkowitz. Ida, Son of Sam, however, was just the opposite of this notorious character.

The grave consequences of Napoleon forcing the name change in Holland resulted in fifteen thousand Dutch soldiers being conscripted to march with Emperor Napoleon Bonaparte to disaster at Moscow. Napoleon began his fatal Russian campaign in June, 1812. Only 25,000 people were still in Moscow when the French arrived on September 14, 1812. Napoleon's army could not be controlled, and they forced themselves into the palaces and rich houses. Some time after Napoleon's army arrived in Moscow, the Russians still remaining in Moscow started setting fire to the city, eventually burning it to the ground. Frustrated by the loss of his prize, Moscow, Napoleon left on October 19, 1812, with 87,500 infantry, 14,750 cavalry and 533 guns with a trail of some 40,000 carriages and wagons. As they retreated, snow bogged them down and most of them froze to death.

By 1825 the French had been gone from The Netherlands for eleven years, but the Dutch continued the French methods of civil registration. "The Royal Decision of William I" declared that still too many people did not use a fixed Christian name and that they had to get one within six months; otherwise there would be a penalty.[26] Exact outcomes of this insistence on a surname may never be known, but records kept in the Sybesma family

---

[26] Willem I, "Staatsblod," (November 1825): 1-4; contains Royal decree, ordering the Dutch to take surnames. Translated by Karin Zuiderhoek, archivist for Province of Groningen, The Netherlands.

Bible show how the Sybesma name changed through the years, although the Sijbes changed their name to Sijbesma in 1811, not all family members had adopted the same surname by 1813. By the year 1844, however, Sijbes had changed to Sijbesma. Since "ij" was often changed to "y" in English, and the Dutch and English languages have many similarities, it is easy to see how Sijbesma became Sybesma.

Some Friesian families kept the old spellings so that Siebesma, Siebersma, and Sybesma evolved into different family groups. The various Sijbesma Families started in the south and moved north, then northwest. They apparently originated in the 1700s in the south of Friesland around Sneek, Tjelleberd, and other small towns. Then they moved on to the north around Dokkum, Hiaure, and Metslawier, where Sijbe was born in 1817. By 1834 they had migrated to the Franeker area near Barradeel, Oosterbierum, Pieterbierum, and Sexbierum, in the lea of the North Sea, as shown on the map at end of the chapter.

Before the Dutch were forced to take surnames, the patronymic rule was used in many parts of The Netherlands, especially the rural areas. The patronymic rule in the northern provinces was to add an "s" after the father's first name for the child/son. This might skip a generation, going from grandfather to grandson. Suffixes used might be "dtr" for "daughter of" and sen/son for "son of." This is seen in the Sybesma family, going back seven generations, starting in 1721. Five generations progress from Sibjes, to Sibje, to Sijbes, to Sybesma (son of Sybe), then to Sybe Sybesma (Sam, son of Sam.) In the two genealogy charts at the end of the book, it appears that the patronymic rule applied to female as well as male names: Auke became Aukes. Bregtje went to Brechtje, then to Bregtje, skipping a generation each time. Frederik went to Frederika, then skipped a generation and went to Frederick. Tracing the progression of these names was confusing because of the repetition of the same names in siblings and cousins as well as in the direct line of ancestors. In addition, the same Dutch word that means cousin also means nephew or niece.[27] See Genealogy Notes and Charts in appendix.

In Holland, the new surnames were referred to as geslachtsnamen: adopted, accepted, or fixed surnames. In defiance of French rule, some Dutch people took facetious names, which they later were stuck with, such as Naakgeboren (born naked) or Dodeman (dead man). Some took names from what they did, from where they lived, or from nicknames. Some were serious about it, while others found humor in taking funny names.[28]

Naming a new generation after the ancestors was a tradition carried on by the immigrants in America. From a handwritten part of "Grandmother Remembers" by Ida Kooi, Denver, Colorado, 1983:

> I named Raymond Kenneth after his two grandfathers, Remko and Klaas, Gladys Irene after grandmother, Grada, and myself, Clarence Frederick after Klaas and Fred, Bernice Lorraine after my mother, Bregtje, Peter Benjamin after Pa's brothers, Peter and Ben. Stanley John after my two brothers, Syne and Sam, and Pa's brother, John. Verna Mae–I just liked that name. Gertrude Mildred I named after my two sisters, Mattie and Gertie. Irene Margaret I named after myself and Maaike, my sister who died at age seventeen, Elmer George after Pa's two brothers, Ellis and George, and Harold Glenn after no one.

My husband and I did not realize how similar the name, Brandt, is to

---

[27] Letters and genealogy charts from Grace Anne Sybesma to Gladys Gritter in the 1980s. Letters from Rinske de Boer, Amsterdam, to author included documents: Begraafplaats (Cemetery) Pietersbierum. Genealogysk Wurkferban Fryskeakademy, pp. 3d, 29, photographs, and information about Friesian graveyards and Dutch relatives, 1995. Oral history from Klaas van der Schaaf, in Aalsmeer, The Netherlands, 1995. Records in the Sybesma Family Bible, Platte, South Dakota. "Family Register" by Gladys Kooi Gritter, 1981. Although documentation exists, it is complicated, confusing, and conflicting. Since I lack knowledge of both the Friesian and Dutch languages, I have been cautious in my use of interpreted documents and letters. Although cousins translated copies of original documents, any errors likely are mine.

[28] "Naamsaannemigen or Name Adoption," Vol. 8, No. 2, pp. 44-45 and No. 1, p. 3, from Quarterlies of the "Dutch Family Heritage Society," Mary L. S. Parker, Ed., 1995.

Brent when we named our first son Brent Douglas Chadwick. His namesake had appeared in three generations. Before my daughter, Nanette Chadwick Furman, gave birth to her second son, she asked for a list of family names from past generations. It included Henry, Gerrit, William, Ralph (Roelf), George, Jacob, Herman, Brant (Brent), John (Jan), Sam, Benart (Ben), and George. She and her husband, Yoel Furman, named their second son Adam Samuel—Adam to honor his Jewish father, and Samuel to honor her Sybesma forebears. "Syne or Sam" comes from "Samuel," which comes from the Hebrew name, "Shmuel," which means, "He who hears God."

The custom of honoring and remembering a dead child by giving the next-born baby the same name continued through many generations. The first child of Brandt and Maaike was a son, Sybe, born in 1813. He died at age four, a month before the next son (their third child) was born in 1817, in Hiaure, and given the same name, Sybe. Their eighth child, Cornelis, died the day he was born, and the son born five years later was given the same name. Both died in Sexbierum, Barradeel, where the last seven of Brandt and Maaike's children were born.[29]

Bregtje Kroese Sybesma named her tenth child, Ytje (same as Ietje), after her older sister, Ytje, who had died as a baby. Mother carried this naming custom with her to the New World and continued it in Iowa thirty-six years later. Ytje, now Ida, gave birth to Elmer George, her seventh child, who died soon after birth. In keeping with tradition, she named her next son, Elmer George. Aunt Mattie also did this. She gave birth to her first child on August 26, 1912. Baby Betty died seven months later, but Aunt Mattie was already four months pregnant, and she named the second baby, born August 25, 1913, Betty.

Fred and Ida Kooi gave names to their twelve children that both go back and forward in time. My father, Frederick Kooi, was named after his grandmother, Frederika (ten Brink) Kastein and after his grandmother's father, Frederik ten Brink. What we children always called our father was

---

[29] Gladys Kooi Gritter, "Sybesma Oral History: Things Mother Told Me," *Family Register*, 1981.

Pa. He and Mother passed on his name to their second son, Clarence Frederick, who in turn passed it on to his second son, Richard Fredrick Kooi, who became known as Rick. He and his wife, Therese, named their son Peter Raymond Kooi. In doing so, they have carried on the tradition of nine generations, perpetuating the names, Remges, Remgo, Reuben, Remko, and Raymond; also Pieters, Pieter, and Peter. It is a wonderful thing, the way the same names, derivatives or similar names, weave through many generations—a heritage of some importance. For example, the Dutch names, Remgo, Pieter, Klaas, Sybe, Geertje, Metje, Boukje, and Bouke have become the American names of many descendants named Raymond, Peter, Clarence, Stanley, Gladys, Gertrude, Margaret, Barbara, and Bernice.

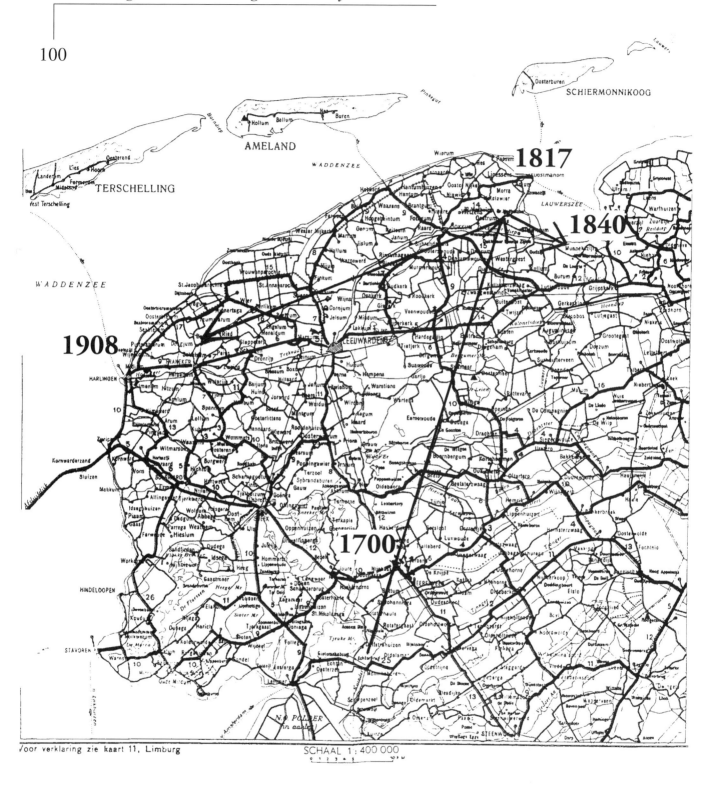

Migration Routes from 1700-1908 of the Sybesma, Siebesma, Sijbesma,
& Siebersma families in Friesland. In 1908, the last three of Klaas and
Bregtje Sybesma's five living children immigrated to Iowa, ending the
Sybesma family line in Friesland.

The Netherlands in Western Europe.

11

Ear Irons

Above the piano in the front parlor of the farmhouse hang two oval portraits. Thick wires stretch from each heavy frame to a nail secured in the top of the picture molding going around the ceiling. Both portraits tilt forward, making it appear as though each face is bulging out. Heavily grained, dark frames accentuate the long, stern faces with unsmiling eyes. Stiff white cloth completely covers the woman's head and ears. Both the woman and the man wear black.

"Why does she wear that white cap with wings over her ears?" I ask Mother. Her answer is vague.

"Are her ears cold?"

"Oh, I guess that was the custom then." Mother's voice is dismissive. She does not appear to want to talk about these portraits. Some sort of enigma shrouds them.

Impertinently, I go directly to what I want. "Who's this man? And who's this woman?"

My parents in the old country.

"Why are her hair and ears all covered up like that?"

Guess that's what they wore then.

"Doesn't she have hair?"

Mother is busy and doesn't reply. She hopes I will go away, but instead I crane my neck for a better look at the portraits high above me and press on. "Well, where are her ears?"

When I turn around, Mother has left the room.

Each time I sit on the piano bench to bang away on the black and white keys, I gaze at these austere, black and white visages. The fading shine of the protruding oval glass covering the portraits magnifies the stern gray of their taut skin and makes the whiteness of the cap with wings stand out. I study the faces before turning away. As I leave the room I shrug my shoulders to shuck off something that feels faraway and faintly threatening. I try to dispel their daunting gaze and the puzzling intrusion of foreboding into my carefree thoughts. Like Mother, I turn and leave.

The grandmother wearing the curious cap with her ears ironed into white wings was Bregtje Syne Kroese Sybesma. The portrait next to her is grandfather Klaas Sybesma. Travel guides written at the time they lived in Friesland, plus current books on Dutch art, discuss the emergence and history of these head coverings, called Dutch muts [cap], flodder muts [soft cap], oorijzer or earizer [ear irons], and casque [helmet]. The reasons these caps with wings came into being is not entirely known. Probably they came into use for decoration, feminine artifice, the necessity of a practical expedient—all of these reasons or some of them. Hendrik de Leeuw tells us "These odd headdresses were worn by the women working in the fields to keep off the flying sand; but as time went by, they became the fashion." Apparently they denoted where the particular person came from, and gave an idea as to the age and religion of the wearer.[30]

> First of all the hair was drawn back and coiled round a pad of cotton wool, under a cap of black sateen. Over this, the oorijzer, the golden casque of the Friesians, was worn, and the ornamental ends of that hung down below the ears. The foundation of the Deutsche muts was a white lace coiffe of especially fine texture which was stretched tightly over the gigantic wire brim of the cartwheel or tambour, so that it fell like a fringe all round the brim. The Friesian ladies in their cartwheel hats had a walk and a carriage conditioned by their fantastic headgear.[31]

The grandmother above the piano was the fifth child of Gerrit Synes Kroeze and Brechtje Sjoerds Kramer, and she was named Bregtje Syne in accordance with tradition. Their sixth child, Bauke, died at age fourteen. The seventh, Rensche (1864-1935), married Jan van der Laan (1864-1934). Although Mother had no recollection of any grandparents, she did remem-

---

[30] Nico Jungman, text by Beatrix Jungman, *Holland* (London: Adam and Charles Black, 1904), 60, 61.

[31] Sacheverell Sitwell, *The Netherlands* (New York: Hastings House Publishers, 1974), 83, 88.

ber her Aunt Rensche van der Laan. "They had five children and lived in Harlingen by the Zee." The two families would visit back and forth. Mother's family lived in Franeker, and it is likely that they walked the six or eight miles back and forth. It was probably an all-day expedition with a picnic along the way in the countryside. The books of that day paint bucolic descriptions of such all-day family outings. Apparently they would prepare for the outing many days beforehand and leave quite early in the morning. Along the way, songs were sung, games played, and conversations engaged. Unexpected occurrences became family lore. After spending the day with the van der Laan family in the Zeedyk, they likely would have returned to Franeker on foot. The van der Laan parents lived to be seventy-nine and eighty years old. Their home is now gone. "We had to leave because of restoration (making it more sturdy) of the zeedyk," their daughter, Ytje, wrote to her American cousin, Ietje. Both had been named after the same aunt.[32]

Of the five van der Laan children, the oldest, Geertje, died in 1960. She had married Klaas van der Schaaf, who died in 1969. They had a farm and two children, Rinsche and Doerke, whose son, Klaas van der Schaaf of Amsterdam, visited Mother in Denver in 1982. Mother was pleased to see him. The second van der Laan, Ynskje, married, had one son, and died when she was 55. The whole family is deceased. The third, Ytje, married Sjoerd de Groot and died in 1984. They had two children, Pieter, who lives in Sint Jacobiparochi, and Rens, or Rinske, who lives in Sneek. The fourth van der Laan was Cornelis who, in old age, lived in the same place as did his sister, Ytje. He left a farm to his one child, a son. The fifth, and last, van der Laan, Sientje, was named after Sijne, her grandfather. She married Dirk de Boer, who had a painting business in Sint Jacobiparochi. Their three daughters live in Holland. The adult van der Laan family is shown in a studio photograph taken about 1930.

When George and Gladys Gritter traveled from their home in Michigan to Holland in 1982, they visited two of Mother's van der Laan cousins,

---

[32] Ytje de Groot in Sint Jacobiparochi, Friesland, to Cousin Ytje (Ida Sybesma Kooi) in Denver, Colorado, letter dated November 1982.

106   Sientje de Boer and Ytje de Groot, also Ytje's son and his wife, Pieter and
Tietje de Groot. Mother was thrilled that her oldest daughter, Gladys, could
visit these Dutch cousins that Mother had not seen since she was eight
years old. Gladys recorded the trip:

> We had an address of Mother's first cousin in Sint Jacobiparochi, but
> we didn't know if she was alive. We met her son, Pete de Groot. With
> him and his wife we had tea and rolls that she had baked. They had
> just finished reading yellowed letters received by his mother, Ytje (Van
> der Laan) de Groot, from Uncle Sam and Aunt Mattie in America
> many years ago. Pete then took us to see his mother in Tzummarium.
> Ytje was then in an old folks home, but she remembered Mother and
> the whole family of her Aunt Bregtje and Uncle Klaas. She could not
> believe that someone had come from her Aunt Bregtje's family in
> America to see her 75 years later. She remembered when the three
> orphans left on the boat in 1908. When I said who I was, she couldn't
> get over it, saying, "Ach Heiden! I can't believe it!" But, I had pictures
> to prove it, ones of Mother's family and Mother and Pa, also one of
> the five Sybesma couples taken in 1930, which she really liked. She
> was so surprised—and very glad we came. She remembered when
> Metje, 21, Sybe, 12, and Mother, as Ietje, age eight, left for America.
> She and her Mother cried, but Metje said, "In the U.S. we'll have
> more food." She never saw any of them again.[33]

Not only was Ytje surprised to see her niece from America, but Piet
and Tietje de Boer also were surprised by this unexpected visit from George
and Gladys. Tietje said, "As we say in Dutch, suddenly you fell out of the
air and there was no time to prepare." Pieter de Groot took them to see a
younger sister of his mother, Ytje. This sister was Sientje de Boer. She did
not remember any of the Klaas Sybesmas. Her husband was a painter. She
served coffee and cake to George and Gladys. After that trip to Holland,
Gladys wrote to these cousins for a few years, and they also wrote to Mother
and sent pictures. Sientje was then learning English. Mother's namesake,
Ytje, died in 1984. Ytje's twin brother had died right after their birth in

[33] Gladys Gritter, "Our Trip" (August 26, 1982), p. 31.

1898, and another small child had died four years previous to the birth of these twins.

In 1995 I was able to visit three van der Laan cousins: Klaas van der Schaaf (of Geertje), Pieter de Groot (of Ytje), and Rinske de Boer (of Sientje.) We share the same Kroese great-grandparents. Countless Sybesma cousins now living in America also share these same grandparents and great-grandparents. As mentioned previously, in 1995 my daughter, Nanette Chadwick-Furman, traveled from Eilat, Israel, to Amsterdam with her baby son, Benjamin, and I met them there. One day we went to visit Mother's nephew, Pieter de Groot, and his wife, Tietje de Groot, who live on part of their original family farm at the edge of the village of Sint Jacobiparochi, Friesland.

The barn adjoins the house, lovely in its appointments, generous in amenities, commodious. Lighted candles are set on a coffee table with fresh flowers. Silver tongs for sugar cubes are set in their bowl next to the pitcher of cream. Coffee cups match the saucers set out next to a platter of sweets. Slices of chocolate-frosted, chocolate-chip cake are artfully arranged next to cookies. The napkin holder shines next to silver spoons. Little comforts are respected. They make us feel at home. Their gracious, crusty-Dutch conservatism and sturdy composition feels good, as right, familiar, and settled as the Iowa farm. In my bones I feel as though I am he, I am she.

Piet gets out World War II correspondence between two cousins—Brand Sybesma in Sint Jacobiparochi and Sam Sybesma in Platte, South Dakota. They had been friends in Friesland and started corresponding after Sam went to America in 1908. He would always share these letters written in Dutch with his sisters, Ida and Mattie. After Sam's death in California, his daughter, Carol, apparently continued this correspondence. In March of 1976, both Brant and Jantje were still living, at age 87. The correspondence spans half a century and I was happy that Piet de Groot of Sint Jacobiparochi, Friesland, loaned some of these letters to me in 1995.

Piet and Tietje show us around the lovely, rustic peace that is their farm. We walk on gracefully winding paths. The cultivated wild is made mannerly with narrow paths of newly laid sawdust. Benches are at scenic bends in the path. Reflected in the green waterways, the barn adjoining the house is just as it has been for centuries. The tall reeds that continue to grow out of the narrow waterways provided the thatch from which the roof of the barn was made. Tietje points out that the thatched roof of the barn, the shed, and the house appear as head-neck-body (kop-hals-rump.) When we return to the doorway of the shed, Piet obliges us by putting on his well-used wooden shoes. Replicas of such klompen have come to characterize Holland, lining the shelves of souvenir shops. I feel so pleased that today we are not tourists, but family.

My daughter, Nanette Chadwick-Furman, recorded Mother's memories of what had happened in Friesland when she was young. Some discrepancies exist between her records and those made by my mother and sisters and the data I found in original documents. This is understandable. Mother was very young when she left Friesland, and her memories were recorded toward the end of a long life. However, Mother kept in her mind an incredible number of names of relatives and endless details about their lives. She could, it seemed, go on forever about which relative was living where and doing what, the prospects, whereabouts, and welfare of second and third cousins. Growing up, I could not have cared less, but now I see the wisdom of recording names, dates, and places of interest. Mother was an uncanny chronicler of things like how many bales of hay or jars of tomatoes were put up, and what was always important to farmers: the weather. Even in her last years of life, Mother kept track.

During my 1995 trip, I was curious and sensitive about the reason the two orphans, Ietje and Sybe, with their older sister, were not taken into the homes of their Friesian relatives after their mother and then their father died. The customs of generations of ancestors prompted me to assume that related families would honor, protect, and support small children, orphans particularly. The love of children seemed to be a deep-seated teaching, handed down, and certainly not simply an individual thing that my parents possessed. Predictably, I did not find any answers during 1995. I think part of the reason may be that immigrating was then quite popular. At that time Europeans were flocking to America, Metje had been instructed by her dying father to keep the family together, and their only siblings already were in America.

While I was in Holland, my second cousin, Rinske de Boer, living in Amsterdam, took me to see her mother, Sientje de Boer, Mother's last living cousin. In her home in Sint Jacobiparochi, Friesland, we sit around the dining room table and sip coffee. As we talk, my eyes stare at a shining helmet behind the glass doors of a locked cabinet. "Yes," I am told, "that is an oorijzer, in the Dutch language, an earizer in Friesian. In English, you say ear irons."

Van der Laan family in Friesland, Netherlands, 1930.

Five Sybesma immigrants with mates L-R: Sam and Carolina, Fred and Ida,
John and Mattie, Gertie and Watse, Syne and Stena, Iowa, 1930.

Family reunion of Remko and Grada Kooi's nine children with mates
L-R: Adrian and Jennie, John and Gertie, Ben and Lura, George and Grada, Pete
and Gertie, Case and Grace, Gerrit and Bertha, Ellis and Christine, Fred and Ida.
Sioux Falls, South Dakota, 1938.

Tietje with husband Piet de Groot wearing klompen (wooden shoes shown below), while author's grandson tries on her eye glasses, Friesland, 1995.

Silver oorijzer (in photo above) is worn by author (in photo below) with second cousin Sientje (van der Laan) de Boer, Friesland, 1995.

Portraits above piano: Klaas and Bregtje Sybesma,
Franeker, Friesland, 1903.

Bregtje Syne Kroese and Klaas Sybesma, Franeker, Friesland, 1903.

116

Gravestones in churchyard for
Bregtje Kroese's brother and sister,
Wijnaldum, Friesland, 1995.

12

Friesland

Before we meet, I feel her presence. This cousin was born three years later than my mother so they only could have known each other as toddlers between 1903 and 1908. Now, Sientje van der Laan de Boer is eighty-nine and frail. Her house is surrounded by blooming flowers on the edge of the village of Sint Jacobiparochi in Friesland. As her daughter, Rinske de Boer, and I enter, I see that Sientje has the same smile as did my Mother, and the same kindly, quiet temperament. Nothing is hurried. Out the window fields stretch into the flat space of green distance. Conversation is contained by familiar polite constraints and the same circumspect looks from eyes I know. They are as comfortable as my own body, as though I am revisiting childhood. I am touched by the daughter's bustling concern for her mother; in many ways Rinske is so much like my own sisters and their manner toward my mother as she aged. My sister, Vicki, wrote this about our Mother:

Lineage

too frail
almost
for this world's use
like the chrysalis
that the moth leaves
after summer's molting
paper-thin
and vulnerable—
she set her skinny shoulders
sharp against each new day's
hurt

and yet
there was a quiet strength
that filled her every way
a line of steel
connecting

118

her frail existence
to eternity
and me.... [34]

We sit on chairs around the end of the dining room table. Coffee and cakes are spread on a Friesian table covering, which is a stiffly thick carpet with a pastoral design in the deep, rich colors of forest and sunset. In the dining room, traditions are observed. So much is conveyed without words. So much is known in silence. So much has come from the landscape of Mother's body when I was in her lap in the rocking chair, sensed in the moment, once. Sientje is like Mother in movement, manner, and nuance. With us, their children, they sing the same dependable lines.

From my home in California, I carried copies of two hymns from *The Psalter Hymnal*, the book we used to sing from at the church in Lebanon and Hospers. "We Praise thee, O God" and "We Gather Together" use the melodies of Netherlands folk songs from 1625, translated in 1882, and arranged between 1838 and 1914. Together, Sientje and I hum the tunes and sing a few words, she in Fries and I in English. We are kept going by Rinske. In starts and stops, our voices blend to carry music from the past into the future. Singing with this grand old lady lets me experience what it might have been like to have a grandmother. Soon, I will return to America with my daughter, Nanette, and her baby son, who will travel with me to Michigan for the Fred and Ida Kooi Family Reunion. Here, three generations of our family will gather to sing hymns, play games, and share stories.

Back home, my husband's eyes sparkled when he heard a beautiful melody coming from a recording of a Haydn quartet. As I hummed along, he looked awed. "Do you know that tune?" "Sure, it's the melody of a hymn." "Can you sing the words?" Of course, in church in Iowa we often sang the words to this melody composed by Franz Joseph Haydn in 1797. John Newton wrote the words for "Glorious Things of Thee Are Spoken." I remember

[34] Vicki Peterson won Second Prize for "Lineage" in the 1984 Annual Bards Poetry Contest, Grand Rapids, Michigan.

most of the first verse, but have to get out the old *Psalter Hymnal* from the piano bench to sing the words for the second and third verses. As I sing, memory straightaway pipes in the plaintive voice of another hymn that Mother sang softly to herself: "I come to the garden alone / while the dew is still on the roses. / And the voice I hear / falling on my ear / the Son of God discloses. / And, He walks with me / and He talks with me / and He tells me I am His own." I hum along-side the voice I hear in my head as the shadow of my mother dances around the room to a tune remotely familiar to one my own shadow sings.

In Friesland with Sientje and Rinske, through the glass doors of the locked cabinet, I see trophy spoons, photos, and the shining helmet. Is this helmet the same kind of odd headdress that was used to cover the hair of my grandmother in the portrait? From the unlocked cabinet come old pho-tos of distant relatives. Out come silver trophy spoons won for keatsen, and this game played by our great-grandfather in 1835 is explained. I am so moved by emotions that whether keatsen refers to the spoons or the game is lost on me. Neither do I grasp the details of how the game was played. Eagerly I wait to touch the shining oorijzer, the treasure. But then, when it does come out of the cabinet, our different language, and my own memories of that white cap on the dark grandparents in dark frames above the piano in the front parlor, get in the way. And so, the when-where-how-why of this cap remains a mystery. Quite quickly the visit is over, and it is time to leave.

Rinske and I travel on to the Rembrandt statue in the center of the village of Sint Jacobiparochi. A KOOI sign in the next village becomes a Bierma connection, linked to Mother's new parents and new life in America. Across the road is a large old home with a windmill where we enjoy a lunch of tasty smoked eel. Good coffee and sweets end the meal, and we resume our trip, passing villages on country lanes under the vastness of the land and sky painted by seventeenth-century Dutch painters. There are only ten to thirty houses in these villages, no McDonalds or Texacos. They are built around terps: large man-made mounds thrown up long ago in the people's constant endeavor to secure living space clear of marsh and flooding. At first they were simply homes, but then the Friesians built farms on these terpen and entire villages gradually grew up around the mound. In today's Friesland the church

120 remains central—highest on the terp, ringed by a moat of grass and a road, and then homes. Roots were left in these mounds—gravestones in the churchyards next to the churches, spiritual havens, the remains of a people inclined to the earth for sustenance. While walking in these churchyards, I feel as though time is standing still. The clotheslines on the Iowa farm carry me back to "Washday," by Friesian poet Durk Van Der Ploeg.

Washday

Our mom did the wash every Monday on the doorstep
Never was the sky lighter than on those days
And by noon, with everything on the clothesline
Up in the wind, our terp was highest of all
She emptied a little box of blue into the water
Never was blue as white as then
When our mom rinsed out the washing with blue
And made the whole terp rise
Then our house was a ship at sea
That set full sails and hurried off
Hard into wind to the churchyard
Which is why, I think, the evenings were sad
When our mom was folding the clean clothes
We were being destroyed under heavy skies
The lamp was beating yellow and I could smell
The light, the wind, the blue from the washing [35]

Today, Friesians produce thirty volumes of poetry per year in a language that is submerged under the official language, which is Dutch. Friesian can be read by 65 percent but written by only 10 percent of the Friesian people. They have a Friesian Academy, a community of scholars that has produced some 700 scholarly volumes in its fifty years and is at work on a 20-volume Friesian dictionary. They really do ice-skate on canals and eat cheese for breakfast and argue about the nationalism they are supposed to have lost 500 years ago. And hun-

[35] "Washday" by Durk Van Der Ploeg in *The Sound that Remains: A Historical Collection of Frisian Poetry* (bilingual ed.), translated by Rod Jellma, (Grand Rapids, Michigan: Eerdmans Publishing Company, 1990).

dreds of them every week use the Friesian Dial-a-Poem service.

Another country lies within Holland. Friesland is a country of farmers, something of a pastoral kingdom, a land apart. Historically, the Friesians seem to be the real indigenous tribes of Holland. As far back as we can go we find them in the province that still bears their name and is occupied by their descendants. The first permanent settlers between 6000 B.C. and 4000 B.C. were seafarers, farmers, artisans, hunters, and merchants. Around the fifth and sixth centuries B.C., the Friesians arrived. Their territory extended from the present Dutch-Belgian frontier to the River Weser in Germany. The northern part of this country, a fertile region because of the deposits of clay, was the center of the Friesian settlements.

Tradition says that in the fourth century B.C., Frisio and his two brothers fled from an insurrection. After many adventures, the three brothers landed in and built a temple to Thor—in their language, the god Stavo. Very soon a town sprang up around the temple and was called Stavoren. This seaport reached the height of its prosperity in the thirteenth century and is the ancient capital city of the Friesians and the oldest city of the Netherlands.

A Greek explorer named Pytheas, in 325 B.C. reported seeing along that "Coast of Awe," to be known later as Friesland, a strange rising and falling that suggested to him, aptly, a sea lung. The climatic and geographic oddities of the place, wind and fog; shifting mud and silt; tide water creeks and gullies like wheezing bronchial tubes; sand dunes walling in dismal swamps and flat green land, much of it below sea level, has, from the start, made Friesland and Friesians strange, mysterious. When the Romans came, about 50 B.C., they found the Friesians living on artificial mounds called terpen, the earliest versions of modern dykes. Eyewitness Pliny the Elder with the Roman legions gives us this view:

> This miserable race occupy elevated patches of ground built up by hand above the level of the highest tide ... resembling sailors in ships ... shipwrecked when the tide has retired. They catch the fish escaping with the receding tide.

Another view comes from Max Schuchart:

> To get out of the floods and tides, they spent twelve centuries moving mud, building terps (mounds of earth, five to forty acres each, sometimes thirty feet high), building 2,260 of them. It is estimated that the Friesians moved 100,000,000 cubic yards of clay for no other reason than to raise themselves out of the water. Compare with this the feats of the Egyptians, who raised (to the honor of the pharaohs) only 3,500,000 cubic yards at Cheops, 4,000,000 at Mycenium. The terps are not registered as one of the wonders of the world, but perhaps the stubbornness of the workers ought to be.[36]

Friesland is only 1,277 square miles, including its four North Sea islands, and it has more black and white Holstein-Friesian cows than people, more bicycles than cars. Most of the 600,000 inhabitants live in no less than 450 villages and will tell you that they are not Dutch, or that they are only secondarily Dutch, and that their language is not a dialect of Dutch but a separate language.

When Rinske and I drive into the village of Holverd, a farmer on a bike leans into the window of our car and engages Rinske in a long conversation in Friesian. Meanwhile, I enjoy his ruddy face, square sturdiness, and smiling eyes. At Metslawier we search for names on tombstones. We talk while we drive on through the glorious green, past flocks of sheep, black-and-white Holstein cows, fields of vegetables—red cabbage, green cabbage, potatoes, more potatoes, golden grain—water everywhere, and bridges. We are never out of sight of farms and windmills and of villages nestled on the gentle green terpen. Names, places, and people get linked. Generation to generation, connections are made.

The ancient language, Friesian (Frysk), is the only blood relative that Old English has, and has been the vehicle of Friesland's survival, despite the various languages that rulers tried to impose on them. Historically, the Friesian people have resisted absorption into the Dutch language and culture of the Netherlands. The motto, "Frysk en Frij" (Friesian and Free), is

---

[36] Schuchart, Max, *The Netherlands*, (Great Britain: Walker Publishing Company, Inc., 1972), p. 50.

a potent slogan still used, perpetuating freedom and pride in Frysk. The slogan goes back to the times of danger from the Vikings and to Charlemagne's granting of liberty to the Friesian people.[37]

123

> Friesian is spoken in most rural areas, but in the larger towns, a compromise language, half-Dutch and half-Friesian, the so-called "Town Friesian," is commonly used. Prior to 1500 the Friesian tongue was not only the natural medium of the inhabitants of Friesland but also the usual language for official purposes. After the alien House of Burgundy was established in 1524, a mass of Dutch-speaking officials entered the area, and Friesian was ousted from official use. Since the language of the Church now became Dutch, even the countryside lay wide open to Dutch penetration. Not until the early 19th century did a Friesian Movement begin. The formation in 1844 of a "Society for Friesian Language and Literature" marked the beginning of the organized Friesian movement. The path of the would-be restorers was not a smooth one. The church, for one, was most unsympathetic, and it was not until 1943 that a Friesian version of the whole Bible appeared. Since the Second World War it has been usual for street names to be posted in both Friesian and Dutch, e.g. Ljouwert—Leeuwarden.[38]

Mother emigrated from Friesland when she was age eight and learned English right away. Pa was second-generation Dutch. However, we never

[37] Charles V. J,. Russ, ed., *The Dialects of Modern German* (Stanford, CA: Stanford University Press, 1989), p. 1.

[38] Lockwood, W. B., *An Informal History of the German Language* (Cambridge: W. Heffer & Sons, 1965), pp. 221-222. Fisher, Raymond. *Frysk-Ingelsk Wurdboek* (Frisian-English dictionary). That the Frisian word, "wurdboek", sounds so much like the English "word book", demonstrates the practical and close similarity of the Frisian and English languages. Other examples include Forward and Foarwurd, cigar and sigaar, character and karakter, freeze and frieze. Indeed, Fisher states that "at an earlier stage in their development, Frisian and English were more closely related to each other than any other surviving language." (Source: Fisher, page iii) Wurdboek is woordenboek in the Dutch language. People in the countryside and the villagers speak Frisian, while the official language in the schools and cities is Dutch. Friesians loaned money to American rebels against King George, and they recognized the new country early—and officially.

124 heard them speak Dutch or Friesian except for the rare occasions when they wanted to discuss something that they did not want us to overhear. Mother did occasionally sprinkle her English with Dutch words, as recalled by her oldest daughter, Gladys:

> Like salt on food gives it seasoning, so the Dutch words gave a rich ethnic flavoring to her speech. It took years before we kids knew which words were Dutch. Two words I remember well were 'snookie' and 'sonicky.' Never mind the spelling-I have never seen them in writing. 'Lief snookie' or 'kleine snookie' or simply, 'Oh, you little snookie, you' were endearments and said in the most endearing way. 'Lief' means darling and 'kleine' means small, but what 'snookie' means I have no idea. If it is not Dutch it is probably a Mother-made-up-word. She would look lovingly down at her nursing baby and coo 'lief snookie.' Or, pat a two-year-old on the head and exclaim, 'Oh, you little snookie, you.' As she kissed a little daughter who had managed to pull a sock on, she would murmur, 'kleine snookie.' The word, 'snookie,' makes me feel soft and tender and warm. I like the word. Then there is 'sonicky'—a very different word than 'snookie.' 'Sonicky' means crabby, hard to please, ornery. I can still hear my Mother say, 'Oh, what sonicky children you are today!' and shoo us all outdoors. Small kids who were tired were called sonicky and big kids who were difficult were called sonicky. The word, 'sonicky,' reminds me of Mother's hard, angry—and patient—look. I did not like the word, but I used it when my kids were small, and they didn't like it either.

"Kids," we were told, meant baby goats, so instead we were supposed to use the word "children." Vernacular usages such as "I ain't" were out. Some words were considered proper nouns and therefore capitalized: God, of course, Mother and Pa, church leaders such as The Consistory of Elders, the Deacons, and the Pastor. At that time and in that place, elders held a capital place and expected to be honored and obeyed. "Capital" and "capitol" came up in spelldowns at school or word games at home where their uses and meanings were explained. The word "ass" was a word in the Bible that meant donkey. Expressions such as "the hell with it" or "dammit" were never heard. The nearest to a swear word was "heck" or "gee" or "golly," but we were taught not to use such words because "heck" was too much like "hell," and "gee" or "golly" like God. "Oh!" was the word to use, but not "Oh my God!" since we were not to take the name of God in vain or to disobey any of the other nine commandments. It was okay to use, "For Heaven's Sake!" or "Heavens to Betsy!" Often used was the word, "ya", like "yeah" in the dictionary, but I never saw it written and did not know that "ya" was really the Dutch word, "ja."

Certain words had hidden meanings. On icy winter mornings when snow covered the path to the two-hole toilet outdoors, smaller children used a potty in the kitchen. The Friesian word "vies" which sounds like "feas," was Mother's denigration of dirty pants, but "vies" meant more than dirty. It was a derogative implying something bad, obvious to us as small children because "vies" was the look of disgust on Mother's face and the smell coming from an uncovered potty that we had forgotten to cover and shove out of sight behind the far end of the kitchen stove. Mother's turned-up nose greeted other things she did not like, such as filthy hands at meal times or dirty rags that were not put away. "Vies" was applied not only to what came out of our little bottoms but also to our fingers when we touched anywhere "down there." With the passage of time, "dirty," "filthy," and "disgusting" became associated with lower things.

After every meal Pa read a chapter from the Bible to the family around the kitchen table so that, from an early age, I heard the Old Testament phrase, "and he laid with her." This meant that husband and wife got into the same bed. What more happened I could only guess from the looks in adult eyes or the shuffling of feet under the table. In the world I knew, all boys and girls grew up to marry and have children; every mother and father had their own bedroom and closed their door at night.

Leeuwarden and Franeker are places in Friesland that Mother knew when she was a child. Most likely she saw the same landscape studded with windmills that we did as Rinske and I drove around Friesland: enormous low farmhouses standing among clusters of out-buildings thatched with moss-covered straw, land immensely fertile, and fields a matchless green. The farming people cluster together in small groups of tiled farmhouses surrounded by acres of pastureland and thousands of sheep and cows. The day before Rinske and I visited her mother, Sientje, in Sint Jacobiparochi, I had been in Franeker with my daughter and grandson to see where Mother lived as a child and to look for the gravestones of her family. It was easy to see how the house Mother was born in would have fronted on a canal. The large cemetery is nicely landscaped, but we found no graves for the nine family members Mother left behind when she came to America. Neither had my sister and her husband found any graves when they looked for them in 1982.

When I tell Rinske that we enjoyed a picnic lunch on a hillside lawn in the graveyard, she gets a very surprised look on her face. "Do you picnic in graveyards in America?"

"Sometimes, yes."

That night I tell my daughter how Friesians eat off a thick brocaded rug they put right up on top of the dining room table—a carpet just like we walk on! That same night Rinske is phoning her news to friends. "And you know, those crazy Americans, they picnic in graveyards!"

"No. Really?"

"Yes, that's really what they do."

The next evening, Rinske and I laugh about our separate misconceptions while we enjoy a delicious dinner that includes fish's tongue. A few years later a visitor from Holland tells me that "fish's tongue" is actually "tong," which is Dutch for sole.

13

Dutch Traits

"Where did you ice skate?" I ask Mother. I am five and the only skating I know about is roller skating at the Roller Rink in Sheldon. The only ice is icicles hanging from the eaves of the house, growing longer each wintry week, nearly reaching the ground before Spring. I know nothing about bodies of water larger than the creek trickling through the cow pasture and the black water at the bottom of the well. Those rare times when the pump breaks and is lifted off the well to be fixed, we belly flop down around the edge of the well and look down. The black water reflects a circle of dark eyes in little faces, and we stare, awed by the dark spaces between our pairs of eyes in the faraway water.

"You fell in!"

"Look."

"Do you see you down there?"

We giggle and chatter, poking each other, elbowing one another to keep our place in the crowded space around the rim of the well. Only seconds elapse before the dark mirror of water is broken. One by one, pebbles are shoved over the edge. Plop. Plop. Each pebble sinks. Then a tiny twig floats.

"Stop. Mother said not to throw things into the well."

"Don't be a sissy."

"You dummy, we drink that water." Another pebble hits the water, and another, then a stone. Ripples grow into shimmering waves and distort the faces looking up at us. "Look at your face!" We make fun of each other in the wavering images we see below us until we hear a stern voice. "Now you kids, you know better than to play around that open well. Stay away from there." Off we run, breaking away from the mysterious reflections and glittering light.

The black pools in Mother's eyes wear a whimsical crinkle as they look beyond me. Her voice is lilting into a rhythmic answer to the question I impatiently repeat. "Where did you ice skate?"

"Zuider Zee, you know, Zee the sea, the Zuider Zee." She pauses to see if I pick up the rhyme and rhythm. As I nod, she continues, "Maybe it was called something else too. I think so. We skated on canals too." She pauses to let that sink in and then notices that I don't know what a canal is. Her explanation comes in staccato breaths as she kneads bread dough. "Like streets—only made of water—ice in wintertime, many canals all over, right in front of the houses."

Incredulity raises the tone of my voice. "Just down your front steps you would be right on a street of ice?"

Ice. I belly flop on the sled as it begins to go down the hill in the schoolyard. Ice glints off the steel runners of the sled as it picks up speed. A patch of ice races by close to my face—too close. The fear of falling pulls me back to an earlier image of Mother in winter. I am getting ready to go outdoors to play in the snow, engrossed in untangling the long yarns that dangle from the sleeves of my snowsuit so that I can pull on my mittens. The long strings are there to keep the mittens from falling into the snow and getting lost when we pull them off, as we always do. As I strain for the door, trying to pull on the jacket, Mother sing-songs a rhyme, "Three little kittens lost their mittens, and they began to cry, 'Oh my, oh my, our mittens we have lost.' Lost your mittens you naughty kittens? Then you shall...." I don't hear the rest, because now both of my rubber overshoes have been pulled, pushed, and tugged on over my shoes and I am out the door, lickety-split.

Little Ietje learned to ice skate on canals as soon as she was big enough to grasp the back of a chair and push it along on the ice. This was not unusual.

As soon as they can walk the little Hollanders are encouraged to skate, and children of four or five years are adept in the art. During the rigors of a Dutch winter, the people, rich and poor alike, keep themselves warm by vigorous skating. The frozen canals become the roadways to all parts, and all the world is out on skates, on business or pleasure bent. It is wonderful to see a many-skirted peasant woman gliding airily along, sometimes balancing a heavy basket on her head, sometimes pushing before her a sleigh evolved from a packing-case and containing a freight of laughing babies. Then glance at her skates: the blades are probably rusty and notched, and kept on her feet with bits of string which appear to be utterly inadequate. [Note: Bone tied to a shoe also served as a blade for skates.] The Dutch skaters do not, as a rule, practice the intricate figures so beloved by enthusiasts in other countries. Distance and speed are the qualities they strive after, and for these, handsome prizes are given in the skating competitions that form the chief amusement of the winter. Frequently the fields are flooded for acres and acres, providing an excellent skating-ground, which has the advantage of being perfectly safe. The ice in the smaller canals gets very much cut up; but in the great centers armies of workers are employed to keep it in the best possible condition. In Groningen and Friesland Dutch skating is to be seen at its very best.[39]

The inland sea Mother knew in the gentler cadences of childhood as "the Zuider Zee… and something else too…" is the Ijsselmeer, created in 1932 by blocking the Noord Zee with a 20-mile-long dam. For six hundred and seventy years this inlet of the sea had been periodically reclaimed by dams and settled as *polders* on farms clawed out of sea water. Friesland is reached by a causeway over this great dike that seals the entrance to the inland sea, known as the South Sea, from the North Sea, or in Dutch: the Zuider Zee from the Noord Zee.

Though not often mentioned as such, this causeway is among the great engineering feats of modern times. It is our conviction that the Dutch alone are capable of this continual and methodical surveillance, without which their country might disappear at any moment beneath the sea. It is owing to their perseverance, the skill of the engineers, and the enormous outlay contributed to by all the citizens that Holland strives against the waves, and still floats on the surface.[40]

[39] Nico Jungman (text by Beatrix Jungman), *Holland* (London: Adam and Charles Black, 1904).

[40] Louis Keymeuler, "The Country", from *Holland*, collected and edited by Esther Singleton (New York: Dodd, Mead and Company, 1906), p. 22.

Driving over this causeway into Friesland in 1995, I began to realize the tremendous impact that such continual watching must have had on the emergence of the Friesian people, their character molded and continually buttressed like this long dam—reinforced like the terps to withstand flooding by an angry, relentless sea. Control of the elements meant control of feelings, and the self presented to the world became poker-faced, stodgy and stout, dour and careful. Out of necessity, a strong will was developed to control raw emotion so that the elements of nature could be kept in check.

How geography and history color the landscape and the character of the Dutch has engaged the imagination of various historians, reporters, novelists, poets, and adventurers. Also, guidebook writers at the turn of the century did not hesitate to comment on the manners, customs, and personality of the Dutch while recommending what sights to see. Some of the many character traits they mentioned rang true to my own experience, while others did not. I doubt if their neatly laid-out streets reflect neatly-ordered, interior lives. But yes, thoroughness may contribute to being critical of self and environs. I agree that the Dutch tend to be a weighty people, physically and psychologically, with much religious pondering and many cautious business dealings. The Dutch people were known for their bargaining and merchant skills. The housewives in Sioux County, like their *huisvrouw* forebears, tended to be substantial women, sometimes wearing a bit too much weight. Although Mother tended to be quietly substantial in spirit rather than body, I recall that she, like my aunts, was slow to anger, patient, good-natured, kind and generous.

Dutch women were characterized by early writers as having homely virtues, their thrifty and modest households having no debts; as industrious, house-proud, chaste women. The men were characterized as hardworking, plain speaking, and soberly dressed, God-fearing burghers who honored contracts and obligations.[47]

[47] Simon Schama, *The Embarrassment of Riches—An Interpretation of Dutch Culture in the Golden Age* (Berkeley: University of California Press, 1988).

Early travel writers described dutch-clean habits:

> Servants are deluging the windows with water, and others are
> even brushing off the lamp posts. You will notice, as you extend your
> walks, that the same mania for cleaning exists in the rich as well as
> the poor homes.[41]
>
> With the Netherlands huisvrouw, clean has become a reli-
> gion. In Veere I saw the girls even wash and scrub the pebbles in
> front of their houses. In the Holland hotels, the first thing that strikes
> one is the snow-white linen, with windows as transparent as the air,
> furniture that shines like crystal and floors so clean that, as my mother
> always said, they were clean enough to eat from.[42]
>
> I call this obsession with cleanliness the sacred life of things!
> In Dutch, schoon means beautiful and at the same time clean, as if
> neatness was raised to the dignity of a virtue. Every day from early
> morning, a psalm of washing, bleaching, sweeping, carpet beating,
> and polishing hovers over the whole land.[43]

On the farm, spring and fall housecleaning were major undertakings.
Pictured on the ever-present can of Dutch cleanser in the kitchen was a
housewife attired in a long blue dress, white apron and winged cap. She
wielded a broom. Gladys recalls that:

> Housecleaning on the Lebanon, Iowa, farm was a twice-a-year
> job. Until I was through grade school Ma had a hired girl for house-
> cleaning. Perhaps she stayed a month or more. Every room in the
> house got a thorough cleaning. We had a system. Early in the
> morning we hauled the mattress outdoors, laid it on three or four
> saw-horses. It would air all day and before taking it in we'd beat
> all the dust out with a carpet beater. Then we took everything from
> the windows. Curtains were probably washed later, but we washed

[41] Keymeuler, op. cit., pp. 46-52.

[42] Hendrik de Leeuw, *Crossroads of the Zuider Zee* (New York: Arco Publications Limited, 1957), p. 166.

[43] Zbigniew Herbert, *Still Life with a Bridle* (NJ: Ecco Press, 1991), p. 9.

the shades, laying them flat on a big table or clean floor. Then we would sweep down the wall-papered walls and ceiling. Next, wash all furniture with clear water and the chamois skin. Then the windows, mirrors, etc. and finally the floor mopped and waxed. In the evening, before supper, the mattress was brought in and the bed made. All done! It was a big day's job for one room—but then it was "deep" clean for another half year.[45]

A glance at a topographic map of The Netherlands shows it in the northwest corner of the continent of Europe where the North Sea laps at a massive mass of sand and alluvium. The land rises almost imperceptibly by gentle inclines to join itself to the plains of lower Germany and the moorlands of Belgium. Holland is the muddy delta of an inland sea, three great rivers, plus numerous waterways. In addition, relentless as the tide, the North Sea keeps gradually rising over the gradually sinking lowlands of Northern Europe. So, to protect this delta against rivers flowing down toward the ocean on the one hand, and from the North Sea off the Atlantic Ocean on the other, means that strict attention must be given to the solidity of the dikes and the efficacy of drainage arrangements. A system of sluices is combined with that of the dikes as a means of defense against the waters. This phenomenon appears to have had the most influence on the character of the Dutch.

> In their struggle against wind and water, they have become as unbending as the elements themselves. The will to remain upright throughout any ordeal translates itself into the Dutch character: direct, stolid, unrelenting; some call it stubborn, others say resolute and enduring.[46]

The national motto, *"Luctor et Emergo!"* literally means to bend the land from the sea—to come up out of the water—which is exactly what

[45] Gladys I Gritter, *My Memories* (Grand Rapids, MI, 1984), p. 28.

[46] Max Schuchart, *The Netherlands* (Great Britain: Walker Publishing Company, Inc., 1972), p. 70. Written in the postwar Holland of 1945 with notes added for 1972 revision.

the Dutch did and continue to do: grapple with physical forces and emerge to the light. Unless they persevered, the powerful, pervasive sea would submerge them.

Heredity seems to play a role in the evolution of national character, as it does in families. Much of the present-day structure of Dutch society and the national character of the people can be traced back to the late sixteenth century when the nation was born. While creating land from sea, the early Friesians earned a reputation for being stiff necked and argumentative. To describe the geography of Holland as a body allows metaphoric insight into the Dutch character. A body of land, a vertebrae of islands, arteries of water, and veins of mud, mark the substance and subsistence, the persistence and flow, of Dutch history.

The Zuider Zee, which has been in existence as an inland sea some six hundred and seventy years, created the peculiarly recessed coastline of the Netherlands, with its outline of islands like the vertebrae of a spine. Without the stiff spine of the people, there would be no Netherlands today. As children we often heard these remonstrations, or variations of them: Stand up for yourself! Where is your spine? Figure it out for yourself!

On the map the Friesian Islands appear bent to shield the lowlands from the blows of the North Sea. In reality the islands act more like a sieve the sea shoots through to periodically flood Europe's low countries; more like a string of delicate pearls lying on the heaving bosom of a landed lady dressed in delicate lace. Canals crisscross the land from terp to terp, water towns surrounded by reeds stand in wet sloughs, and wind buffets clouds that scud overhead. In the face of this, the Dutch became cautious and resourceful. Their success in drying the polders, some of which are twelve to fifteen feet below sea level, necessarily inspired them with great confidence in their resources. The force of the sea also served as a means of defense against foreign invaders. Several times in their history the Dutch chose to undo the patient toil of years and let loose the all-devouring waters rather than to deliver themselves into the hands of the enemy. Always, the Friesian people rode the edge of the European continent, and the edge of their existence as a nation as well as their village life. This attached the Dutch to what is, rather than what might be.

134   The physical peculiarities of Holland have influenced our domestic life to a great extent. What I mean to say is that the necessity for constant labor and struggle and perpetual sacrifice in the battle against the sea have always kept us to a sense of reality and have made us a highly practical people. Because of this, and because of our qualities of prudence, phlegmatic activity and love of conservation, we prefer to stay put or hang on to what we have got, since we do not know what we may get. That is why we cling so stubbornly to our age-old traditions and why we have preserved these customs and traditions despite the fact that we are surrounded by so many nations.[47]

Although the "Free Friesians" movement was active before the American colonies were free, it was more acceptable to their nature to resolve their worries by arguing than by using guns. In 1626, Dutch settlers bought the island of Manhattan from Native American Indians for the legendary price of sixty guilders. In New Netherland, they were reluctant to use arms at first, preferring to engage in the lucrative fur trade. However, by the 1630s, they were brutally crushing the "River Indians." In 1664 the Dutch lost New Netherland to the English and it was renamed New York.

    Throughout our American struggles, Friesland and its freedom-loving burghers were always in close touch with us. Friesland was the cradle of liberty and not only was the first to show its resentment towards Britain, but also the first to show its heartfelt sympathies for the American colonies.[48]

The Friesians had their own language, own flag, and even their own breed of cows. They are—even today—characterized as an insular, self-sufficient, and in-control people. A Dutchman's habitation, be it the merest hovel, is very much his castle, and in the small villages anything short of extreme courtesy is liable to meet with a severe rebuff. A villager is

[47] de Leeuw, op. cit., p. 249.

[48] de Leeuw, op. cit.

quoted: "We cherish that home so well that we rarely leave it, but spend our time there amidst those we love. That may also explain why we drink much, eat much and smoke much and," he chuckled, "why we have children much."[49]

They take religion seriously and abhor idleness. "When they meet in council to deliberate upon the affairs of the village, each man brings his knitting in order not to have his hands unoccupied."[50]

On Reading Dutch History

How limited. How small.
What islands our minds really are—
so much boundary—
when all around us lies a sea.
We in the Netherlands,
where the North Sea must invade,
keep plugging dikes with fingers,
The past is a sea
invading our landscapes
our art, customs and dreams.
Through and through I am Dutch.
I read not about the past
but about myself.[51]

[49] Jungman, op. cit., p. 250.

[50] Sacheverell Sitwell, *The Netherlands* (New York: Hastings House Publishers, 1974), pp. 13-14, 143.

[51] Poem by author appeared in *PenWind*, newsletter of the Modesto Chapter of the National League of American Pen Women, Linda Sawyer, ed., 1996.

14

Ietje in Friesland

Klaas Sybesma was twenty-four and Bregtje Kroeze nearly twenty-three when they married on May 19, 1883. Bregtje Kroeze's family was against the marriage. Mother's memory of this is that "He was thought to be a TB (tuberculosis) person." Whatever the case may be, we know that Klaas sold coffee, tea, and cheese from a cart pulled by two dogs. The family had meat only when a farmer gave them the head of a pig or a cow. Carts drawn by dogs were not unusual then. Carts were used to transport cheese, cream, or other farm produce and also were used by vendors.

> On the narrow roadway of the dikes trundled gay little handcarts propelled by men or drawn by dogs and loaded with large cans, painted light blue and red. These were on the way to the farmhouses. And everywhere, as far as the eye could roam over these flatlands, were hundreds of cattle—the finest I have seen anywhere in the world—ruminating, chewing their cud and snuffing the sweet, moist, early-morning air.[52]

Between 1884 and 1904, in the space of only twenty years, Bregtje gave birth to twelve children. The couple gave each baby the middle initial of K. According to the family Bible, "K" stands for Kroeze. However, in common use then was the use of the father's initial for a second name. And on burial records, the second name for each child is a K. for Klaas, S. for Sijne, G. for Gerrit. So, the middle initial, "K", was given to distinguish the father as K. Sybesma, and not the children of his brothers, Sijne or Gerrit.

During the first two years, Klaas and Bregtje lived in Pietersbierum, where their first two babies were born. Apparently, sometime during 1886, they moved to Osterbierum, where two more babies were born. Sometime between the fourth

[52] de Leeuw, op. cit., p. 20.

child in 1888, and the next one in July 1891, they moved to Franeker. Here, eight more babies were born. The three villages where they lived are in the Province of Friesland near its capitol, Leeuwarden, near the North Sea and the Friesian Islands. They are also close to a large inland sea variously called the Zuider Zee or Waddenzee.

Immediately outside the front door of their one-room house in Franeker was a sidewalk with a canal right next to the sidewalk. According to Mother, "Beds were built into the walls, two on each side. I guess the babies were put on a top bunk. Potatoes were stored under the beds. There was a table and a cabinet. In the evening we went outside to shut the blinds on the windows."

> Friesian family members slept in the typical old-fashioned, hole-in-the-wall-style bed found in nearly all Friesian dwellings. At night they would open the double doors of the spooky aperture, place a chair in front of it, kneel by the chair to say their prayers, and then step on the chair to climb into the high and chilly bed, drawing the doors almost shut behind them. Ventilation? What did those good-hearted old Friesians know about oxygen and the like?[53]

The typical Friesian farm had the cowshed attached to the house, similar to attached garages in America. I saw this kind of attached cowshed at the ancestral farm of Pieter and Tientje de Boer in Sint Jacobiparochi, Friesland, in 1995. In this northern land, the climate for most of the year is not congenial for being outdoors because of the rain, fog, wind, and snow. Here, animals as well as people must have protection from the elements, and so, it is practical to have the shed attached to the house.

The first baby born to Klaas and Bregtje Sybesma was a daughter, Geertje, on March 17, 1884, known to us in America as Aunt Gertie Bierma. Next came a son, Syne, born the next year on June 25. Another daughter, Metje, arrived a year and a half later, on January 27, 1887. Born the next year, on August 10, 1888, was another daughter, Maaike. With these four small children the parents

---

[53] John Monsma, "Farewell to Windmills and Dikes," *Origins*, XIV, no. 1, 1996, pp. 32-38.

moved to the town of Franeker, where the next two sons were born. Sybe came on July 21, 1891, when baby Maaike was three years old, and then another son, Bouke, was born in April of 1893.

That same year, the young couple saw the death of two sons. In August, Sybe died at the tender age of two, and then in December, Bouke, their eight-month-old baby, died. Three years later, when another son—the seventh child—was born, they named him Sybe to honor their deceased son. The second-named Sybe lived a long life, growing up to become a mischievous lad in Franeker, and then later on, our beloved Uncle Sam in Platte, South Dakota, known for the merry twinkle in his sky-blue eyes.

During the last three years of the nineteenth century, a baby was born every year in the Sybesma home. In 1897 the first of these three babies was named Ietje, but the next year Ietje died in February at the age of seven months. Bretgje was already pregnant. The second of these three babies was named Bouke. He died in January of 1899 at only five months of age, the second boy named Bouke to die as an infant. Again, Bregtje was already pregnant, and she named her third baby Ietje, who became Ida Sybesma Kooi, our Mother. Born in the Friesland of 1899 on September 6, this tenth baby for the Sybesma couple perpetuated the name of Ytje, the baby who had died a year and a half earlier ("ie" and "y" being the same, pronounced with a long "e"). When their eleventh baby was born in 1902, they feminized Bouke, (the name of their last two sons who had died as babies) to become Boukje, by adding a "j".

That same year Klaas and Bregtje Sybesma said goodbye to their oldest son, Syne, who emigrated to America sometime during 1902. In Friesland, the Sybesmas were very poor, and they believed that there was no future for their children in Holland. They hoped for a better life for them in America. Ietje was two years old when her oldest brother left to make a new home and life for himself; and when she was three, her oldest sister left as well.

Friesians in the area of Barradeel were severely hit by the agrarian depression of the late nineteenth century, which gave a substantial impetus to mass emigration. Almost 10,000 people left the clay region of Friesland between 1880 and 1914. Most emigrated because of economic and social burdens, although some left to escape military service or be reunited with family who had gone ahead.[54]

In 1979, my daughter, Nanette Chadwick Furman, recorded the memories of her grandparents for a paper that her sociology professor required about a major group of people in the making of America. For this paper, "The Dutch in Iowa," she asked her grandmother how it happened that she came to America. "Well, Aunt Gertie was the firstborn, you know, who wanted to go to America. And she saw to it, and my father did too, that there was no future at all in Friesland, the wages so low and the country wasn't prospering." Then, in that confidential tone of voice of someone remembering something revealing, she went on, "So, she must have come here second then. I heard that Syne dodged the draft! When he was eighteen years old, my brother would have had to go, and he hated that so much. So, when he was seventeen..." This memory made Mother's voice drift. "One came, then another one would come. As soon as one had earned a little money, he would send it over. They helped each other that way.

"Syne came to the United States with two other boys in 1902. His Uncle Gerrit had died in the army, so our parents were glad to send him to the United States. Then, a year later, the oldest daughter, Geertje, went to America. She was nineteen and had a boyfriend who had come two years earlier, but when she got to America, people told her not to marry him because he couldn't stick to a job. So she didn't. Instead, she became a housekeeper for an old man in Sioux Center. Later, she met Watse Bierma and married him." Apparently, the boyfriend, Klaas Meyer, was upset about being jilted and demanded the return of his sponsor money. So, after Geertje married Watse Bierma some three years later, Watse put together the ocean fare and paid off the debt.

In Franeker, the year after the two oldest of the family had left for America, the twelfth, and last baby, was born. Daughter Egberta lived only

[54] Annemieke Galema, "Frisians to America, 1880-1914, With the Baggage of the Fatherland," *Origins V*, no. 1, 1997.

six months, dying in September 1904. The week before her parents buried Egberta, their fifth baby to die, Ietje turned four. Maaike was ill with tuberculosis, and at sixteen, she sometimes came home from the sanatorium. Since she was contagious, she had to sleep in a separate bed. Not much else is known about Ietje's life before she was seven, except that she played with her little sister, Boukje.

Two years later, in 1906, death claimed three more of the family. In March, Maaike was the first to die, at age seventeen, from tuberculosis. In August their mother, Bretgje Kroese Sybesma, died, at age forty-six. In November their little sister, Boukje, died at the tender age of four, of whooping cough. Already dead were two sons named Bouke, and now Boujke, the daughter named after them, was dead as well. A succession of birth, sickness, and death had been in the life of the family, but the year of 1906 must have nearly broken their spirits.

Seven of the twelve children—and the mother of the family as well—were dead. Except for tuberculosis and whooping cough, the causes of these deaths are not recorded. Perhaps they were "failure to thrive," malnutrition, other diseases, or a combination of causes. Four had died as babies, two before the age of five, and one at age seventeen. Two of the twelve children had emigrated to America. Only four of the family of fourteen were left in the Franeker home: the father, Klaas, the older sister Metje, little brother Sybe, and little sister Ietje. Like her own mother, little Ietje would become a mother of twelve children, but only two of her children would die while still young. Later in life, as Ida Sybesma Kooi, she told her children that she remembered very little of her own mother except that she was always sickly, had a poor back, and was in bed a lot, and finally, the doctor coming every day.

Absorbing these stark facts gives me an understanding of the mother I knew when I was little, particularly her fears for our safety. Many times she warned, "Watch out!" She nursed us through many childhood illnesses: two types of measles, mumps—first on one side, then on the other side of the face—chicken pox, ringworm, impetigo, the seven-year-itch, sprains, colds, and fevers. When all four of us youngest came down with the hard measles, Mother made the front parlor into a hospital. Each of us had our own bed, on the davenport or some sort of cot. Our older sister, Bernice, home from wherever she was working, became our nurse. Drawing the shades to protect our eyes, she would make rounds every morning and evening, sticking a thermometer under each tongue, applying a damp washcloth to a hot forehead, giving a backrub, or relieving the angry red of itching bumps with a special salve. The dishes of ice cream she brought were a rare treat. She wore a halo. Her touch was that of an angel.

During the same year of 1906, after three family members had died, Klaas became ill. On December 29 he went to a hospital in Leeuwarden, the capital of Friesland. This town was then quite a distance from Franeker for the children to go to see him, but all three found a way to visit him twice. Metje was older and able to go more often. Mother recalled, "Our father was never strong. He had had tuberculosis when he was young. He was always sickly that I knew, the doctor coming every day—socialized medicine, you know."

As the year, 1906, ended, Metje was in charge of her little brother and sister. Sybe was eleven and Ietje seven. Metje was nineteen, turning twenty at the end of January in 1907. The doctor in Franeker wanted to adopt little Ietje because he and his wife didn't have children. However, their father, Klaas, in the hospital with bladder cancer, said, "No, the family should stay together." Mother recalls that "The doctor was a tall man with a cane." In the hospital, Klaas wrote to his children.[55]

Leeuwarden, Jan. 23, 1907

My dear beloved children.

Well, here is a letter from me. Right now I am in the Bonevacius hospital in Leeuwarden. But you probably know this already. I was admitted December 29 and have been here almost four weeks. Well dear children I haven't improved much, there is still blood in my urine. I have to pee every hour. The doctor is afraid he may have to operate on me, he told me this twice al-

---

[55] Twelve Sybesma family letters written between 1907 – 1975 were translated at Heritage Hall, Calvin College Archives. Curator H. J. Brink returned these letters with translations to Gladys Gritter on May 17, 1993.

ready. Well, my dear children, I leave this up to the Lord and the doctor.

They take good care of me, the food is very good. Sometimes I get bored laying in bed all the time, and when the doctor examines me, then I have a lot of pain. Pray to the Lord to give me strength and grace to carry this heavy burden. I remember our Lord telling Paul: "My grace is sufficient for thee." Well, dear children, I don't know when I will be operated on (the operation is dangerous) but I know if the Lord wants to take me away from here I'll pray his grace will bestow upon me. I know you understand that this life doesn't mean much to me.

Oh, children if mother was still alive she would have cried a lot; but on his wisdom the Lord took her away. In the meantime, it is now Monday January 28, a week later, and I better finish my letter. I don't know anything, the doctor said nothing about the operation, maybe he is not going to operate after all. There is here a gentleman with the same problem. He has been operated on for the third time so he is worse than I am.

Well, dear children, Metje visits me every four days. I think she will come tomorrow. Seibe and Ytje visited me twice. I am laying in a ward with 8 other men, they all have their problems, what a suffering! This is a Catholic hospital and the nuns take very good care of us, they are so sweet.

Well, dear children, I have told you all about myself. Now you know how I am doing. My sincere thanks for the 20 dollars. If it is God's will to take me away from here, I am ready to go to Him. I pray that the Lord will strengthen you when I depart from you; and that the Lord will take care of dear Geertje. This letter is also for my Son Syne. Dear children, may the Lord bless you and give you whatever you are in need of—body and soul, that is my wish.

Loving wishes from your father
K. Sybesma

Klaas Sybesma wrote a last letter to his oldest child, Gertie, in America, and Mother read this letter to my daughter and me in 1979. "Who would have thought that the Lord would give us such a heavy load to carry? But, He will give us strength also." Then, her father quoted from St. Paul: "My strength is sufficient for you." Mother added, "He knew his Bible. That 1907 Bible I have yet. Gertie gave it to Syne. Then Sam got it. Now I have it." Today, that family Bible is kept by Clarence Sybesma, Sam's son, in South Dakota.

In the spring the doctors operated on Klaas, but he got worse instead of better. The three children's last visit with him was shortly before his death on May 5, 1907. He wanted them to sing a Dutch hymn he liked called "Ga niet alleen door't leven." Apparently he was aware that this might be their last visit. When she was eighty-two years old, Mother translated, and then sang, this hymn in Dutch. She emphasized that she was translating it, "As I remember it."

> Go Not Alone Through This Life
>
> Go not alone through this life
> The burden is too heavy for you
> Go to your Savior now
> There is so much to grieve for
> And so many tears
> And so much sorrow to bear
> Go not alone

Klaas Sybesma was forty-eight when he died. His youngest son, Sybe, later became our Uncle Sam in South Dakota, where he wrote a letter, dated December 18, 1961, to his cousin, Brant, in Friesland:

> Burial spot of my parents, if I remember right, is in the second block on the left side and on the northeast side when you enter the cemetery. My sister, Maaike, and my mother are in the same grave, and a Roman Catholic girl was buried there too, but later they moved her to the back. The grave digger has all the records. The location of the other graves I've forgotten. We buried so many loved ones there in such a short time, but with the confidence that they're now in glory and there's no burden, no grief nor sin nor parting.

In 1995, in Franeker, Nanette, Ben, and I went to a huge graveyard with woodland hills lovingly sculpted into gardens—but found no gravestones for Klaas Sybesma and Bregtje Kroeze Sybesma or their seven children. The search for these graves has led to what appears to reflect not only customary Friesian burial practices but also the poverty of the Sybesma family, evident from various sources. Since land was scarce and valuable then, the practice was to bury one body on top of another. In this manner, one grave could contain several members of one family. By 1907, however, there most likely were not nine members of the family stacked one above the other in a common grave. Each time the grave was opened to be re-used, any body that had decomposed to bones would have been taken out and disposed of in order to allow space to receive another body. Only a casket and a layer of earth would have separated each body. If no one paid for the upkeep of the grave, the burial plot could be sold to someone else. So when the Sybesma family's common grave was needed, their bodies and bones more than likely were dug up and disposed of.

> For lack of space in that densely populated land, people are often buried two in a grave. A little girl was buried right on top of Grandfather. Many of the graves receive bodies every fifteen years or so. That is about the length of time it takes a body to decompose and molder to dust in that soil and climate. Some of the larger bones may be left at the end of that period, but if they are, and if the "bodily remains" of some other burgher have to be stowed away in the same grave, the grave digger simply collects the old bones and dumps them in the charnel house back of the church building. I took a peek in that charnel house once upon a time—and shuddered. A veritable hillock of bones! The skulls, femurs, and hipbones of a thousand or more Friesians—men, women, and children—must have been collected there.[56]

Metje became solely responsible for Sybe and Ietje after their father died. "She saw to it that we kept together," said Mother. Metje was age twenty and she turned her mind to getting the last three members of the family in Franeker to join their sister, Geertje, and brother, Syne, in America. During the time that it took her to find money to buy passage to America, she had to find ways to feed them day-by-day. Families then were very poor. Apparently, farmers would "dig peas and thresh them" (take them out of the pods). They would bring a 100 pound sack into town so people could clean the mud from the peas and put the peas into smaller bags. This made money for Metje, Sybe, and Ietje—both during the time their parents were

---

[56] Monsma, op. cit., p. 34.

146

very ill and dying, and then afterwards. To feed her two small siblings, Metje also did what her father had done: sell cheese from a little cart.

With a spirit of adventure made inventive by necessity, Metje devised ways for small Ietje to help earn money. She taught Ietje several verses to sing while leading the dog pulling the cart filled with cheeses. Ietje was quick to learn. Metje made up more verses, which she taught little Ietje to sing as she pushed the cart around. The dog was docile. Money came in, however slowly. They ate. They waited. In September of 1907, Ietje turned seven. As it got dark in the evening she often heard her older sister call and call, then call some more, for Sybe to come home. Finally, dark would close in, and Metje, afraid that Sybe might have drowned in a canal, would take Ietje by the hand and go look for him. As a young woman, Metje had already closed in death the eyes of nine family members. The fear of another must have been on her mind often. Everywhere there were canals and waterways. I asked Mother if she and Sybe could swim. She said she did not remember ever swimming in a canal, but she did recall that when the canals froze over, she would sell suckers, two for one cent, to the skaters. "I can remember going to a nursery when I was about four where I could play with sand and toys. We played 'Ante Ante Over,' the game where a ball was tossed over the outside toilet."

Although enough money to buy food for the children had to have been a worry for Metje, an even greater worry must have been their health. The letters from the two siblings in America and also from common knowledge, would have let Metje know that if she took the two orphans to America when they were not in good health, they would either be held in quarantine on Ellis Island or be sent back to Holland. Of course, American immigration authorities might not accept them anyway, but to go without being perfectly healthy—having lice, tuberculosis, or any kind of injury or ailment—was unthinkable.

Sybe had a fascination with the outside world. Apparently he had inherited good looks and a charming disposition, and he made good use of them. When he took off in the morning to see what the world was made of, he inevitably would come upon an adventure beyond his ability. He hurt his ankle swinging on an iron door. They waited for Sybe's ankle to heal.

When that healed, he got injured again. In Mother's words, "First, Sam got his hand in some machinery and was injured, then he was burned badly when a kettle of hot water tipped on him." For a while, the doctor came every day and they had to wait some more. The winter of 1908 was nearly over before his burns healed.

Evening came. Metje and Ietje put down the shutters on the outside of the house. Still, ten-year-old Sam was missing. Metje ran into the street and called for him, frantic. Where could he be? The words of her father, "Keep them all together," rang in her ears. Sybe tended to disappear while out playing, as kids will. Ietje got dragged along by older sister, Metje, as she hunted. They looked in every nook and cranny. Finally Sybe was found. Ietje never forgot what a frantic feeling it was to have to look for her lost brother in the dark, to worry that he might not be found. The anxiety about safety and health left its mark.

Of the events during this time, Uncle Sam wrote in his letter of December 8, 1961, to his cousin, Brant, in Friesland:

> I think your mother always felt a little sorry for us, especially during illness and the death of my parents and sisters, and demonstrated that by giving us the choice of what we wanted to have for our last meal in the Netherlands, and that was fish, of course. I can still remember Cornelis and Sientje. I remember also my mother saying that Aunt Renske had a little girl, and I wonder if Cornelis still remembers that the four of us went boating and that a neighborhood boy fell into the water while we were way out, and how we hollered for help!

Metje also had the responsibility of disposing of the things that she could not take on the boat to America. Mother recalled that "During the wait in Franeker in the winter of 1908, Mattie got a carpenter, who made a big box and painted our name on it, so we took woolen blankets and some things of value." Probably there was not much to take from the one-room house with its one table and one cabinet. The large wooden box was hand labeled:

ROTTERDAM
S. S. RUNDAM .18 April.
MEJ: METJE.SUBESMA. 2/de KLAS
ORANJE. CITU. SIVUX. JOWA. N.A.
Mr. W. BIERMA

Into this box went anything they could take to America, including their Psalm Book, Bible, any photographs or treasured mementoes they had of their family.[57]During the ninety-plus years since then, this box has become known in the Sybesma family as, "The Blanket Box." Cousin Henrietta Bierma, who lives in Sioux Center, Iowa, sent photos of the box and wrote, "You are wondering what the '2 de' in front of 'Klas' means on the snapshot of the box. It means 2nd Class. The address can be seen on the top of the box. Klas means class, but Klaas is the name translated as Clarence. What you see is all there is. It is quite a large box. Height: 32 inches, width: 41 inches, depth: 26 inches." Box was in Henrietta Bierma's attic until 1995, then at her daughter's home in Ontario, Canada: Rosanne & (Rev.) Jack Van Marion.

On April 18, 1908, Metje was twenty-one; Sybe, twelve; and Ietje, eight, when they sailed on the Ryndam, from Rotterdam to New York City. They had earned part of the money for their voyage, part had come from the church, and part came from their older brother and sister who helped them in the time-honored way that immigrants have often helped one another: by sending money back home. There was likely a time of waiting in Rotterdam to go aboard the boat. Imagine what it must have been like on the dock for Metje, the young woman, as she watched over the two young children. Sybe had the kind of energy and boyish curiosity that kept him out on the streets of Franeker after dark. He had shown a propensity to get into the kind of trouble that could keep them from leaving for America.

---

[57] The Musuem at Ellis Island has displays of such "valued items" immigrants took from the old world to the new. When I walked past these displays in 2002, my eyes clouded over with the mists of memory. How few, valued, and cared for must have been the things Aunt Mattie packed into that box to carry from the old to the new world!

Ietje was probably eager to leave behind the house of sickness and death, and was sticking close to Metje. Perhaps Ietje, as a small child, felt lost in the big city, tightly holding onto her big sister; dough-cheeked Metje with her apple-pie heart.

A year had passed since their father's death, and now the three of them were on their way to America to join their two older siblings. Perhaps, once they were on the ocean, their ancestors became birds and fishes, sticks and stones, bodies and bones whirling away. And Ietje looked ahead to another world of myth and sky, sea and sand.

On the wings of birds and fins of fishes, they fly into view. Carried spider-spin on angel strands, bouncing beyond the Milky Way, bodies swaying, climbing, to the great beyond. Standing at the railing of the ship, gazing at the night sky, Ietje may have felt a precognition of the Biblical rock of Kooi families that she would meet in Lebanon, Iowa.

S.S. Ryndam sailing from Rotterdam to New York.

Only known photo of Sybesma family in Friesland before Geertje
immigrated to America: Ietje, Bregtje seated holding Boukje,
Geertje, Klaas seated, Metje, Maaike, 1903.

15

Coming to America

An enormous influx of immigrants—8.8 million—entered the United States of America during the first decade of the twentieth century. The peak immigration year was 1907, when 860,000 entered New York City through Ellis Island. Once settled, their first priority was to bring the rest of the family over to this wonderful new place, known literally as the Land of Milk and Honey. Here, everyone had enough to eat, and they could buy several kinds of food that were ready to eat without cooking. Houses had many bedrooms, closets, and cupboards. Anything would grow on the land. All one had to do was find a way to cross the ocean. And so, one went, and as soon as he had earned a little money, he would send it back home so that another one could come; helping each other this way was a common practice.

One out of every three Americans alive today (March 2004) are descendants of the 17 million men, women, and children who came to America through Ellis Island between 1892 and 1954. Disastrous crop failures in Ireland and elsewhere triggered this migration, the largest one in history. Conditions in steerage were awful on the aging vessels, called coffin ships, pressed into service in order to turn a quick profit off the thousands of Irish escaping the potato famine. Overcrowded, often lacking adequate water and food, and without even basic sanitary facilities, many of the emigrants on these ships perished in the filthy cargo holds below deck. Still, they preferred such vessels rather than to face almost certain starvation at home.

About 175,000 Hollanders entered the U.S. between 1860 and 1910, with a peak of nearly 10,000 in 1882. The number of U.S. citizens who are descended from Dutch immigrants is estimated at seventeen million, two-and-a-half million more than the total population of the Netherlands. According to Dena Boer, "The first large Dutch settlements beyond the East Coast were Holland, Michigan, and Pella, Iowa. Later strongholds of Dutch immigrants were Grand Rapids, Michigan; Roseland, Illi-

152 nois; Sheboygan, Wisconsin; southwest Minnesota; northwest Iowa; and the southeastern section of South Dakota." [58]

Before Ellis Island in New York Bay became a port of entry for immigrants, it was used for the storage of ammunition. A similar ammunition dump was located at Hercules, California, near the West Coast immigration station on Angel Island in San Francisco Bay. After the Ellis Island immigration station closed in 1954, it became a national monument. Similarly, after the Angel Island immigration station closed in 1940, it became a National Historic Landmark. However, only 175,000 Chinese immigrants had been detained for processing on Angel Island, a mere fraction of the millions who had passed through Ellis Island. Metje, Sybe, and Ietje were quarantined and processed at the infamous Ellis Island immigration station.

Aboard the T.S.S. Ryndam in 1905, letters, dated 28-3-1905 and 2-4-1905, were written by Doeke van der Schaaf, probably intended for his parents in Friesland. Doeke was a brother of Klaas van der Schaaf's grandfather. He was on his way to Orange City, Iowa, but not to the Sybesmas, his cousins. He returned to Friesland within the year and died a year or two after he returned to Pietersbierum.

> Second Class is quite satisfactory. Steerage was about 1000 Poles and Russians. A real mess there, some with big boots, others with no clothes, treated like cattle. The bow of the ship is very cold because there is no shelter. In Second Class we always have shelter. Rose early to see new land, saw it at ten o'clock, was impressed with Rotterdam but really impressed with New York. Arrived March 28 in New York.[59]

In contrast, young Lubbigje Schaapman's letters home, written in 1911 while aboard the S.S. Ryndam, describe good times. She spells out details of musical performances twice a day and storytelling during the thirteen days

[58] Dena Boer, "The Dutch Among Us," *Stanislaus Stepping Stones* (Quarterly of the Stanislaus County Historical Society), Vol. 10, #3 (Fall 1986).

[59] On July 16, 1995, Klaas van der Schaaf, in Amsterdam translated and paraphrased these letters while my grandson, Ben, was fussing, so I could have heard some of the translation incorrectly.

she was at sea.

> I was not bored one minute. Waiters go over the whole boat to call
> people to come and eat at eight long tables and a larger one in the
> dining room. The chairs had each one leg, fastened to the floor,
> although you could turn around different ways with the chair. The
> food is fantastic. We can get anything we want; there are eggs,
> cheese and meat. Everyone has one bed. I am sleeping on the top
> bunk. If you fall out you will wake up. I should have a ladder to
> climb in. In the morning when we get up we quickly get dressed
> and we go on the deck because if you lie too long you are sure to
> be seasick. Many people are seasick. They do not eat because
> they do not feel good. Beer and lemonade can be purchased. There
> are a couple of Friesians on board who are big drinkers. They say
> that one spent ten gulden (dollars) the first day on drink. I think
> that is a lot of money for just drink! Lemonade is a quarter. The
> Friesians wouldn't care about that. One time a little boy was pes-
> tering him and he gave him one gulden. Then we arrived in New
> York! There was a beautiful big statue. One hand was held high in
> the air just like she was the boss of all the countries of the world.
> Beautiful! The Dutch flag was pulled up and we stepped off the
> boat with music in our ears and were brought to a big area where
> the trunks had to go through customs.[60]

Inscribed on a bronze tablet in the pedestal of the Statue of Liberty
in New York Harbor are these lines from "The New Colossus" by Emma
Lazarus:

> Give me your tired, your poor, your huddled masses yearning to
> breathe free. The wretched refuse of your teeming shore. Send these,
> the homeless, tempest-tost, to me. I lift my lamp beside the golden door!

Mother's smiling eyes in the year of her death, 1984, were lit by
childish wonder as she recalled being on the deck of the Ryndam in April
1908 and seeing the Statue of Liberty coming into view. "Ah! America—

---

[60] Dena Boer, "The Diligent Dutch," *Stanislaus Stepping Stones*, Vol. 10, #3, (September 1986), "Letters From Lucy," pp. 525-538.

the land of milk and honey!" On Ellis Island, the American Immigrant Wall of Honor contains the names of 200,000 immigrants including George Washington's grandfather, Miles Standish, Priscilla Alden, the eight great-grandparents of John F. Kennedy, Irving Berlin, Frances Cabrini (the first American saint), as well as Ida Sybesma Kooi (1908), Peter Kooi (1854). and Peter Kooi (1859). The name, Peter Kooi, is listed twice on the Wall of Honor on Ellis Island: Pieter Kooi immigrated in 1854 and his brother, Wilem, with son, Peter Kooi, in 1859.

During the eleven days at sea, the three Sybesmas were in "2nd klas." The captain of the Ryndam had the ship's surgeon do a physical and oral examination (29 questions) of each alien on board as he filled out a detailed document titled "Manifest of Alien Passengers for the United States Immigration Officer at Port of Arrival." On arrival, these affidavits were sworn testimony by the First Officer before the Immigration Officer on Ellis Island, F. B. Machat, attesting to each alien's fitness to enter America. None could be feeble minded, a pauper, likely to become a public charge, have tuberculosis or any other contagious disease, have any criminal record of any kind, be a polygamist or anarchist, be a prostitute, or be coming to engage in any other immoral purpose. F. B. Machat then signed the manifest. An affidavit attested, as well, to the medical training and experience of the surgeon. One of the questions asked of each female passenger before reaching port was, "Are you accompanied by a man?" Metje's "No" to this question meant they could not disembark at Battery Park as most First and Second Class passengers did, but had to go through Ellis Island. Ferries and barges brought all unaccompanied women, any ill person, and all steerage passengers from the S.S.Ryndam, docked at Battery Park, to Ellis Island for processing.

The three Sybesmas arrived on Ellis Island on April 29, 1908. Imagine how bewildered Metje must have felt to hear not only English but a host of languages being spoken around her. Although she had the harrowing experience of not knowing the English language, she had met a man on board the Ryndam who befriended her and he became her interpreter on Ellis Island. They walked down a wooden ramp toward American soil, then went into the main building. Once inside this imposing three-story structure that looked like a castle, they entered the sixty-feet-high Great Hall crowded with immigrants being viewed from above by doctors. One newcomer reported that on entering, "There was a man shouting at the top of his voice, 'Put your luggage here. Men this way. Women and children this way.'" The doctors who were walking on the walkway above and looking down at the crowd of immigrants, pointed to any person with obvious medical problems or those who appeared likely to become public charges. Twenty percent failed this immediate clearance and officials among the crowd would mark such immigrants with a chalk initial on their clothing: E for eyes, L for lameness, X for mental disability, and so forth.

Being processed on Ellis Island was terrifying for Sybe. The sexes were separated, and he was sick and alone. He said it was the most fearful time of his life. It haunted him for the rest of his life. We do not know how long the three immigrants were held on the island. In a letter to his Friesian cousin, Brant, written thirty-eight years after Ellis Island, he wrote: "Those beginning days are days we will never forget in our life time. Probably we will never have to experience them again."

When they finally did leave the nether-land of neither land nor sea and got into New York City, the three were separated again. In taking the streetcar to the train station Metje had put the children in the streetcar with some baggage, and as she turned to pick up more bags, she heard the loud "All Aboard" and away went the streetcar. Frantic, she ran after it shouting, "Ach, mijn kinderen, mijn kinderen! Var is mijn kinderen?" over and over. This attracted quite some attention, and the boat friend who had helped her earlier calmed her down with, "We will get on at the next stop." He helped her from then on. Soon, the three immigrants were off the strange streets of New York and aboard the train bound for Orange City, Iowa.[61]

Ietje's new parents in Iowa were her oldest sister, Geertje, and her new husband, Watse Bierma. When Metje, Sybe, and Ietje arrived at their Sioux Center farm, the couple had been married only two years. Five years had

[61] Catherine Feikema De Bie, "The Life and Times of Catherine Feikema De Bie," n.d. Received from her in June 1995. The parts adapted for use in this book were carefully edited.

passed since Ietje had last seen Geertje and six years since she had seen her oldest brother, Syne. Doubtless, Ietje had no recollection of them from Friesland since she was then only two or three years old. Now, the three immigrants saw not only their brother and sister but also met Watse for the first time. The couple had a baby who had been baptized with the Friesian name of Geertje's mother, Bregtje, but they called her, Bertha. Ietje was now an aunt. Her sister, Geertje, spoke to little Ietje in Fries, but English was spoken almost everywhere else, except at church, where services were in the Dutch language. True to their father's last wish, they had stuck together through tough times and now were together in the home of Watse and Gertie Bierma.

"What did you do first?" I asked Mother. Since she hesitated, I added, "Everything must have felt so strange." Mother answered with a bit of a bristle. "Well, of course Gertie showed me what to do. The first thing was, we took a basket and she showed me how to gather dry corn cobs, sticks, and things like that for the wood box next to the stove."

"And then?"

"Well, each morning she would show me something new to do. I liked it. It helped me forget." As her voice trailed off, I nodded, imagining her as a child who was used to life in a town with canals and new to farm life but quick as a whistle to learn how to do things. She was the kind of person who would one day expect her own children to take action without first being asked to. "Just go, see what there is to do, then do it." Probably the three immigrants quickly adopted the habits and style of their new country. "Before you know it, we are doing just what the style is here," wrote one immigrant to her friend in Holland—just as Geertje must have done when she came five years before.

Geertje Sybesma met Watse Bierma while she was keeping house for two widowers, Pelskamp and Levankamp, in Sioux Center. The farmer for whom Watse worked had some egg customers in Sioux Center, and the widowers were two of them. Watse volunteered to take the eggs into town, and this way he met Geertje. His volunteering went on for a few years and ended in marriage at the church parsonage in March of 1906. After the wedding they settled in town until they could find a farm. They were there only briefly when tragedy struck the Rensink farm family. Tony, the younger brother of Henry and Bill Rensink, was building a basement barn on his intended farm. He was about to marry and was getting ready to settle in when, while fetching a load of sand from the Rensink property, a massive cave-in came without notice and Tony was buried alive. His brother, Henry Rensink, became the owner. The tragedy left the farm vacant, and Watse was in the right place at the right time. He rented the one hundred sixty acres on the site of the buildings and forty acres across the road. In March of 1907, they moved onto the farm and lived there for nearly thirty years. Their daughter, Bertha Bierma Geels, wrote about that time:

> When I was about a year old, Aunt Mattie, Uncle Sam, and Aunt Ida came to the U.S. to live with us. Aunt Mattie, who was about 19 or 20, worked out some as a hired girl. Uncle Sam and Aunt Ida went to the Christian School in Sioux Center. Even though they were eight and twelve, they had to start in the lower grades in order to learn English. By the time I started school, Uncle Sam had to help my father, but Aunt Ida still went to school when I did.[62]

My oldest sister, Gladys Gritter, recorded the following account of Mother's first years in America:

> She went to school for five years in the Christian school in Sioux Center, Iowa, finishing seventh grade when she was fourteen years old. In Holland she had gone to a kindergarten from age three to age eight. When I was small, Mother had a box of very pretty books she had made in kindergarten. She learned to knit there one night a week and sang while knitting. Aunt Gertie Bierma was fifteen years older than Mother. They talked in Friesian, but Mother learned English in school. She did not retain a Dutch accent because she was so young when she came to this country.

Why Watse came to America and the personalities of this couple who became Ida's American parents is described by Syne Bierma:

---

[62] Bertha Geels, *The Life of Bertha (Bierma) Geels* (Sioux Center, IA: n.d.)

Watse Bierma had come to America from Friesland in 1890. He immigrated with two buddies who were also 23 years old— Unema and Dykema. Their first stop was in Grand Rapids, Michigan. Watse stayed there for less than a year, long enough to despise the stifling factory work; so he went on to Lebanon, Iowa, in 1891. He realized that if he was going to stay in America, he would have to learn English. He decided that the best thing he could do was to be a hired man for a farmer who didn't know the Holland language and so he hired out to Remko Kooi, a land-rich maxi-farmer with more than a dozen hands to help work his sections of land. [Author's note: Remko later became the father of Fred Kooi who married Ida Sybesma, who had had Watse as her American father.] Remko had advanced his passage money, so he worked for him until that was paid. Watse then went to work at Rock Valley and hired out to Evert Hulshof. Evert was also a big-time farmer, and judging by the number of times Hulshof's name came up in later years, Watse was impressed by him. After working there for a few years, Watse rented five acres from him to raise potatoes, a job he knew well since that was the Biermas' main crop in Friesland.

Just why Watse came to America remains vague. He was tightlipped about his motives, and the children never dared to ask him. He did remark that the economic stress and a desire to start anew in a new country were pushes. Of course there were guesses why he really came: (1) he was disappointed in love, (2) he was preparing a place for his secret bride, or (3) he had a quarrel with his father, but that did not jibe with the fact that Watse's mother always spoke of the Bierma family as very closely bonded, and they pleaded for him to stay in Friesland. Whatever the reason, Watse did return to the Netherlands in 1895 to see his family. He was there only briefly and felt out of place. He longed for the wide-open spaces, the freedom and the opportunities that America offered. After he got back, he worked for Hulshof again and, once more, rented land to raise potatoes.

During the span of 1895-1899, Watse went through a period of spiritual turmoil. He was never a total atheist, as were his buddies back in the old country, but Watse proclaimed himself an agnostic, uninterested in church or its related activities, although he did attend the old Sioux Center Reformed Church for a year or two. He then went to the Christian Reformed Church where Reverend Henry Beets, first and always an evangelist, was serving as pastor. He confronted Watse about the matter of salvation. That was finally the answer to Watse's restlessness. After this time, he was on fire for his Lord and Master. He served as the first president of the Sioux Center Christian school and became a strong advocate for Christian education from grade school through university. He lived the dedicated life with a passion. He breathed Christianity. He was also active in community affairs and was especially absorbed in the cooperatives (the creamery, elevator, and lumberyard) and the funeral home.

Watse wore a semi-walrus mustache, which was a rust color with gray sprinkled throughout. On his Friesian brow was a patrician dignity that folks respected, but there were times when he could be seized by fits of laughter that would bring tears from his eyes. He also had a microwave temper. Nothing could light him up quicker than to watch one of the milk cows jump the fence and pirate the corn.

Syne Biersma's memory of his mother strikes a chord in me, since it sounds true to Aunt Gertie and much like my own Mother.

As a family, we never had a memory of Geertje ever running or walking rapidly. She never had the strength. Yet she worked early and late. No one could ever imagine Watse playing with the children, but Geertje would often play different games with the children, including checkers and dominoes, while Watse read. She always wore her hair in a chignon or Psyche knot. At night we were amazed how far her hair dangled down when she unpinned it. Geertje was a background person who never dominated a group, but she quietly influenced relatives and friends by her strong common sense and practical wisdom. She could "read" people's character more accurately than anyone I ever knew. Feminine intuition was highly developed in her, and she was never wrong about people and never fooled about their motives. She probably talked less and said more than any other family member.[63]

The aged Aunt Gertie I knew was always frail. Her big eyes had a

[63] Syne Bierma, "Bierma, Watse Family," *The Centennial History of Sioux County* (Sioux Center, Iowa, 1991), 235-7.

curious light in them—like Mother's eyes. Before going to visit them, Mother would caution us, "She's so thin now, so you be good. Don't jump on her lap or play rough at their house, you hear?" I came to view her as old and small, as fragile as a china teacup. I was sure she would break if I came too close to the chair where she remained seated, welcoming us into her living room.

The first of the five Sybesmas to emigrate was Ida's oldest brother, Syne Sybesma in 1903. He married Christina Brock in August of 1910. The next year, on the day after Thanksgiving, Mattie married John Feikema at the home of Watse and Gertie Bierma. Soon afterwards, the Biermas received word that their Grandpa Bierma had died in The Netherlands, but their Grandma Bierma and her five daughters and two sons were still living. Bertha Bierma Geels recalls:

> In September of 1912, I started kindergarten in Sioux Center Christian School. I would have liked to have gone to high school at Western Christian High in Hull, but I had to stay home and help my mother. During my grade-school years, only the first few, I and Ed, who started two years after I did, were taken to school and gotten after school by my father or the hired man. When Ed became old enough to drive a horse in front of a buggy, we would go to school by ourselves. The horse was blind, and a clumsy, old slowpoke. When it was very cold or snowing, my father would usually take us to school with the bobsled. We were very comfortable with heating stones under our feet and many blankets thrown over us. But the driver would have to face the wind, and it was sometimes necessary to get out and lead the horse through the snow drifts. It was seven miles to school and home again.[64]
>
> My parents and I, about five, and Ed, about three, left in December on a boat trip to Holland, while Uncle John and Aunt Mattie took care of Uncle Sam and Aunt Ida, and did the chores. We got back to America and Orange City sometime in February. Uncle John and Aunt Mattie were there to get us with the carriage. Aunt Ida was also there to meet us, and when I saw her I said, "Goein dag"—Good day. But she had become quite Americanized after going to school, and said, "Don't say that. Say

---

[64] Bertha Bierma Geels, op. cit.

'Hello.'" After being in Holland for a couple of months, "Goein dag" came natural.

Mattie Sybesma married John Fiekema three years after she immigrated. They had nine children. Her oldest surviving daughter, Catherine DeBie, now lives in Artesia, California. After teaching full time for many years, she did substitute teaching. The Fiekema families still get together for family reunions as does our Fred and Ida Kooi family. Catherine has recorded her memories of growing up on the farm and says that her grandchildren have a hard time believing that she walked six miles to high school on the dirt roads each day, hoping a farmer would come along and give her a ride.

Bertha says, "My mother used to tell me about a day when Ida came home singing, 'Gore night ladies.' My father, who knew English quite well, said, 'No, it's Good night, ladies.' But Ida insisted that the teacher had said, 'Gore night ladies.'" Bertha's younger brother, Syne Bierma, recalls that:

> For 29 years the same kitchen table, swaybacked and rickety, served the family as it swelled and shrank in numbers. We never owned deep-bottomed breakfast dishes but ate our cereal out of flat dinner plates. That posed an engineering problem for those on each end of the table. I always sat at the end. In order to keep the milk from cascading downstream, I had to stick a knife under the inclined plate as a shim to keep it on an even keel. With nine people around the table, it called for some impromptu ingenuity. The eating table doubled as a discussion table, which at times was dominated by Watse, Eddie, and Bertha. The rest of us did a lot of listening. The names of Teddy Roosevelt, Coolidge, Hoover, Henric Colyn, and Abraham Kuyper came up frequently; the latter two were Calvinist Prime Ministers of Holland. Eddie sharpened his argumentative beak on the bark of those discussions. Although Watse and Geertje were separated in age by 17 years, there was a love and understanding present, and all the children felt a deep sense of belonging and feeling of worth that had nothing to do with money or personal success. Their pervasive sense of right steered the family through all circumstances.[65]

---

[65] Syne Sybesma, op. cit.

162

My oldest brother, Ray, recalls that "Uncle Watse was a leader, which his children appreciated. When I was ten or eleven I was sitting in their living room and recall his talking about the Boer War, when the English fought the Dutch settlers in South Africa. He hated the British going after the farmers. He planned his boys' education." This was during the Great Depression, a time when clothes had to last a year. It was a time of dust and drought when, according to Syne Bierma, "There was just as much real estate in the air as on the ground. Depending on which way the wind blew that day, one could see South Dakota go by one day, and Minnesota fly by the next. So much of Dakota flitted by that they were in danger of losing their statehood."

Ida Sybesma (9) and Sam Sybesma (13),
Sioux Center, c. 1909.

Sam Sybesma around age 15 in Sioux Center, Iowa, before 1911.

Mattie Sybesma before she married John
Feikema in Sioux Center, Iowa, 1911.

16

Dinner for Threshers

On hot nights I lie listening to freight trains laboring through the San Joaquin Valley. Long-winded, long whistling they lumber over a wooden trestle going over the river. In the dead of night they groan through orchards, cross vineyards and fields, enter farmhouses, and break into my reveries. Far away is childhood and Iowa, farther yet is Friesland and *keuken, kinderen, kirk*. The rhythm of freight trains is the monotonous click of heavy wheels passing over steel tracks, rumbling into the distance. At last, an eerie whistle sends a whimpering echo—a last breath, and as the weighted freight of memories dwindle, so do I. Moving on, carried off, I fall into dreams.

Here, along the creek in the San Joaquin Valley, are stands of bamboo. Their stalks sport sword-shaped leaves, like long leaves of corn growing longer. The fresh green feel is Iowa. I am five and the smell of growing corn fills my nostrils. Milk is poured over cornflakes that crackle in the bowl. Warm milk with spice cake or gingerbread warm out of the oven tastes oh-so-good! The smell of bacon fat sizzling into supper is tantalizing, as are slices of potato frying with slices of onion going limp into white rings. Bacon and eggs with bread or oatmeal is breakfast, rarely pancakes. Boiled beef, mashed potatoes, and a vegetable, such as beans or peas, is dinner. There is always dessert—a jar of peaches, pears, or apricots from the cellar; pudding, pie, or sometimes bread and milk, which is simply bread broken into a dish of milk with a sprinkle of cinnamon. On the supper table is the beef left over from dinner. A plate of homemade white bread, and the butter dish and jam jar are always on the table. Sunday dinner is special, maybe chicken, maybe cake for dessert. The food is about as plain as you can get. Boil-bake-fry is the rule; the black cast-iron fry pan always sits on the stove, as does the heavy tea kettle steaming with hot water for dishwashing. On the end of the stove stands the dented metal dishpan, slowly heating more water for washing dishes. Gladys relates that:

The only person I ever knew who was on a diet was Aunt Gertie Kooi, and she was a diabetic. Otherwise, I never heard the term diet—even though I had plenty of plump and mature-looking aunts—and a few uncles and cousins who, by today's standards, were overweight. But no one talked about it. I never heard anyone say, "I shouldn't really eat this piece of cake," or "I have to lose ten pounds." Eating was more a part of life. And, like sleeping, it was just not discussed. No one went out to eat. Men discussed crops, politics, livestock, and the weather. Women talked about children, canning, and house cleaning. My Mother had no recipe book, and I can't remember following a recipe for anything. Everyone knew how to make bread or cake from scratch.[66]

Spek was hot bacon fat that was sometimes substituted for butter on pancakes, or simply put on fried bread before adding syrup from the pitcher. At the table, Mother instructed, "Dip the bread in spek. It's good that way and you wipe the plate too. See?" Fat and meat in abundance defined the rich diet of the immigrants in their letters back home. From Mother we heard glowing praise for oliebollen—a sort of spice doughnut eaten at New Year's in Holland. She didn't mention *hutspot*, a Dutch stew with pureed vegetables, much like the overcooked vegetables we had at meals. In Holland it has been a Dutch tradition for the last 400 years—ever since 1574, when the Dutch fleet chased the Spanish besiegers from Leiden—to serve *hutspot met klapstuk* on the third of October. Accounts vary, but we can assume that the pot was not abandoned by the Spanish as they retreated, and that the starving Dutch actually had stewed human ribs during the long siege.

Mother kept enough laying hens to provide eggs, and someone got the chore of gathering eggs from the chicken coop every day. We drank hot cocoa made by Droste or Hershey. Holland Dutch Rusk was a staple, like graham crackers—so, too, was Cocoa Wheat, Cream of Wheat, and cornbread. Food was very simple. Curatives were even simpler: liniment, castor oil, and the teaspoon of cod liver oil, thick and yellow. "Just open

---

[66] Gladys Kooi Gritter, "Our Family Register" (Grand Rapids, MI, 1981).

your mouth and swallow it. C'mon now. Don't make such a face. It's not that bad." Rarely did we go to a doctor. He was so unimportant that I did not even know his name.

When our youngest son, Timothy Randolph, was in third grade, he brought home from school the recipe for Pigs in Blankets. He continues to love it. A recent Christmas letter from an Iowa cousin tells about the continuing popularity and production of this homemade treat:

> Our Golden Hour Ladies have been busy making Pigs in Blankets (sausages), a Dutch thing. A roll of meat wrapped in dough. Our bakery handles them, and December is especially busy although we make them year round. We made around 300 dozen last week and ran out so had to get right back at it.[67]

In her garden, Mother grows enough vegetables to feed us during the summer, and enough extra to can tomatoes, beans, beets, and make cabbage into sauerkraut. Once there was a surplus of tomatoes, and by February we all were tired of home-canned tomatoes. Sacks of flour, salt, and sugar in fifty— or hundred—pound cloth sacks came from the store in town. To get to town, we crossed the Floyd River and the train tracks. In California, I once again hear the train whistle working its daily cycle: yawning into the gap of silence at two a.m., hooting short puffs across country bridges at noon. Wooden trestles creak. Rivers ease away. Seasons pass. The long coil of a rattlesnake loosens its sinuous body under dried brush. Walking along the tracks near the river, I find its entire skin shed: parchment-thin, transparent, its symmetry a beautiful thing to hold in my hands. From the distant north comes a low, long whistle, dimming into nothing, disappearing—only to meet the train traveling south, coming fast across the trestle. Then suddenly there is silence.

Pa is getting ready to go to town when he asks Mother, "By and by I'm going to trade in Hospers. I'll take in the eggs. You need a sack of sugar, or anything?"

"Well, I guess we can use a couple sacks of flour. Be sure you get

---

[67] Henrietta Bierma to author, letter dated December 1993 (Sioux Center, IA).

170   two flour sacks with the same print so there will be enough for a dress."

"Okay, I better be going then."

Baking bread at home was customary, as was putting by something freshly baked in case someone came by for coffee. Cookies, cake, or something sweet usually was baked once a week. If no one came by, it was eaten anyway. The nine o'clock and three o'clock lunch times were coffee times. "The coffee pot is on" meant "come by our place to visit." An expression that was a holdover from the old country was *"koffie klets,"* a time around coffee drinking for women to exchange gossip and news. So, Pa would often offer Mother a ride into town to go to the Wednesday afternoon Ladies Aid Society at church, but she rarely went. Mother never learned to drive. "Oh, I think Pa can do that."

Milly hands me my first stick of gum. "Here, you can have one." I chew it until the sweet taste fades, then swallow it like candy. She jeers, "You're not supposed to swallow it!" I'm alarmed: "What will happen to it now?" Off-handedly she retorts, "Probably come out or get stuck somewhere." A week later she consents to giving me another stick, declaring, "This is a waste of good gum." I chew and chew, take it out and examine the uneven gray lump, noting each tooth mark, experimenting with how far I can stretch its sticky strands before one breaks. Finally, I put the lump back into my mouth and chew and chew some more. It becomes tasteless. Perplexed, I consult Milly: "It doesn't go away. What do I do now?"

"Come here with me; I'll show you." I follow her to the kitchen where only the drone of flies fills the room. Silently, she ducks under the oil tablecloth falling over the four sides of the table. Hidden underneath is a ledge running around the entire table. The ledge has become a storage place for unwanted food stealthily discarded by hands reaching under the tablecloth to hide it. Among the lumps of gum as hard as little fists stuck fast to the ledge are dried up crusts and a few dead flies.

Farm implements not in use were parked behind the machine shed, tool shed, chicken coop and corncribs. We were not allowed to play on these interesting contraptions, but we did. We examined the cultivator, plows used to weed the rows of corn, the seeder, harrow, mower, sickle, binder, hay-loader, hayrack, the disc, baler, binder, and the manure spreader.

Not a favorite chore of any big brother was pitching manure into the manure spreader, driving it out to the field, and spreading manure over the field. No one acquired an appreciation for the aromas of the various kinds of manure. On our explorations into forbidden places, we played on farm machinery, climbed up into metal seats, pulled at gear sticks, and tried to turn the steering wheels, but we left the manure spreader alone. The dump rake had huge semi-circular tines lifted with a lever. When the tines got full and the hay was let down in rows—or when the rake came to the end of the row—the tines were lifted, so that the whole unwieldy contraption could turn into the next row. Rows of hay were pitchforked into a hayrack, which then was taken to the haystack, or to the haymow in the barn.

Once, Elmer, Glenny, and I were riding high on top of the hay in an overloaded hayrack when it tipped over at the exact moment it came to a full stop before the gate into the farmyard. The high stack of hay slid slowly to the ground, cushioning our ride down. Not until I heard the frantic shouting of the big brother, who was driving the tractor pulling the hayrack, did I realize that I was under the hay, not on top of it. Pete yells: "You kids okay?" "Ja, just smothered and itchy." "You hurt? Come here. Let me see you." I walk over to him. "You're all right, just a little scratched up. Don't you tell Pa I let you little kids ride on top of the hayrack. You walk home now. I have to stay here and take care of this mess. See that Elmer and Glenny get home alright." When we get home, Mother is in the garden, her face shielded by a worn, floppy, straw hat, her apron fallen forward. She is leaning on a hoe at the end of a row of radishes, easily identified by the bright red seed packet impaled upside down on a stick. Stan is helping her hoe weeds. The three older brothers are helping Pa in the fields. He wears his long-sleeved blue work shirt and overalls and stiff yellow straw hat.

Outside the kitchen porch's screen door, on the front stoop, is the place to clean up before coming inside. Off to one side is a metal scraper embedded in the concrete. Here the men stand to scrape most of the dirt from their boots. On the other side, near the board where the wash basin sits, is a metal milk pail half full of clean water. Above it, a wire holder for soap and a mirror is nailed to the outside wall. A circular towel runs around the towel roller. As it gets used, the towel swerves off to one side. During threshing, baling, corn picking, and at other times during harvesting, when several men are working in the fields, Mother puts two wash basins out on the stoop.

Before Pa comes in for meals, he takes off his hat and hangs it on a nail just inside the screen door. He rolls up his sleeves, leans over the white metal basin of water and scrubs, splashing his face and neck, rubbing his red eyes with his knuckles. Water flies out of the basin. Straightening up, he pulls on the once-white but now-gray towel with its fraying, blue-striped border twisting around the roller. The roller squeaks. He wipes himself, then lifts the basin and flings out the dirty water. The whirling arc splats into the dry ground, scattering the dirt into arrows. Chickens jump out of the way, protesting. He lifts the pail of clean water and pours some water into the basin to leave it ready for the next man coming in from the fields to wash up before going inside to eat. For Pa, the basin and pail are as light as one of the toothpicks in the holder on the center of the kitchen table.

Briefly he looks in the small framed mirror hanging lopsided on a nail, replaces his glasses, straightens himself and snorts. The wire in back of the mirror is twisted. The cardboard backing is bent. A crack runs across a lower corner of the glass. At the end of the summer, it will land in the dump. Next summer we will quarrel over who gets to hang it on the trunk of a tree in her playhouse. Pa's forehead is red below the hat line, white above. Two inches of iron-gray hair stand straight up from his forehead. The heat of his body radiates power. His gait is straight forward. He knows where he is going. Seeing me standing there watching him takes him by surprise, and he pauses momentarily. I slip out of sight.

Between 1901 and 1935, the artist, Grant Wood, lived in Cedar Rapids, a town across the state of Iowa from where we lived. He painted "Dinner for Threshers" in 1934. It was so large that the easel broke under its weight, damaging only the wallpaper in the background, which he had to repaint. He accurately depicted details in the farmhouse kitchen, among them the match holder on the wallpaper, the dab of butter on the mashed potatoes, even the piano stool one man sat on. Eventually, Nelson

Rockefeller acquired the painting.[68]

Decades later, I bought a print of "Dinner for Threshers" from the De Young Museum in San Francisco. I studied the half-red, half-white foreheads of the men around the dinner table, and remembered Pa's half-red, half-white forehead.

A threshing party was held on a night sometime in August before harvest time when the threshing machine would be needed. During the party, business was taken care of by the threshing ring, a small group of farmers who hired the man or the farmers who owned and maintained the threshing machine.

Some farm families at the threshing party were not church members, which made them outsiders. A party at night with outsiders was unusual. It's a time for sweets, dressing up, and staying up late unsupervised since the older ones are not "watching out." I get to see what the older sisters and brothers do! For younger to watch—and older to not have to watch out—was rare. Also, since threshing occurred around the busiest time of the year, during canning and the harvesting, the older ones were occupied with more important things than telling us what to do.

One year, the party was at the Houtsma farm near the corner where the mailboxes stood. On the appointed evening, the tone is business-like and serious in our kitchen. Supper is over quickly. Mother covers her pies with a damp dishtowel to carry to the car. We run upstairs to put on clean clothes. I watch Verna Mae pull a slip down over her head, then her cotton dress with the red, white, and blue collar matching the skirt. She must have put that bra on after she told me to go get something. Someone calls up the stairway, "Ready to go!" Downstairs, we comb our hair and pile into the back seat of the Chevrolet to drive to the Houtsmas' farm. The older kids have already walked to the party or gone somewhere else. Approaching the Houtsmas' driveway, we hear their dogs, tied up somewhere, going crazy. Pa parks in the middle of the yard under a tall yard light

[86] Nan Wood Graham, *My Brother, Grant Wood* (Iowa City, IA: State Historical Society of Iowa, 1993).

casting a wide arc of yellow into the dark. Shadows jump out from the edges of the pool of light. We don't know the Houtsmas very well because they don't go to our church. "Well, as far as I know they don't have a church," Mother told us when we pestered her for the name of their church. We feel awkward around the Houtsmas, shy, like we do around other outsiders. The nearest we get to their farm is when we play at the creek in the cow pasture, or walk past their place to go to the mailbox. They must be those "heathen going to hell" the preacher gets excited about on Sundays, but the only heathen we have ever seen are their dogs—barking, growling, and running out onto the dirt road to bite at our heels when we walk past their driveway. We carry sticks to fight them off.

As we tumble out of the car trying to behave ourselves, we stick close behind the folks as they move toward the Houtsmas' front stoop and knock on the screen door. Mrs. Houtsma takes her time coming to the door. In the kitchen, Mother sets her pies on a table that has begun to fill up with good things: pitchers of lemonade, frosted white and chocolate cakes, peanut butter cookies. A five-gallon pot of coffee sits on the cookstove. For the adults, there is a stack of glass plates indented with circles where matching glass cups will be placed. There are no paper plates or napkins and no plastic spoons. When the time comes for dessert, we little kids will take goodies in our hands and go outside to eat.

Now we hang around Mother's skirts, trying to behave while she helps Mrs. Houtsma get the coffee ready to pour. The women are going to serve the men first so they can have their coffee in the parlor and start the business meeting, but then the men decide to meet first and eat later. Into the parlor they go, closing the double doors behind them. The men take their places, regarding each other with respect while finding seats. Each year they take care of routine business matters first: whose farm the threshing machine will stay on when threshing is finished, who will maintain and move it, how the costs will be shared, on whose farm the threshing party will be next year. The suspense in the room is palpable as they wade through the usual business, waiting for the end, when the most important decision will be made: the order in which each farmer gets to use the threshing machine. They will pick straws to see who gets to use it first, second, third, and so on. Profit from the harvested grain stored in the tall towers of the "Farmers Co-op" will depend on timing—getting in the crop at the right time so that early rain or other bad weather does not ruin the crop. The timing is everything.

The tone among the wives in the kitchen is also serious, even reverent, closed, and set—like church where we must keep quiet and stay in our seats until the end when the doxology is sung and the last Amen uttered. The women are strangers to each other and they, too, have business to transact. At first, their talk is hesitant and intermittent, and then it is about inconsequential things. As they warm to each other, the talk turns to the business at hand. Large cooking pots and other kitchenware that is infrequently used will be borrowed from each other when the threshers go to each of their farms and the threshers' dinner must be prepared and served. Two five-gallon coffee pots will be needed and a big roaster for the meat. Mother, it appears, has plenty of pie pans to lend.

With both hands full of cookies, I go outdoors. Under the yard light, the boys look at beautiful Verna Mae, my sister. How much I envy her Elizabeth Taylor face, the breasts filling her new, red white and blue, cotton dress. How much I want to be noticed like that! Howie Houtsma is talking to Verna Mae. Milly and Elmer have wandered off somewhere. When Verna Mae tries to get rid of me, I hang back in the shadows to watch. Howie wants her to walk out toward the corncrib, but she hangs back. Pretty soon brother Stan comes along, and then Pete, carrying a watermelon from the cornfield where they grow among the rows of corn. Seeing me, he says, "Now you don't go tell what we got and you can have some." I follow them out behind the corncrib. A knife slices it clean through with one stroke. Someone hands me an end chunk and warns, "Better not drip that down your front." Next day Pa is mad because somebody's big boys had a watermelon fight, throwing, cracking, demolishing—and wasting—watermelons. No one admits doing it. "Must have been those Van Kalsbeek boys down the road." Pa grunts, turns away mad, and goes outside.

For several days before the threshers come to our farm, hired girls help Mother and the older sisters bake, prepare extra food, and make special foods. Everything will be made from scratch: the sauce for sliced beets, string beans from the garden, applesauce, various kinds of pies, mashed potatoes and gravy, boiled beef, breads, butter, jam and apple butter. Wedding dishes come out of the glass china closet in the dining room for relishes such as pickles and radishes. Thin slices of cucumbers with white rings of onion in sweetened vinegar will go into the fancy pickle dish that was a wedding gift. Mother worries about whether there will be enough string beans ready to pick. She picks the best. This is the biggest dinner of the year.

Shocking comes before threshing. During shocking, binder twine is tied around sheaves of grain that then are thrown upright into shocks by the shockers. Three or six bundles of the hay, called sheaves, make a shock stand upright and able to shed rainwater until the threshing machine comes.

When the brothers, a same-age cousin, and Pa are shocking grain, they wear long leather gloves with stiff cuffs that Pa buys in town especially for shocking. The cousin catches a bundle of grain, jerks the baling twine into a knot around it, then throws his shock against two other shocks as they are being grabbed, tied, and thrown upright by Ray and Pa. All three are covered with a fine spray of chaff, sweat, and dirt, their faces and necks itchy red. Every half hour the driver stops and comes back to share the canteens of water. Looking back at the shocks, up at the sun, then forward at the waving grain, the men calculate how long to lunch, dinner, lunch and quitting time, hoping the machine will break down. The driver takes his turn shocking. Earlier, Mother told Pa, "Ray's got hay fever and can't take all that chaff blowing into his lungs." Pa grunted and turned away. Now the sun is past two o'clock and Ray is driving more often than shocking. Later in life, Ray recalls that he hated shocking barley, and oats too, but not as much as barley. Barley was terrible because briers would get inside of shoes and clothes.

The threshing machine was loud, even from far away. When it rumbled through the farmyard on its way to the fields, it was an attractive nuisance. We were told to go run, play, stay out of the way. But how could we do that? We were enthralled by this behemoth that harvested our parents' hopes. Cumbersome and slow moving, the thresher was the biggest machine we had ever seen. The big people were consumed by threshing for several days. Oldest brother Ray says:

The thing about threshing I remember is stamping on the straw stack after the straw was blown out of the blower. I hated that. I recall that I was too young to drive the horses. The first threshers were run by a steam engine on wheels; that engine went one or two miles an hour so it took forever, one hour actually, to go the one mile to get to the next farm. In the threshing ring I had my first taste of beer. I was helping our neighbor, Mr. Houtsma, out in the field. At noon he got out the beer and gave me a taste. I hated it. He wasn't from the Reformed Church, so he could do these things. No beer was ever around our house or around the houses of anyone we knew.

The threshing machine separated the grain from the straw. Wheels and pulleys, cogs, gears, and sprockets made the big machine clatter and rattle whenever it was moving. Once the thresher was in place in a field, it was stationary. Using a wagon, men pitched the sheaves of grain up to a man who would neatly stack the sheaves in the wagon until it was full, and then drive over to the thresher. Here he tossed the bundles, one by one, on the conveyer belt that carried them into the threshing machine. Beaters knocked the grain from the straw, and a sieve separated it from the chaff. The straw was blown up a long spout and fell out high in the air to make a haystack. The shiny pipe that blew out the golden flume of straw could be seen from miles around. On the other side of the thresher, the grain went up a tall angled pipe and dropped down into a box wagon and was hauled away to the barn, silo, or the Farmers Co-op for storage. By the late 1800s, steam engines powered most threshers, but later on, engines were used. The wagons pulled by horses or a tractor were eventually replaced by diesel or gasoline trucks. By 1936, combines began to replace threshing machines.

Once in a while we little kids got to carry lunch out to the men in the field, and the noise of the threshing machine was deafening. Grains flew out of a fat tube into a wagon so fast that they were a blur. Pa had to yell really loud at the driver to cut the engine before the noise stopped. Only then could we hear Pa yelling, "Lunch time!" Lunch time in the fields came at mid-morning and mid-afternoon.

Cornpicking usually came later on, in September. Farmers around 1900 cut their corn by hand to provide winter feed for cattle, using the dry stalks first. Then silos came and farmers like our grandfather, Remko Kooi, put silage in either silos or pits. He cut 150-200 acres of corn a year with a single-row binder. Then he shocked all that he had cut, and finally, with the help of a crew, he chopped the corn into silage. This was a neighborhood operation, much like threshing. The bundles were hauled on flatbeds, hayracks with one side off. The men would throw the bundles of corn onto the flat-bed, and then off into the cutter at the silo. One man was up in the silo, tramping the silage down and packing each door carefully with mud to make it air tight to prevent spoilage.[69]

Mother's niece, Bertha Bierma Geels, writes about the extra field work and kitchen work that harvest time meant:

> For the little kids, threshing meant a lot of excitement, but for the older people it meant a lot of hard, hard work for a couple of weeks because all the threshers would go from one place to another until all of it was done. I helped my brothers shock grain sometimes, but otherwise I didn't do much spring or summer field work. In the fall my brother, Ed, and I would have to start picking corn until some neighbors' boys or boys from Minnesota came to pick people's corn after their own was out. When they came, it meant that my corn-picking job was finished, but it also meant helping my mother. The big job of the summer was the harvesting of the oats and threshing it. The days before they started threshing were busy baking cakes and bread and making preserves. They would need lunch coffee, sandwiches, and cake at 9:00 in the morning and at about 3:15 in the afternoon. As soon as the morning lunch was done, we had to wash the dishes and begin to clean vegetables and prepare the rest of the meal. The table usually had to be set for about 14 hungry threshers. After they had eaten, the rest of the family could eat their dinner. Then we had to wash the dinner dishes and get the afternoon lunch ready. Some threshing rings served supper, but we didn't. The only time I was glad to see a threshing rig was when it was leaving the yard.[70]

[69] Mike Vanden Bosch, ed., *A Pocket of Civility, A History of Sioux Center* (Sioux Falls, SD: Modern Press, Inc., 1976), 57.

[70] Bertha Bierma Geels, op. cit.

From the table in the dining room Gladys has cleared away the dress she was cutting out. Extra leaves have been brought from the back of the bedroom closet and put into the table. Mother's special-occasion, creamy-lace tablecloth hangs far down over the sides of the long table under which we little kids are playing unnoticed. From under the tablecloth I take quick peeks. My gaze travels up the front of the oak china closet door to the place where there is a keyhole. Mother has turned her back to the table, taken the key, and turned it in the small, curved S brass plate, and then hidden the key in one of the cubbyhole drawers. The right half of this china closet has slotted cubbyholes and small drawers behind a pull-down door that serves as a secretary for Pa. Its door has the same S keyhole as does the door to the china closet. Important things like the wedding china and bills are kept locked here. The door is a curving bay window, the keyholes brass, and the four curved, stubby legs have claw-shaped feet. Above the pull-down door is a mirror framed by oak carved with swirls and flowers.

High above and well out of reach in the china closet are plates shaped like an artist's palette, with a turned-up edge to keep in melting whipped cream on Jell-O or ice cream on pie ala mode. Delicate and thin as an eggshell, a ridge rises up to define the place where the small cup sits with its small, ear-shaped handle. The plates are translucent. Only the inside of the cup is a different color—burnished gold. There are other cups with saucers in soft hues, but I stare at the one that is sky blue. The cerulean glaze shimmers. What remains of a young couple's wedding gifts include sherbet glasses—five perfect half moons of crystal above long stems, three shooting stars etched into each crystal moon. Mother tells us to keep our hands off. "Believe there were eight, once. That's why you keep out of there."

Only an older sister may take out the pickle dish of heavy glass with its deeply cut design, or the long cut-glass relish dish with its delicate design. By the time I am seven I am told, "If you're really careful, you may carry that pickle dish in here to the kitchen table." Like shooting stars, the beams of light in my eyes watch the sherbet glasses etched with crystal moons being taken down. Dinners with the lace tablecloth covering the oval oak dining room table lengthened by all its leaves were an event to remember, build dreams around, and let imagination leap. "One day, when I grow up..."

Talk about crops permeated even the conversations of us little kids. We asked where linen came from, since we often overheard Mother say to one of the older girls, "Just go put those sheets in the linen closet," even though the sheets were made of cotton. In the linen closet are stacks of pillowcases with crocheted edges and embroidered flowers. Embroidery thread is tumbled together into a jumble in the cigar box kept in the linen closet next to the button jar. Sewing things are also there, next to the long ivory tablecloth made of linen and lace.

"What is flax? Like alfalfa?"

"No, flax is seed that makes linseed oil."

"Oh, like the linseed oil in the can in the tool shed?"

"Ja, well, the flax is seed that makes oil, I guess."

"Pa grows flax?"

"Sometimes, it's just a small crop, like soybeans. Sometimes he grows it, but not every year. Fine flax is like the linen used to make cloth."

"Like the stuff stacked in the linen closet?"

"Like that."

In the dining room, Bernice sets the table. Extra chairs are carried in from the kitchen and the piano stool from the parlor. Gladys counts to be sure there are enough places. This is the only time of the year when the women and children eat separately from the men. In the kitchen, our hurry-up meal must be over before the men start coming in from the field. Mother is nervous about having enough food to serve the hungry men. We finish eating and are ordered to run and play outside. Instead, we hang around to watch.

At noon the men come trudging in from the fields. They hang their straw hats on the hooks on the porch wall, nod to the women as they pass through the kitchen, and to go through the swinging door into the dining room. Each man finds a place to seat himself at the table laden with large bowls of food. This is the only meal when coffee is served, brought out when the men are ready for dessert. The pies are made from fresh peaches,

cherries, apples, and Pa's favorite—rhubarb. "That pie plant is sure good,"
he will say several times. After the men go back to the fields to thresh,
Mother goes into the bedroom to lay her weary body down. Tonight's supper is good leftovers. In two days the threshing is done, but Mother is still
tired.

> The unsung heroes of threshing day were the ladies who prepared
> the meals. A large bowl of mashed potatoes would disappear be-
> fore it got half way around a table of men. (Ladies did not sit
> down to eat with these threshing crews). Homemade pies were
> cut in gargantuan pieces and devoured like so many peanuts. The
> only dishwashers to wash the mountain of dirty pans and plates
> were human ones.[71]

---

[71] Vanden Bosch, op. cit., p. 56.

17

Fireflies

Pa too feels it tonight, as we speed by with the windows open, on our way home from the church program. Mother's eyes look wistful. Fireflies shoot up like sparks in front of the windshield and in the ditches as we pass by. The July soil is alive with insects hopping, buzzing, and mosquitoes biting. The earth seems to be growing larger even as we pass by. Elmer faces an open window in the back seat, his hair blown back flat. "See 'em? See 'em jump?" I pull myself closer to a window, get a firm grasp on the window frame, and look again. Sure enough, the longer I look, the more fireflies I see jumping up out of the black night.

"How come they jump up like that?"

"I dunno," says Elmer dreamily.

"Kind of night they're coming right at you," Pa observes. Sure enough, fireflies keep on popping up, right in front of the windshield, then fly up and disappear. When we slow to turn into the driveway, I think I hear the same popping sound that is made by kernels of yellow popcorn popping in the beat-up black popper that is pushed back and forth over the top of the wood stove during the dark, cold nights of January. We pile out. Milly wanders toward Mother's vegetable garden, and I follow her. "Think they're in there too?" She doesn't answer. Mother calls, "Time for bed now."

"Dancing—they're dancing!" I tell Milly, who informs me, "That's bad, you know."

"How come?" But Milly is lost in reverie and doesn't answer; so I say to myself, as much as to her, "Don't see why." Her terse reply is meant to shut me up. "Like playing cards and gambling, it leads to other things, not suppose to do it." Mother calls again and we go in.

All night long, fireflies pop up in my dreams. The next night we are playing Kick The Can when Mother calls, "Time to come in. Bed time now." Instead of going in I walk down the driveway toward the dirt road, scared of being alone in the dark, but hoping to see the fireflies again—those elusive flashes, here-and-there, now-and-then sparks from the ditch. I must watch closely because I don't know where one will jump up until I see it start to jump, and then it's gone before I know it. As I walk out the driveway, insects land on my arms and legs, biting before I can bat them off. The rare occurrence of a car going by surprises me. I wave. When the cloud of dust dies down, I walk onto the road and get as close to the ditch as I can without falling in. Weeds choke the ditch—dandelions, red clover, white clover, the lucky four-leaf clover, milkweed, pigweed, and thistle. During the day the weeds in the ditch are familiar, but now it's dark, and I can't make out which ones are stinging nettles. I draw back and step another way. The whole ditch is singing with a kind of droning singsong, louder than Pa's sing-song long prayer after meals but with the same lilting cadence. The pitch grows higher as I get closer. Lesser voices join into the melee at intervals. Another bug bites me and I run home to find Mother.

"Do bugs sing to the fireflies?"

"Say, snookie, you got some big bites there." She shoos me off to bed with "Fireflies are really bugs, you know." I call back at her, "Do they start fires?" But she's around the corner by now, out of sight. "Shimmer, glow little glow worm, glimmer, glimmer," I mutter to myself, half singing, half remembering the tune on the radio. Slowly, I climb the stairs to bed seeing flashes, shimmers, and dives. All together bugs sing the same note loudly, all night long, every night. Upstairs I look out the window at the stars. The long Milky Way sways like the wood swing in the grove. Wondering why, I dive between the sheets. One of Mother's favorite hymns sings itself inside my head, again, almost putting me to sleep. "I come to the garden alone, while the dew is still on the roses, and the voice I hear, falling on my ear..." Singing along with Mother, I drift off.

Years later, I visit cousins on their farm near Sioux Center, Iowa. Their farmhouse is set back a short ways from the road, like our farmhouse was near Hospers. Supper is over. While cousin Margaret (Mike) Kooi is putting away food and doing dishes, her husband, Bill, and I walk down the driveway to the road. Fireflies are jumping out of the deep ditches ripe with tall weeds, appearing and disappearing with the speed of lightning, and I wonder if what I am seeing is real.

Idyl

Please bring me back my childhood
in that Iowa frame farmhouse
My Mother's flour-smudged cheek, and
apron pockets filled with this 'n that
Her mason jar of buttons
Cigar box full of thread
The gopher holes along the creek
The pasture where we went for cows
our bare feet circling fresh cow pies
And spreading out at dark—
one yellow circle of farmyard light
that made black lines weave in and out
from vacant, slatted, long corn cribs
to where we kids played Kick The Can [72]

Besides the indoor games we made up during the long winter nights, we had some store-bought games like Monopoly and checkers. Caroms and checkers were played on the same side of a game board we called the carom board. On the other side of this board were Chinese checkers, or perhaps backgammon, but we rarely played these games. The carom board was kept standing against the wall behind the davenport until after supper. Then Pete or Stan would set it on a bench, group the caroms in the middle, position the special shooter-caroms behind the lines, and find the sticks. Invariably, one or another of us little kids would beg, "Let me play too." Invariably, a big kid would reply, "Wait'll you get a little bigger," and then—later on—give in to our begging and stand by, impatiently waiting, while we tried it.

Setting up the game took awhile. The trick was to balance the board properly so that it would stay level during play. Four green pouches at the corners of the board were made of heavy net, and each pouch had to hang freely. Equal numbers of red and green wooden rings called caroms were grouped in the center of the board with one black carom at the exact center

[72] Poem by author.

186 of the group. Round sticks like pool cues were held just so in two hands and the end of the stick was moved back and forth. Aim was taken at the caroms with a white carom, called the shooter, which was placed on the red line by the player's bank. When the shooter carom hit the centered caroms, they scattered. This was called breaking the caroms. Then, each player got a turn at trying to bounce one carom off another carom to send it into a pocket. Only accurate aim by a player could do this. At each turn, a player had to carefully gauge the placement of the wooden rings on the board before he aimed at a carom. The goal was to be the first team of two people to fill two pockets with either the red or the green caroms. Of course, there were rules:

1. No throwing caroms since lost caroms are not as easily replaced as lost checkers. A button or coin could replace a lost checker, but replacement caroms had to come from town, and it could be quite awhile before Woolworth's Five & Dime got them. New caroms also might come from the Sears Roebuck or Montgomery Ward catalogs by mail order, but that took months.
2. When finished playing, pick up every single carom and put them all away in the tin can.
3. Put the sticks away with the board. We lost or broke the round sticks, then begged Mother to let us use the flat sticks at the bottoms of window shades. She always said, "Be sure to put them back in the shades when you finish playing." Sometimes we forgot to do this, and in the course of time we had to use a thumb and forefinger to shoot caroms.
4. Not fair: sneaking a hand or knee under a pocket just as an opponent's carom was sliding into it, so that the carom jumped back onto the board.

We played card games such as Old Maid, Rook, and Authors, but there were always some cards missing from the deck. Sometime after the deaths of my parents, I was in Denver visiting my sister, Bernice. In the basement of her home, next to the furnace, was a box of old things that no one had wanted. In it was the worn deck of cards for Authors with many cards missing, but I found the four cards for Nathaniel Hawthorne, each card showing the title of one of his books. On the farm, four of us would play Authors. Four cards listing four titles by the same author made a book, and whoever got the most books won. The titles of the books were by authors such as Edgar Allen Poe, Charles Dickens, William Shakespeare, James Fenimore Cooper, or Sir Walter Scott. I took the cards home with me to the San Joaquin Valley in California.

Early one day in April of 1990, I take the long way home from a poet's home near the town of Linden. The rural route is along Fine Road, through walnut groves. Twisting into Hewitt, at Peters, I see Hawthorne's *House of Seven Gables* set high upon a hill near long chicken coops. Across the road are neatly stacked piles of junk—rusting pillories around a rotting farmhouse that is framed with boards painted by fungus, lichen, and mosses, revealing Hawthorne's *Scarlet Letter*. Again, I am a child in Iowa and we are playing "Authors" around the kitchen table.

Along the rural roads in central California are redwing blackbirds, lined up post to post, like the birds that sang on fence wires in Iowa. Around the orchards there are no fences at all to contain the joy of wild mustard, grasses wet with diamond dew, and fields of upturned loam. Below the long reach of white egret wings, country bridges romp across broad-shouldered canals. From the mud beneath almond orchards, to the giant hands of valley oak, there is a black tracery of memories tangling eye to acorn in apple-balled branches bared to winter's instructions. As I cross another bridge, into the country of childhood, I see how true were Pa's tired words, "When the cows come home..." As they always do, as they always did at milking time, every morning and every evening. Going home, I am taking the slower way home: Fine Road running past riparian haunts where almond blossom snow powders the ground and scarlet hawthorns tell *Twicetold Tales*, replaying fire lit card games when I was six or seven, maybe eight, meandering into Authors, Old Maid, checkers, and caroms on snowbound nights during the war, when *The Wonder Book* could win, but not *Tanglewood Tales*.

The cows came home single file, tramping a trail through the pasture as they slowly plodded to the milk barn. Scratchy grass and cow pies littered and bordered this winding trail of worn dirt. Someone would be sent to get the cows while they were still munching on grass in the far pasture. Pa would yell to Stanley or Verna Mae, "Go get the cows." One of

188   them would walk out along the trail, dodging cow pies, calling over and over, "C' bos, C' bos." Pa's expression, "When the cows come home," implied forever, since cows come home to be milked twice a day every day of the year whether it is Sunday, Monday, Tuesday, or Christmas. "Forever," said Pa's long whistling and his singing, "There's a long, long trail a-winding into the land of my dreams." The cows are forever with us, like the air we breathe, the dirt in the fields, and the gopher holes in the pasture. We poked into gopher holes with sticks. We pushed dead gophers, armless dolls, and other broken hopes through the culvert that went under the road. As with many things, we learned how to kill gophers from the big kids. My sister, Gladys Gritter, tells how to drown out gophers.

> Clarence and I used to hunt gophers. Apparently gophers were a menace to cows feeding in the pasture, who might stumble into a gopher hole and break a leg. Probably we were between four and eight years old when we did this. For every gopher we killed, the folks paid us five cents. I guess they took our word of honor, since we didn't bring the dead ones home. The gophers made holes all through the pasture. In digging up the pasture, they left dirt mounds. Our long, winding, one-half mile of pasture followed the long, winding creek. Gopher mounds were all over. Every spring there were lots of them. They multiplied easily. We'd take a gallon syrup pail, a club of some sort, and getting water from the creek; we'd pour it down some likely looking hole. This was called "drowning them out." Pretty soon, up came the drenched gopher. Then we'd club him to death—unless he made it to another hole first. We also trapped them, setting our traps by the mouth of the hole, securely staking the trap to the ground. Some mornings we'd have two or three gophers in our traps. If they weren't dead, we'd club them. Now, at age fifty-eight, I wonder how I could do this. But then, I can't ever remember thinking about the killing part. The creek was a very enjoyable part of childhood.[73]

A culvert carried the creek under the road to the next farm. After trickling through this corrugated-metal tube, the water disappeared into a

---

[73] Gladys I. Gritter, "Gophers," in *My Memories* (Grand Rapids, MI, 1984).

slough, drying up each fall. The road and creek had no names, and there were no signs at the corners where the roads met to section off the land. Perhaps the creek was one of the tributaries flowing into a branch of the Floyd River. A Lynn Township map shows the landowners on 36 sections of farmland, but does not show our creek. However, a map titled, "Dutch Settlement in Sioux County, Iowa, about 1900," does show several tributaries flowing into the Floyd River. Perhaps the creek we loved flowed into the slough, and then underground into one of the tributaries that flowed into a branch of the Floyd River (maps at end of chapter). The culvert made a slight bump in the road, if that, but not enough of a rise to be called a bridge. The nature of bridges is such that they shrink distance and extend the neural maps of memory. Like spider webs, they cross at differing angles into shifting planes.

Even before we went to school, we knew that what Pa jokingly called "the crik" was really the creek. We studied the character of the creek as the seasons changed, watching it as closely as the farmers watched the weather. On the way to church in the winter, we pressed our noses against the car window to see if the deep snow still held a trickle of water bubbling along inside the banks of the creek. By March the snows and rains cut deeply into the rich, black land, cracking and crumbling chunks of bank into the muddy water. During the spring, the culvert clogged, and the creek reared up to run over the road. In summertime, the lazy meanderings of the creek became endless bends holding treasures. Beyond each turn, who could tell what surprise awaited us?

The culvert caught all kinds of debris and became a storehouse of twigs and sticks that became the source of makeshift toys. The creek and culvert were the sites of games and contests that we made up as we went along. Miniature rafts were built, tied together with the supple stalks of weeds, to carry sheaves of grain downstream to the twin towers of the Farmers Co-op in Hospers. At harvest time the culvert held the slender arteries of used-up creek water. Now and then, it hid a stray cat that had been clobbered by a car, a bird with a broken wing, or a bird's nest. All sorts of familiar things got caught in the culvert. We found a pile of ragged clothes that either had been abandoned by a hobo or had blown off a scarecrow, but we did not find the hobo who we imagined slept in the ditch next to the culvert. Such scary finds were part of playing along the creek, in the pasture, or in the weed-choked ditch along the road.

To get sluggish water to flow through the culvert we stuck long sticks into it. An older kid would prod a younger kid. "I'll push the sticks through the culvert if you crawl to the other end of it and pull them out the other side." The creek ran through the pasture and in it, fresh cow pies were circled by the buzzing of bugs trying to land on them. They dried up quickly and got so hard that we could not even poke sticks through them. I was poking at a thick drop of milkweed milk on my skin when I saw Elmer running away, across the ditch, through the tall grass, toward the culvert. Then I saw Milly running, so I too ran as fast as I could to see what was happening. A big kid was daring each little kid to crawl into the long, cavernous mouth of the culvert and go clear through the dark, damp, dirty debris to the other end. "Hands first, belly down. C'mon, don't be a sissy."

But, the middle of the culvert was no place to get stuck. Something might bite you when you got half way in. You might be sucked into the long throat of whatever was in there. Snakes lived deep inside and dead mice were caught in old leaves. The creek could rush down at anytime to drown you. Dead cats were buried in the culvert, wrapped in a rag and laid in a shoe box.

"Fraidy cat! Fraidy cat!"

"You're just a fraidy cat."

"Run! Run! Bet I can beat cha home!"

Then the older kid would run. Although the creek was far enough away from the farmhouse and mother's eyes and ears, so that we could do as we pleased, her admonishment, "Watch out for each other," was with us. Even so, out of her sight, the bigger and smarter kids governed whatever happened, and their tricks and threats kept us in line. If a bigger kid got in trouble, he or she could run home for help, but it was a long way for a little kid to run for help. Elmer or Glenny would need more than ten minutes to cross the cornfield and get home. Who would go for help if I took the dare and crawled into the culvert? What if I got stuck half way through?

"Double dare! I double dare you to crawl through!" I didn't take the dare.

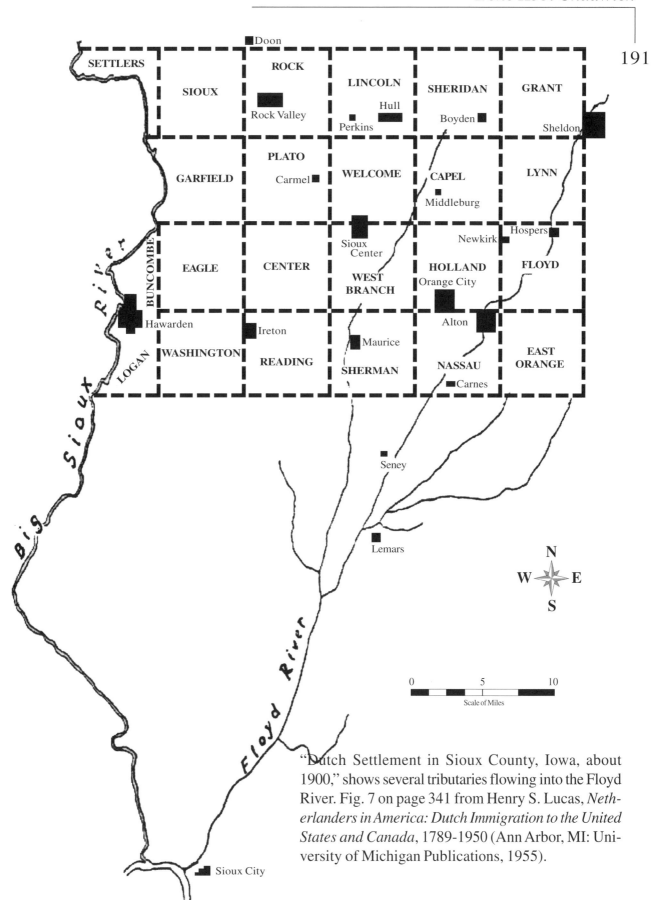

"Dutch Settlement in Sioux County, Iowa, about 1900," shows several tributaries flowing into the Floyd River. Fig. 7 on page 341 from Henry S. Lucas, *Netherlanders in America: Dutch Immigration to the United States and Canada*, 1789-1950 (Ann Arbor, MI: University of Michigan Publications, 1955).

LYNN PLAT

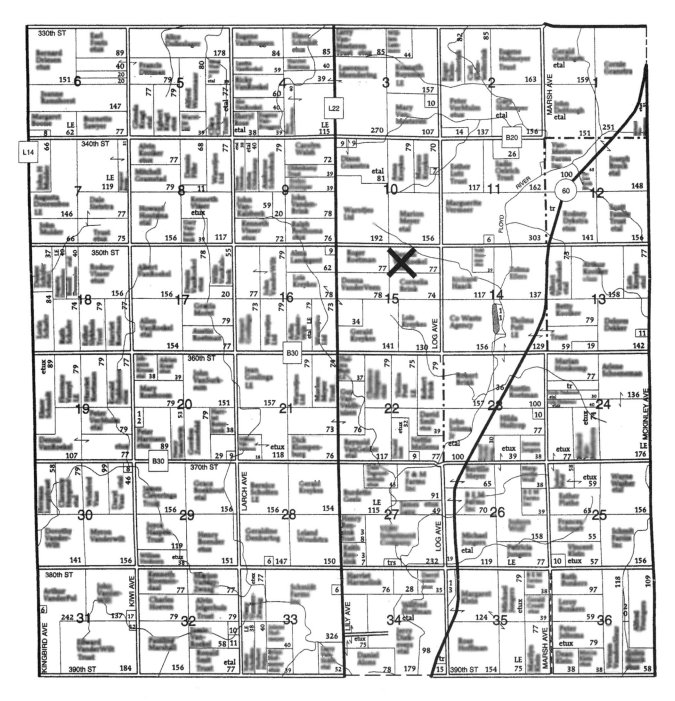

Lynn Plat shows the 36 sections of Lynn Township in Sioux County, Iowa, but not
the creek on our farm. The Floyd River roughly parallels Route 60. "X" denotes our Hospers farm
from 1939-1947.

Five Kooi brothers at reunion: John, Fred, George, Ben, and Ellis, Rock Rapids, Iowa, 1936.

Two oldest sisters, Bernice and Gladys, in new housecoats, Lake Okoboji, 1941.

194

Peter Kooi on Hospers Farm, 1942.

Clarence Kooi on Hospers Farm, 1943.

18

Will the Child Say Grace?

Aunt Jennie, Pa's youngest sister, and Aunt Gertie, his oldest sister, married Haverhals brothers, settled on nearby farms, and raised large families. Both kept family records. When Aunt Gertie passed on, Aunt Jennie carried on, keeping many drawers full of documents, records, photos, and memorabilia. She often wrote long, detailed letters that included genealogy. Once when I was visiting Aunt Jennie, she told me that her mother, Grada Kooi, often made the things needed by her family. In those days, things were not so easy to buy or were not well made, and she had the choice, energy, and joy of doing things herself. After her mother's death, Jennie kept several things her mother had made or used. Among them was the shoemaker last she used to repair shoes, also the simple wooden desk that she built for Fred's bedroom, so that when he was sick he would not have to come downstairs but could read in his room.

Aunt Jennie said: "We knew very little of any early Koois until recent years, when we were contacted by far-off Koois who see, meet and learn of connections; also by nieces and nephews who travel to the Netherlands and elsewhere. Generations go back, side-by-side, down to the 1700's, always to the Province of Groningen, north, near the sea borders there, in the Oldenzyl area." The town's name was Uithuizen, which means houses standing away from other houses, not out houses. The Province of Groningen is in the northern part of Holland, to the east of Friesland and adjacent to it. These two provinces have a separate and distinct character from the rest of Holland, since waters surround them. The city of Groningen is important historically for its guilds, and as a communication center linking places via its extensive waterways for far-reaching commerce.

Groningen is not only a fine large town, populous, rich and flourishing, but it is, moreover, the most ancient in the country. Ancient chronicles date it as founded 500 years B.C., some by a person called Grunus, who gave it its name; according to others by a

German race, the Gruines, mentioned by Tacitus. But neighboring towns, jealous of its pedigree, affirm that the name is derived from the Dutch adjective "groen" (green), and from the substantive "inigen," which in the Drenthe and Over-Yssel patois means "field" or "meadow," and that really she takes her name from the green pastures with which she is surrounded.[74]

The first main migration of Europeans to the South Chicago area and to Wisconsin occurred in the 1850s. Both Fred Kooi's mother, Grada Kastein, and his grandfather, Pieter Kooi, were a part of this migration. Many Kasteins emigrated to Wisconsin in the 1860s, and some even before that. In 1854, Pieter Kooi and Geertje Abbenga, sailed to America from Groningen. On arrival in South Chicago, they got married and had eight children. Four babies died, all by the age of fifteen months, and are buried with their parents in Graceland Cemetery. Peter and Geertje Kooi bought a family burial plot there in 1869. Cemetery records show:

> John P. Kooi d. 1857, age 15 months
> Jane Kooi d. 1870, age 1 month
> Jeneke Kooi d. 1872, age 11 months
> William Kooi d. 1873, age 4 months

Their first-born son had died in 1857, ten years before they bought the family plot, so in 1869 they had his body moved to this plot. Between 1870 and 1873, three more infants were buried there. The names on the gravestones are John, Jennie, Jennie, and Willie. Four more babies were born between 1858 and 1866. In 1873, Pieter Kooi, the father of these eight children, died, and in 1874 the mother, Geertje, died. Their deaths left four orphans: Peter, age eight, Remko, age ten, Barbara, age twelve, and John, age sixteen. In the large Dutch families of that time it was not uncommon for nearly half of the children to die, and to die quite young. In both the old and new world, early childhood diseases took a heavy toll.

Burial records at Graceland Cemetery (section 133, area 108) show

[74] Op cit, Singleton, p. 86.

that the name, Pieter, had changed to Peter, but his wife had retained her Dutch name, Geertje. She died at age 40, Peter at age 50. She had spent half her life in Groningen and half in Chicago, and he had spent his first thirty years in Groningen and the last twenty years in Chicago. In 1920 or 1923, when the four orphaned children were adults, they placed headstones on their parents graves and maintained the headstones. Listed by the cemetery as owners are the three brothers, John, Remko, and Peter Kooi, and their sister, Barbara Smithson. Two burial plots are not in use. Aunt Jennie says, "We surmise that they were intended for Barbara and her husband, Robert Smithson, but later on they moved to California, and are buried in the Forest Hills, Hollywood Cemetery."[75]

The Graceland Cemetery is known historically for perfectly cared for, well-known gravesites, with notable tombs, memorials, and fitting tributes for some of the biggest names in the city's history. George Pullman, the railroad magnate after which Pullman Cars were named, is under a fortress designed to stop angry union members from digging him up. Marshall Field, founder of the Department Store by that name, was also buried here.

> If you want to commune with the king of rock and roll, you go to Graceland; for merchant princes and emperors of architecture, you want the other Graceland, the one in Chicago. Only Elvis Presley and his immediate family are buried at the Memphis Graceland; Chicago's is a 116-acre cemetery open to anyone who can afford the price of a plot. Since it opened in 1860, Graceland has been the final address for many of the richest and most powerful Chicagoans— and often for the architects who designed their tombs. It has Egyptian pyramids, Greek temples, assorted statues, and even a giant stone baseball for National League founder William Hulbert. It also has one unmarked grave. World heavyweight boxing champion Jack Johnson bought a family plot when his wife Etta, died in 1912. He gave her a headstone but didn't get himself one.[76]

[75] John Haverhals visited Graceland and sent records and photographs of our ancestors' gravestones to his mother, Jennie Haverhals, in Sioux Center, Iowa.

[76] Excerpt from Associated Press story in unidentified newspaper, n.d., titled *Graceland: where death is king,* subtitled *Chicago cemetery the final home for city's rich and powerful,* dateline: Chicago, by F. N. D'Alessio.

198   According to Aunt Jennie, "Only the oldest of the four Kooi orphans stayed in the Chicago area. John Reuben Kooi, 1858-1926, married Elizabeth Hermann and they had two children. Their son, Elmer, and his family lived thirty miles northwest of Chicago in Marengo, Illinois. Elmer had one brother, Eddie. Seems he met death as a young man involved with the crime element in Chicago. That is the only sad incident I know of. More, I'm sure, but there was general well being from all indications and appearances." Since there are no descendents of the John Reuben Kooi family, when all John's heirs died, the last one left the "Kooi Family Bible," photos, and memorabilia to Jennie Haverhals, the youngest daughter of John's brother, Remko. Aunt Jennie gave this large illustrated Bible to her grand nephew, Terry Kooi, and his wife, Julie, in Iowa, the son of Peter and Nella Kooi and the grandson of John Kooi, my father's brother.

What happened to the four orphans in Chicago is oral history from Aunt Jennie:

> Barbara was twelve when she went to live with my Aunt Lizzie Kooi Groot, a close-knit cousin of Remko Kooi and the other siblings. Lizzie was one of the six daughters (and one son) of Willem Kooi, the older brother of my grandfather, Pieter Remgus Kooi, who had come to Chicago five years later than my grandfather. He came with his family of five girls and one son, Peter, whose only son, Will, 1895-1918, was a World War One casualty in France. Several of Willem Kooi's daughters had large families, mainly girls, but no male heir named Kooi has originated in either Peter's or Willem's line, except for the male heirs in our Remko Kooi Family. In the early 1900s the Remko Kooi family knew Uncle Willem Kooi's family very well, visiting back and forth, often traveling to see each other even though they lived great distances apart. Your Aunt Bertha recalls many visits in the early 1900s to and from Chicago. The four siblings, John, Barbara, Remko, and Peter, stayed in close touch.

The favorite relative to visit, and write to, was Lizzie Groots, with whom Barbara had gone to live after her parents died. Barbara became a successful businesswoman in Chicago. Studio portraits of her made in Chicago show a stylish woman with wonderful hats and nice accessories. A reserved and confident air graces her features. She met a rich man, Robert Smithson from Santa Barbara, married him when she was forty-five and moved to Hollywood, California. The Iowa relatives knew very little about him. A snapshot she sent to Iowa shows her holding a bouquet of flowers in front of a Hollywood home luxuriant with flowerbeds. She died in 1937, and in her will she gave $8712.81 to Aunt Jennie.[77] The same amount went to each one of Remko and Grada Kooi's other living children, including Fred Kooi, my father. This inheritance came at the right time—between the spring of 1938 and winter of 1939—at the end of the Great Depression when Pa was hard pressed to keep the insurance company from foreclosing on the farm.

Remko was the third orphan—of interest to me because he became the father of ten children, among them, my father, Fred. Remko Kooi was born on the Fourth of July in 1864. Orphaned at age ten, he went to live with his Uncle Hessel Abbenga, 1842-1911, who was a younger brother of Remko's mother, Geertje Abbenga Kooi. Truck gardens and growing vegetables was the main work in what was then South Chicago. These farms supplied the city tables with vegetables. A job for children on these farms was the clearing of new fields by picking up the stones that stuck in plow blades and tossing or carrying them to the side of the field. This was heavy, tedious work, especially for a child. The family of Lizzie (Kooi) Groots had a store that sold produce, eggs, and so forth, and likely the vegetables were supplied by the truck gardens where their cousins worked. Remko did not like living with and working for his Uncle Hessel. At age seventeen he ran away to Sioux County, Iowa, against the wishes of his uncle. Since Hessel had been appointed the legal guardian of Remko who was still a minor, Hessel got a judge's order to send Remko's belongings to Iowa. Remko went to live with a good family in Iowa, the Borgmans, whose son Jim, age twenty-one, was to become a lifelong friend of the Remko Kooi family. Jim had thirteen daughters and then one son. This well-educated son is the only remaining living member of that family. Their elegant home still stands in Southeast Sioux Center.

---

[77] Letters dated March 4, 1938, and January 3, 1939, from lawyers for Barbara K. Smithson's estate to Jennie Kooi Haverhals.

In Chicago, Peter, the youngest orphan at age eight, grew up and started out as an employee of the Burlington Northern Railroad, apparently as a spittoon hauler for a time. Peter married Mary Helen Brown (known as Aunt Mae), and had three daughters. The family moved to Wyoming, where Peter became prominent in business. He founded a coal-mining camp and community named "Kooi" in the hills near Sheridan, Wyoming. The mine operated from 1906 to 1922, employing two hundred and sixty men in 1913.[78] He built a large home in Sheridan, Wyoming, and sent his three daughters east to be educated. Aunt Mae often returned to Chicago to shop. The family traveled extensively in 1919 and 1920. All three daughters retained the Kooi name for their middle name after marriages. Lorna Kooi Simpson (1900-1995) married a lawyer in 1929 and had two sons. Her husband, Milward L. Simpson (1897-1993), became the Governor of Wyoming and then a U.S. Senator. Their two sons are retired U.S. Senator Alan Simpson and University of Wyoming Vice President Peter Simpson. In 1993, Aunt Jennie related that:

> From all indications, the Hollanders did well after arriving in Chicago, and with a minimum of schooling, maybe three years, my parents, Remko and Grada, both were able to do very well. My father, with all his many projects and political interests, also helped scores of Dutch to come over, to work and farm. In 1881 he signed for 75 Dutch immigrants who worked for him for a year or two before striking out on their own. I see Mother in her chair reading. We had many good papers and books. Also, the children of Willem Kooi, and other Koois in Chicago, apparently succeeded well in their living conditions and business. From the pictures and all, one has this impression.

---

[78] Story and maps of Kooi Mine are in *Black Diamonds of Sheridan, A Facet of Wyoming History*, Chapter 13: Kooi 1907-1922, by Stanley A. Kuzara.

"Will The Child Say Grace?"

I had heard stories about the success and fame of Great Uncle Peter Kooi and Great Aunt Mae in Wyoming; I knew the names of their three daughters, who they married, and what happened to their children. Naturally, I was curious about this famous uncle but had never met him because he was already dead when I was little, just like all the grandparents and the other great-uncles and great-aunts.

After we moved to Denver in 1947, Pa took me in his car on a week-long trip to Sheridan, Wyoming, to visit his cousin, Doris Kooi Reynolds, one of the three daughters of great-uncle Peter Kooi. I was either eleven or twelve when we took our trip. Pa was in his mid-fifties and wore the straw hat he wore on Sundays to church. He had on his long-sleeved blue work shirt. He would not have thought twice about taking me out of school, so it may have been in September. I felt special, sitting alone in the front seat next to Pa in the 1947 gray Chevrolet. Being alone with Pa was a rare thing. Out on the open road he would sometimes let me hold the wheel. I was a scrawny but scrappy pre-teen, dying to drive, although I could barely see over the hood. Pa only spoke in answer to questions. I asked him about the cousins that we were going to see. I gathered that they were not like us, that is, not from a Dutch, Christian Reformed background. Worldly, not Christian, I assumed they would be different. He warned me to use good manners while there. Pa was proud of my ability to read the map and figure out distances and to calculate how long it would take us to get to the next gas station or cafe. It took a long time—all day—to get there, but I was happy. Valued as the navigator, I no longer feared him.

At the Reynold's large home, there was one grown-up daughter named Crew Kooi Reynolds. Mister Reynolds showed us around their house and took us into a big, dark downstairs to show off his hunting trophies. Turning to the bar, he asked Pa what he'd like to drink. Pa seemed confused, as though he didn't know what to say. I remember feeling embarrassed for him and wishing I could disappear under a large table in the middle of the room that was covered with green felt. I had never seen a pool table before, but I knew about pool halls—remembered from Question School at church that playing pool was sinful.

At the large oval dinner table, Mister Reynolds asked Pa if he was used to saying grace before eating. Pa mumbled something that I could not hear. Then Mister Reynolds looked around the table, and his eyes came to rest on me. He asked Pa, "Would the child like to say grace?" Pa's reply was to give me a look that meant, "Do it, and do it right." I sat very still and did not say anything. During the long silence, everyone stared at me and waited. I was so embarrassed that I wanted to slowly sink lower into the chair and then disappear under the long white tablecloth. Mortified, I turned beet red, looked down, and hoped no one would notice that I existed. After what seemed like an eternity, Mister Reynolds said, "Well, Fred, would you like to say a few words?" Pa nodded and mumbled a long prayer in his usual sing-song prayer voice. I was stunned. So that was what grace meant. What a surprise. Of course, I had heard that word "grace" hundreds of times. It meant something like being in a blessed place. More importantly, it was cousin Grace's name, Uncle Pete and Aunt Gertie's second daughter. Grace never meant prayer.

On the farm at the table we did not talk; we ate—unless we needed more to eat, and then we would say, "Please pass the potatoes." Or salt. Or gravy. During the dinner at the Reynolds in Sheridan I said nothing. I kept my eyes on my plate, tried not to spill anything, and tried to use the right manners, not being any too sure just what was right. The adults seemed to be having an awkward time trying to make conversation. Afterwards, someone showed me where the swings were out back, and I played alone outside until the adults took me with them to look around Sheridan. We saw business buildings, a dusty museum in the making, and the fenced-off mansion of the great-uncle Peter Kooi whom I had never met.

We probably stayed less than the intended week, since Pa would have seen what there was to see in a few days, and he was not one to sit around in strange surroundings. I do not remember the long trip home except that I was very glad to get home, and Mother asked me if I had had a good time. I told her that the Reynolds were very rich, lived in a big house, and were different from us, but they were nice to me. She smiled, kissed me, and said "Well honey, I'm glad you're home again."

Illustrated Holy Bible
of Geertje Kooi has
family records, 1870.

Gert, at age 14 the oldest child of Remko and Grada Kooi in Lebanon, Iowa,
visited her father's two brothers, John and Peter, in Chicago, 1903.

Peter Kooi of Wyoming and Barbara Kooi of Chicago traveled to Lebanon,
Iowa, for funeral of Peter, son of Remko and Grada Kooi. Seated L-R:
Grada, Jennie, Barbara. Standing L-R: Fred, Peter, Remko.

Barbara Kooi at age 14 in Chicago, 1876.

19

Butchering

Butchering brought fat as well as meat into the house. The lard rendered from fat was used for cooking and baking. Some fat was made into soap by treating it with lye, a poison that Mother took extreme care to keep away from us little kids. Hot bacon grease was used to fry potatoes, onions, pancakes, and eggs. I loved to chew on the thick slab of bacon still sizzling and curling up on top of pancakes, dripping with hot grease and syrup, but I could chew on the tough bacon rind for only so long before I had to spit out the hard wad. While Mother was looking the other way, the wad got shoved onto the ledge under the table.

On the farmyard, a roof stretched over two slatted corncribs with a wide slab of concrete on the ground between them. Open to the farmyard at both ends, this concrete drive was used to unload corn from the wagons that the cornhuskers brought in at harvest time. Afterwards, this concrete was where Pa and the big brothers butchered a hog or steer. Between two sawhorses, four-by-six boards held the dead animal. Blood flowed freely from the butchered steer and ran down the sides of the boards and sawhorses onto the concrete floor and into cracks in the fine, dry soil, staining the earth. What horrified me was the fat hanging from the flesh of the steer. It fell off the carcass in slippery slabs and slid off the table. The hanging snot of fat tissue in large clots was gory—revolting. I bolted. I had no doubt at all about what this snot brought to mind—the sticky-thick oatmeal that congealed into knots of glue clinging to the sides of my bowl at breakfast. When I gagged on that sticky snot, Mother took pity on me and let me leave the last globs of oatmeal in the bowl, but she cautioned, "Next time, don't take any. Take something else. Eat the boiled egg or take some toast." I felt relieved and grateful to turn away from that gelatinous, gray goop and hoped never to see it again.

Outdoors, in the farmyard, I backed away from the fat slithering off the carcass. Every part of the steer seemed broken, bleeding, screeching, curdling, dead but still pleading. Pa looked nervous. Maybe he too felt savagely out of place, I don't know. He yelled at us. "Now you little kids stay out of the way, ja hear?" Hushed shame hovered over butchering. We backed away to watch from a distance, but Pa saw us and yelled, "Don't stay here." On the ground the blood was mixing with the fine dirt to make mud. The stain became a strain that could not be blotted out. Finally, Pa had had enough and ordered: "Find someplace else to play. Go. Now! Get out of here!" As we ran off, I felt sick to my stomach. Never again did I watch butchering.

Around the year 1940, a butchered steer or hog was brought to town to be stored in the frozen-food locker. Before the advent of electricity and freezers, the meat was preserved in salt or canned. Cousin Catherine De Bie reports that "butchering was usually done in the winter, and it took nearly a week before everything of a steer and a hog was taken care of. Meat would have to be canned, and lard would have to be fried out. This all would have to be done in the kitchen, so when it was finished the floor and the ceiling of the kitchen needed a thorough scrubbing." Sister Gladys recalls canning in the 1930s when she was age twelve.

> The first to be canned was pie plant (rhubarb.) We pulled tons of it and washed and cut it into pieces, put it into kettles, and canned bushels and bushels of it. On canning days—and there were lots of them—I would wake in the morning and Ma would say, "Well, girls, today we can pie plant," or whatever it was. "Get the jars from the cellar." After that we washed the jars, rubbers, and lids. I filled the jars and turned them tight with a two-piece mechanical gizmo. One piece held the hot jar and the other the top of the cover. If the lid was dented at the lip, we would pound it down with the handle of a knife. After pie plant, I think there were beans. We kids helped pick and snap beans when we were very little. It wasn't a dangerous job like cutting pie plant was. Canning meat came later in the fall. The pig was "stuck" in the pig yard. I hated to hear his cries as he died, so I didn't get anywhere near. Then after the men had strung him up with ropes on the rafters in the shed, they would have to have gallons of boiling water to scrape the hair off. Just how they went about cutting the pig up, I don't recall. But pretty soon the liver or the heart would come to the

house to be made ready for dinner or supper. Later in the day we'd start cutting up the meat and putting it in jars. I cut lots of meat in my day! I think we added a teaspoon of salt and a half teaspoon of pepper to each jar and filled it with water and boiled the jars either in the wash boiler on the stove or else in a low pan in the oven. Rendering out the lard took a long time. Maybe it was done the next day. In large cookie-sheet-type pans we put the cut-up fat pieces. After they were in the oven awhile, the lard would be poured off into a crock. We had crocks of all sizes, from large to small. Now I see these kind of crocks in restaurants for decoration. I can't remember butchering a cow, but we did can beef, so we probably got a half or quarter when a neighbor butchered one. When we kids went to the cellar for a can of meat, the dark meat was beef, the light was pork. It had a layer of white fat towards the top of the jar.[79]

At certain times, a bull was let into the pasture. A few months later a cow had a calf. Birth was an event that we little kids were not allowed to watch. We did watch the calf suck milk from the cow. Soon, however, the calf was weaned from the cow to a pail of milk. In this way a cow was freshened for use as a milk cow.

At first the cream separator was turned by hand, but later on it was run by an electric motor. A pail or two of milk was poured into a stainless-steel bowl. The separator worked by centrifugal force. The whole milk was spun around very fast, and the cream rose to the top. One of Gladys's chores was to set the separator, which was done before the men brought the pails of milk to the house before suppertime. It had to be done just right, or the separator leaked when they used it. The separator Gladys used was run by hand. Someone turned the wheel and kept turning until the milk was all separated. This milk went to the little calves and the pigs, and the cream was put into cream cans in the cellar.

After the 1939 move to the Hospers farm, an electric cream separator was put into a separate room in the barn that had a cement floor for the shiny-new machine. A government inspector came now and then to check on sanitary conditions. Mother would often warn us as we ran outside to

[79] Gladys Gritter, *My Memories* (Grand Rapids, MI, 1984).

play, banging the screen door behind us, "Now you little kids watch out for the cream hauler coming into the yard." Apparently she trusted him to watch out for us, because we would overhear her remark, "Well, anyway, he will slow down and look around when he drives into the yard. He better, anyway." On the Lebanon farm, Bernice recalls learning to milk cows at an early age:

> I always tried to get out of it but rarely succeeded. The barns smelled and were dirty. In the winter it was a miserably cold job. In the summer you fought flies constantly, as did the cows. They swished their tails smartly in your face if you didn't secure the tail in the chains placed around their legs so they wouldn't kick the milk pail over. But they got mad when their tails and legs were tied. In revenge they sometimes fell down on top of you. I learned the rhythm of milking: front teat, back teat, and finally stripping each teat while holding the milk pail between my legs. I did it for many years, but I always hated it. Crops were an important source of a farmer's income, but my father also raised cattle for market.

Farmers carefully watched the market fluctuations for hog and cattle prices.

> For weeks Pa comes in at noon and listens intently to the market report on the radio. It is still dark one morning when I hear men talking loudly, excitedly. The yard light is on, and when I look out the window, I see the big trucks. Soon the steers are herded into the trucks for their trip to the slaughterhouse in Sioux City. I go back to bed, but soon light begins to melt away the darkness. We get up, milk the cows, eat breakfast. Pa is business-like. Our parents have made a decision as to who can go on THE TRIP, and this time I get to go! It is fifty miles to Sioux City, a great distance. I have never been so far from home. Pa is driving and is nervous when we enter the city, not quite sure which streets to take. The odor tells us we are nearing the stockyards. We kids are told what to do, what not to do, and where we must go. We obey and, as usual, depend on each other. Pa will be watching the sale. I do not know then how important the day is for him. Last year he borrowed thousands of dollars from the bank to buy these cattle. They have been carefully fed and cared for. Market reports were

studied carefully and the crucial decision made concerning which day to sell. If sold on the right day, he will get a price that will benefit our family financially. If not, hundreds or thousands of dollars will be lost. But this is not my concern. I need a restroom, and I am enjoying these fancy city toilets with a chain to pull for flushing, when I see this strange person. She has very dark skin and tight black hair; only the palms of her hands look normal. I stare at her. This must be a Negro. I have never seen one before. I feel a little afraid of her.[80]

The stockyards in Sioux City and in larger cities, notably Chicago, were the destinations for cattle from the farms of the Midwest. Here, livestock was rendered senseless in mere seconds after being kept in holding pens covering many acres. Not only did the stock bound for these cities experience violence—so did some of the immigrants. Since 1848, immigrants from Groningen had been settling in the southern part of Chicago. The first ones who came from the Province of Groningen were mostly from Uithuizen, Uithuizermeeden, Vierhuizen, and Usquert. They soon made a good living. Attracted by favorable reports, more Groningers came, Remko Kooi's parents among them. As early as 1859 there was a Groningen Quarter in the area between Halsted and Ashland Avenues and Twelfth and Eighteenth Streets. Stores catered to the Dutch and the Hollanders, who made a good living hauling garbage, controlling most of this business.

> The Groningen Quarter (Groningsche Hoek) in Chicago (1848), lacked the religious faith of other immigrants who settled in Roseland and South Holland. The small number that did have the vital spark of zeal struggled to form a congregation, and by 1858 had a mediocre place of worship. The community flourished materially; it became the nucleus of an ever growing Dutch settlement, which for years attracted a steady flow of immigrants.[81]

---

[80] Bernice Afman, "Market Day" and "Milking".

[81] Henry S. Lucas, "The Groningen Quarter (Groningsche Hoek) in Chicago (1848)," *Netherlanders in America: Dutch Immigration to the United States and Canada, 1789-1950* (Ann Arbor, MI: University of Michigan Publications, 1955), pp. 231-232.

212

The South Chicago that was the home of Pa's father, Remko Kooi, for the first seventeen years of his life, is graphically depicted in an excerpt from Carl Sandburg's 1916 poem, "Chicago."

> Hog butcher for the World,
> Tool Maker, Stacker of Wheat,
> Player with Railroads and the Nation's Freight Handler;
> Stormy, husky, brawling,
> City of the Big Shoulders:
> They tell me you are wicked and I believe them, for I have seen
>   your painted women under the gas lamps luring the farm boys.
> And they tell me you are crooked and I answer: Yes, it is true
>   I have seen the gunman kill and go free to kill again.[82]

During the last week of September in 1993, the fifty-first child under age fifteen was killed in Chicago. And "more children had been shot in the Chicago area since the beginning of that year than all the people of all ages gunned down in England during 1991." Gunshot was heard regularly in the streets of South Chicago neighborhoods. "Get your gun off the neighborhood wagon!" shouted the gunman during his regular run through Chicago's South Side neighborhoods. He was selling handguns to minors from the back of a van. The kind of gun the shot came from was recognized by its familiar sound, compared and discussed in kitchens, as though it were a kind of broom or baby bottle—as, perhaps, the kind of cars going by were discussed by neighbors sitting on their stoops in Sioux Center, Iowa. In South Chicago, funerals for young men and boys were commonplace. Hospitals and emergency rooms were full of people who are cut up and shot.[83]

In Sioux County, Iowa, another kind of neighborhood wagon made regular runs. "Get your candy from the peddleman!" shouted the peddler

---

[82] *Chicago* was the title poem for Carl Sandburg's first book, *Chicago Poems*. These poems came from his working-class background, intimate knowledge of urban life based on years as a journalist, a belief in social and economic justice, and his faith in the people.

[83] Joan Beck, "Curbing Violence," *Chicago Tribune*, October 2, 1993.

to draw us in. Playing in the grove, we would race toward the house when we heard the clanging bell and the peddleman's drawn-out yelling, "Get your candeee...." But, there was no hurry to get it. We would have to wait while Mother examined thimbles, thread, home remedies such as linament, and several other things displayed by the peddleman. How many coins Mother had in her apron pockets we never knew. The items on Mother's list never seemed to be urgent. Often she would say, "Well then, next time." Bernice recalls that:

> Every Friday the peddle wagon drives slowly up to our house. Mama comes out with the list in her hand. The peddle-wagon man owns the little store in Lebanon and peddles his wares on regular routes to the farmers. The peddle wagon is gray and is full of fascinating little drawers and shelves with hinges on them. As Mama tells him what she needs, he opens the appropriate door and sets it out. The list completed, we children wait for what we know comes last. The peddle-wagon man acts as though he almost forgot, then smiles and hands each of us a piece of candy.[84]

Another kind of peddler came to the farm as well. Gladys recalls that: "Once a month the Watkins man made a call to our farm. He hauled in his suitcase of items—mouthwash, toothbrushes, aspirin, stuff to gargle with, stuff to put on your hair. We kids sat close, hoping for something free—only once I remember we got a free straw."

"Get your gun off the neighborhood wagon!"

"Get your candy from the peddleman!"

If Remko Kooi had not run away to Iowa, he would not have met Grada Kastein. Perhaps Remko would have married a Chicago woman and his children might have been caught up in the random violence of the growing, brawling life of South Chicago. Chicago's big shoulders might have carried them in another direction than the place we come from.

The path that led to Grada, led to their secret marriage.

---

[84] Bernice Afman, "Peddle Wagons."

20
Secret Marriage

Ancestors of the Bride: Frederika ten Brink

The bride's grandfather, Frederik Wilhelm Joseph ten Brink, from Werth, Westphalia, Prussia, was born in 1797. In 1838, he married Barendina Jansen, age twenty-five, and they lived on an acre or two of land, in a very small community known as Westerdorp, a few miles west of the town of Varsseveld, in the municipality of Wisch, Province of Gueldres, The Netherlands. He had come over the border from Germany. The couple had two children in their small home, known as "De Masse"— first a son, Hermanus, in 1838, and then a daughter, Frederika, in 1840. Hermanus (1838-1914), continued to live in The Netherlands, but Frederika (1840-1897) immigrated to America. She left behind her mother and brother.

The father, Frederik, died in 1855, when Hermanus was seventeen years old and Frederika was fourteen and still in Holland. Their mother, Barendina, was widowed at age forty-two, only seventeen years after her marriage to Frederik ten Brink. Her son, Hermanus, married and had four daughters. The oldest, Hannah, married Ferdinand Schiebout. A small, faint photograph shows them immigrating to Alberta, Canada, carrying large suitcases and wearing heavy coats and hats. In his old age Hermanus, Hannah's father, became depressed and semi-demented while thinking about his four daughters who had migrated from The Netherlands to far-away America, and since he never heard from them again, he assumed they had drowned during their sea voyages. His mother, Barendina, lived until age seventy-three. When she died, Hermanus, in Nyverdal, Netherlands, wrote a letter to his sister, Frederika, in Sioux Center, Iowa. He told of their mother's death, and what he did with her property: "But your spinning wheel I left in storage in 'De Masse' for you, hoping that you will come some day to get it, when we can see each other again." They never did.

Ancestors of the Groom: Benart Kastein

The groom's father, Roelf Kastein, was born in 1811 at Suderwick in Westphalia, Germany, just across the border from Dinxperlo in The Netherlands. He was a subject of the Kaiser, a Prussian. Probably he was a younger son in the Kastein family, who owned Beersendam, a farm two or three miles east of Dinxperlo, province of Gueldres, Netherlands. In 1966, an Arnold Kastein still lived in this farmstead, which was not in good repair. Roelf was described as big and straight, with good judgment. He probably was not a church member. The groom's mother, Elizabeth Te Beest was born in Dinxperlo, in 1809 and she married Roelf in 1835 at Dinxperlo, Gelderland, in The Netherlands. She was described as very pretty, with brown eyes and wavy hair. They lived in the Province of Gueldres, The Netherlands, in a neighborhood known as De (Voor) Heurne, in the municipality of Dinxperlo, and in a house numbered 504. The house had the name "Weversjanshuis," because Roelf Kastein was a farmer and a weaver. The little farm and Weversjanshuis exist yet today, at Casparstraat 21, three miles northwest of the center of Dinxperlo, occupied by a Hengeveld family.[85]

In this home, five daughters were born to Roelf and Elizabeth. The Kastein women were said to have had cheerful, energetic, and outgoing personalities; one was described as "a kindly judge." Also in this home two sons were born, Benart (Bernart), in October, 1836, and a younger brother, Gerhard, in 1845. When he grew up, Gerhard was enthusiastic about immigrating to the U.S. with his parents in 1867, but he was ill. On his death bed Gerhard urged his brother, Benart, and his new wife, Frederika, to follow his parents to America. All of the family advised them to "Go on with plans to go to America." Gerhard B. Kastein (1845-1867) died in The Netherlands at age twenty-two from what was called "brain fever." He died a week after his parents had left for America. His father, Roelf Kastein, born in 1811 in

---

[85] Frederick Nymeyer, *Kastein Ancestors*. "'Weversjanshuis'" can be dissected in part as 'Wevers'—'of a weaver'; and 'huis'—'house'; the jans I cannot translate." This is the last part of a Dutch letter from Gemeente Dinxperlo to Frederick Nymeyer, dated July 28, 1964.

Dinxperlo, Gelderland, came to "N3A," which apparently was Alto, Wisconsin, in 1867, at age fifty-five. He came for economic improvement, classified as a less well-to-do farmer. He came with his wife, Elizabeth Te Beest Kastein.[86]

The Bride's Parents: Benart and Frederika

Within a year after their marriage on May 11, 1868, in Varsseveld, Gelderland, Netherlands, Benart and Frederika (Ten Brink) Kastein followed his parents to America. They sailed to America with their six-week-old daughter, Grada Wilhemina Kastein. Information found in "Ship Sailings, Netherlands to U.S. 1850-1890," shows that they immigrated to the Waupun area, near Alto, Wisconsin, in April of 1869, for economic reasons. Benart Kastein was thirty-three when he came with his wife and baby to the same area his parents had settled a year before. To the newly immigrated couple came four more daughters, Dina, Elizabeth, Hendrika, and Marie, all born in the Alto and Fox Lake areas of Wisconsin, near Waupam.[87]

---

[86] Dutch Immigrant Records, 1835-1880, from Dordt College Archives, Sioux Center, Iowa.

[87] The year Hendrika was born was the year that her grandmother, Elizabeth, died (1876). Roelf was sixty-five. He remarried a well-to-do woman with a dowry of a better farm than his. She was cheerfully dispositioned, a kindly widow. Aaltje Acherhof was well spoken of by the granddaughters, who would accompany their parents on Sunday afternoons to visit their grandfather and his second wife on their farm near Alto. After the second wife's death, Roelf married a third time. The third wife survived him. He may have been calculating in his second and third marriages, from a monetary stand point, according to Fred Nymeyer (1897-1987), his grandnephew, grandson of Elizabeth Kastein. The one known photo of Roelf, at age sixty-eight, shows him to be broad shouldered and dark haired, with horizontal eyebrows and with lips in a tight, straight line. In later years, one of the reasons given by Roelf Kastein for the unnatural behavior of his son, Benart, was that he suffered from the same fever as his brother had died from in Gelderland, possibly a case of encephalitis. Benart was not always sensible. The practical judgment that he lacked, and the reasonableness that he did not display, had to be made good by his extraordinary wife, Frederika Ten Brink. The male Kasteins were long lived, with the earliest, Gerrit Jan, dying at 83 and Roelf and Bernard both at 82. Also, many of the women in Roelf and Elizabeth Kastein's family lived to old age. Roelf and Elizabeth Kastein are buried in the cemetery of the Reformed Church in Alto, Wisconsin, northwest of Waupam. In 1969 Fred Nymeyer replaced the head stones on their graves.

218 The oldest daughter of Benart and Frederika, Grada, was thirteen when the family migrated to Sioux County. In 1882 the Kastein family moved to a farm northeast of Sioux Center, Iowa, and south of Hull. Only one other farm was between the two towns. The last two children were born on this farm. The sixth baby, Aaltje (Ella), was born in 1882. Four years later another baby was born. Kooi relatives tell the story of an enraged Benart, the father, during the birth of his seventh child. While a midwife attended his wife, Benart stood outside the bedroom door with an ax. He paced up and down, saying that he would kill the child if it was another girl. Fortunately, the baby was the long-desired son, Ralph (1886-1973).

The six daughters worked as men, doing fieldwork. Benart bragged that his daughters could outwork any hired man and that they saved him the expense of hiring help, according to Grace Haan, a cousin of Jennie Kooi Haverhals. Lizzie (Elizabeth) left home at age eleven, in 1884, and seldom returned. She was a hired girl until her marriage in 1895. Dina also was a hired girl. My cousin, John Haverhals, the oldest son of Uncle Adrian and Aunt Jennie Haverhals, says the Kastein family lived on a farm one mile north and one mile west of Sioux Center, now known as the Bleyenberg farm.

Ralph (1886–1973)

Ralph married and had seven children in Doon, Iowa. The local newspaper reported that, as he got older, he became somewhat of an eccentric, living the life of a recluse in unusual circumstances, often in a shack, in a cave, or outdoors.

When the roster of Doon's grand old characters is put down, there will be Ralph. He is gone these many years, but the memory of him lingers. Ralph is special in my memory. He was our own Westside character. I can only remember him as an old man, old Ralph. I can see him now in my mind's eye, walking by on a summer day. He did not dress like the beautiful people. He wore a red handkerchief under his cap to safeguard his neck against the mosquitoes. He was forever puffing on his pipe, the lid of penny-box matches slipped over the fire bowl as a chimney. The pipe seemed to propel him, like a little locomotive. Slightly bowed, he plowed into the chore of getting home, for he was then in his later years. Home to Ralph was his jungle two blocks north of the lumberyard. He loved nature, like in trees and shrubs, and he let her have her wild way. Over the years his domain became a tangle of brush and forest. In late spring, lilacs, honeysuckle, and peonies blossomed, and there were beds of irises. A narrow beaten path ended at his shack. It was a scene out of a dream. Few were welcomed into his dwelling. Ralph was a private person. The shack was a single room, maybe 12x12 feet, with an earthen floor, constructed of scrap lumber and allowing the light of day through one small window to the east. A lean-to was built to the west for things saved and stored. The shack was furnished with a small table, a single chair, a small potbelly stove for heating and cooking. He slept on a bed roll on the floor. There was a cupboard of sorts and that was all. All, except for the stacks of newspapers, for Ralph loved to read and save newspapers. He had no electricity, no running water. When the sun was high in the sky in summer, he lived mostly out of doors. He cooked on a crude fireplace. He slept on a bedspring on a bedroll six feet off the ground, suspended between trees. It was his firm belief that four hours of sleep in the open equaled the regenerative power of eight in bed in the stale indoors. There, high among the trees in his bedspring hammock, he slept for as many months as he could, except when it stormed. There in his island jungle on the west side of Doon town, Ralph kept a big garden, including such delights as asparagus and strawberries. Ralph was not rich. He had no slips of paper from the bank, but then his needs were few and simple. He was both a simple and a complicated man. I knew him in my childhood and teens and then lost him in later years. I suspect he was a deeper man than most thought. I sense there was an untold story in Old Ralph.[88]

Sioux Center

The town of Sioux Center began in 1871, chiefly settled by immigrants from Alto and from Sheboygan County in Wisconsin—such as the Kastein family. A decade after Sioux Center began, Remko Kooi and the Benart and Frederika Kastein family came to Sioux County and found that Sioux Center was being rapidly settled. The town developed slowly at

---

[88] Harold Aardema, "Ralph," *Doon Press*, May 4, 1989.

220 first. The first job of the new towns started by Dutch immigrants in Sioux County was to form a congregation and then to build a church. Before they "called" a pastor of their own to Sioux Center and they could build a church and parsonage, a dominie came from Orange City to preach each Sunday. By 1884 the congregation erected a church that seated six hundred. When Watse Bierma came from Holland in 1890, Sioux Center had grown larger. And by 1895, the town boasted sixteen stores, two banks, two lumber yards, and four grain elevators. At the town's twenty-fifth anniversary in 1896, its founding was celebrated with religious services and an official issue of *De Volsvriend (People's Friend)*. This Dutch-language weekly newspaper spread the news of Dutch people migrating to Sioux County. It was published by Henry Hospers to publicize the opportunities for settlement in northwest Iowa. Readers of this newspaper were found all over the country, wherever Dutch families settled, and even in Holland itself. [89]

The success of the immigrants from Holland was remarkable. In the two decades after the hardships of the seventies, they had turned prairie sod into profitable crops and established model farming communities. Towns were settled in rapid succession after the village of Orange City was started in 1871. A congregation formed in Newkirk in 1882. Today, the most famous native of Newkirk is Robert H. Schuller, founder of the Garden Grove Church in Garden Grove, California, which has become known as the Crystal Cathedral. Born in Newkirk, he went to the one-room school and later was married in the Newkirk Reformed Church. The town of Hull began in 1885, Boyden in 1886, Rock Valley in 1895. That same year, North Orange changed its name to Hospers. [90]

The Secret Marriage: Remko Kooi and Grada Kastein

The "Kooi Book," a three-ring binder that annually updated the genealogy of several generations of Koois until 2001, records the following

[89] Op. cit., Nieuwenhuis.

[90] Op. cit., Lucas.

about the Kastein family journey from Wisconsin to Iowa. "Being the oldest, Grada was in charge of a railroad car with their cattle. During the journey, the car was separated from the train for a time, causing some anxiety."

The only story of how Grada ran away from home that I could confirm is from the *Sioux Center News*, which also gives some interesting facts about Remko Kooi.

Before marriage at age twenty-four, Remko had spent seven years in Sioux County and had established himself both as a farmer and as an entrepreneur who dared to take considerable risks. The year 1881, in which Remko came to Sioux County, he broke the prairie sod and began to farm. That same year he signed for seventy-five Dutch immigrants. Coming two or three at a time, or in a larger group, they would work for him for a year or two before striking out on their own. Watse Bierma (Ida's new father in the new world) was one of these immigrants who was sponsored by Remko Kooi. Three-fourths of Section 27 was still prairie in 1888, before the sod was broken by Remko and his men. As time went on, he added other land in adjoining sections. Remko had over twenty horses to till the soil and do the hay hauling. Homesteading was in its heyday.

When Grada Kastein married Remko, she was nineteen and worked as a field hand for her father, apparently against her will. It seems as though Benart did not like Remko and would not let Grada see him. When Remko asked Benart Kastein if he could marry his oldest daughter, Grada, the answer not only was, "No," but also, "Stay away." So, Remko and Grada made plans to marry in secret, meeting at night in the fields to plan their marriage. Little by little, Grada collected a trousseau of sorts—a bundle of clothes tied in a knot. She hid this bundle in a remote part of a field. The other members of her family were asleep on the night of September 24 when she fled from the farmhouse and went to a prearranged spot in a field to meet Remko. Either Remko had previously engaged the pastor in Sioux Center to marry them, or maybe they just appeared at the door of the parsonage and asked to be married. What is recorded in small print in two inches of space in the *Sioux Center News* is that when Benart found his daughter gone the next morning, he went to the sheriff in Sioux Center.

222   The sheriff documented Benart's complaint and promised to investigate the matter. This investigation led to the parsonage. Here, the Reverend James De Pree said that he had married the couple the night before but did not know where they were.

Five years later Grada's sister, Maria, married Peter Niesink, and on August 23, 1893, the *Sioux Center News* reported the event. "Mr. B. Kastein came after the marshal to help him find one of his daughters who had disappeared, taking all her clothes along. Kastein suspicioned that she had left with a former hired man." All six Kastein sisters married, raised families and enjoyed the respect of the community. Five of the sisters stayed in the Sioux Center area and kept in close touch with each other.

In later years, Aunt Bertha and Aunt Jennie often spoke fondly of these families visiting back and forth and of the fun they had had together with uncles, aunts, and cousins. Grada's mother, Frederika, died of pneumonia at age fifty-six in Sioux Center, Iowa. She is buried in Sioux Center's Reformed Church Cemetery.

Benart Kastein

After Frederika's death, Benart continued living for twenty-one more years, until 1917. Benart may have married three times, as did his father, Roelf. After becoming a widower the second time, Benart homesteaded a farm near Conrad, Montana, and died there of cancer on September 16, 1917, at age eighty-two. Probably he was buried in Montana, but no records seem to exist of his other wives. Although it is said that he was buried next to his first wife, no burial records exist for him at the Reformed Church Cemetery in Sioux Center. Neither is there a marker for his grave in the Kastein family plot in the cemetery, nor are there any burial records for him in the archives of the Sioux Center Library.[91] Aunt Jennie shared her thoughts about her grandfather, Benart:

[91] Sioux Center records and the *Sioux Center News*, September, 1888, found in Sioux Center Library, Iowa, 1996.

It seems only negative memories are known about Benart, but Aunt Bertha remembers hearing that he liked to play the organ. Lizzie thought very highly of her mother, "An outstanding person who made the best apple pie I ever ate." However, apparently there are really no memories of our grandfather or mother talking of him. They were not on too friendly terms because he had an attitude about "all girls," and so the daughters had no desire to spend for a gravestone for him.

In 1999, my sister, Vicki Peterson, offers this observation: "My ancestry is starting to come together. No wonder Pa was a little strange. He must have taken after his maternal grandfather, Benart Kastein, and his great-uncle, Ralph. I never once heard our parents talk about them, or about the marriage of Remko Kooi and Grada Kastein. The ghosts are starting to come out of the closet!"

Ferdinand and Hannah (Ten Brink) Schiebout emigrating to Canada, ca. 1860.

Remko and Grada Kooi, ten years after their secret marriage,
Sioux Center, Iowa, 1898.

Author at gravestone of Mrs. B. Kastein, Sioux Center cemetery in 1995. After Aunt Jennie restored this gravestone in 1996, "Thy Will Be Done," appeared above heaven's gates opening to a crown, "MRS. B. KASTEIN, Overleden, Dec. 9. Jan. 1896, Oud 57 Jaar, KASTEIN." Documents show that correct year is *1897*, age is *56*.

Benart and Frederika Kastein with children: Dina, Elizabeth, Hendrika, Marie, Ella, Ralph. Grada, the oldest, is not in photo. Sioux Center, 1891.

21

Homeplace

After the secret marriage of Remko Kooi and Grada Kastein in 1888 at the parsonage in Sioux Center, they lived on a farm west of Lebanon. On this farm, their first child, Gertrude Wilhemina, was born and named after her mother, Grada Wilhemina. In 1890 they moved to a farm called the Studer place and built new tall buildings. This farm lies in the northwest corner of Iowa, in Garfield Township, Sioux County, ten miles west of Sioux Center and three-fourths of a mile west of Lebanon. Nine more babies were born in this farmhouse. The ten children grew up on this farm, and nine of them married in the church a mile away. They raised large families on nearby farms. Ever since 1890, this farm built by Remko and Grada Kooi has been called "The Homeplace" by the Koois.

The first six babies were born approximately every other year. The oldest son was named Benart, after Grada's father, Benart Kastein. The second son was named Peter, after both Remko's father and brother. The next son became the person I knew as Pa. He was born on April 19, 1894, and was named Frederick, after his grandmother, Frederika Kastein, and his great-grandfather, Frederik Ten Brink. The fifth baby was the couple's second daughter, Bertha Jeannette. Born in June, 1896, she died at age one hundred-five, in April, 2002. Her colorful history spans the twentieth century and deserves a book of its own. Six months after Bertha's birth, her grandmother, Frederika Kastein, died in January of 1897.

The sixth baby was named John, after Remko's brother, John. That same year, 1898, a big barn was built on the farm. While the barn was going up, people from all around came to see the largest building anywhere around (56 by 84 feet). At the top of the red barn, "Blue Grass Stock Farm 1898," is painted in large white letters. Today the barn remains as a landmark.

The last four babies were spaced out over longer periods of time: born between 1901 and 1911 were Dreaka Helena, George Remko, Ellis

Daniel, and then the tenth and last baby, Jennie Marie. When she grew up and married, she settled on a farm within sight of "The Homeplace," and not far from the farms of her older siblings. Aunt Jennie recalls:

> Our first farm was rented from your Grandpa, Remko Kooi, who had acquired eight to nine farms for all his children. Grandpa bought land for $250 an acre before World War I, and afterwards the land was worth $100 an acre. It stayed that price for a long time.[92]

Aunt Jennie kept a collection of photographs that show how the house and farm buildings on "The Homeplace" changed over the years.

> The Kooi home was built in 1890 when your Aunt Gert (oldest of the ten children) was a year old, just the middle rooms and stairs to the bedroom, stairway, and two small east bedrooms upstairs with a large, maybe twenty-foot, ballroom. In the early 1900s the kitchen to the north was added. In 1913 a big addition was made to the house: the pillared porch, living room, and bedrooms. The southwest bedroom and bathroom, laundry room, etc. followed. The pantry on the northeast corner was likely added in 1920.

As Aunt Jennie got out more old photographs, there was one with an addition spreading out from the house toward the north. Aunt Jennie's eyes flickered and grew wistful. This was, she explained, a playhouse that her father built for her. A later owner either replaced it, tore it down, or converted it into an attached garage. She pointed to a second-story bedroom window. "Your father, Fred, was the only son to have a room alone; his health was the reason, I think. He had hospitalizations in Sioux City since there was no local hospital then." I was curious about what kind of illnesses he had had, but Aunt Jennie did not know. He was sixteen when Jennie was born, and he left home for the Army when she was only six. Aunt Jennie paused and then went on to say:

[92] Conversations with Aunt Jennie in Sioux Center, 1992, and letters from her. Corroborated by other relatives and information from other sources.

When she was young, Dina Kastein, my mother's sister, worked at the homeplace. In the early 1900s, Ella also worked at the Remko Kooi home. She was still a young girl, playful. She would lean far out from an open upstairs window to tease and scare us little kids playing below. When the first-born daughter, Gertie, was between eighteen months and two-years-old, she wandered off. Mother sent Ella to search the water tanks that the animals drank from, which were across the road in the yards. When mother found Gertie floating in the creek face down, she yelled for a hired man to take a team of mules to fetch the doctor from Hudson. They came back in twenty minutes, going straight through three to four miles of fields, since there was then no bridge over the Rock River. By that time, mother herself had used desperate efforts to help Gertie and had been able to get her breathing again.[93]

Gertie was the oldest, twenty-two years older than the youngest. As the youngest child tends to be, Jennie was favored in the family. According to Jennie's oldest son, John, "Little Jennie loved to go along with her father as he went out to visit the various farms he was buying in the Lebanon area. Some of her older siblings sometimes thought she was a bit spoiled from the attention she received." By age eleven she was already driving the family car. When her father died in 1924, she began to drive regularly for her mother. Her son, John, says that his mother told harrowing tales about driving the car over muddy roads between the homeplace and Sioux Center to shop or visit relatives. At that time, however, it was common for farm youngsters to drive by age thirteen. Within sight of the homeplace was the tiny town of Lebanon, started by Remko Kooi.

On November 21, 1903, the Christian Reformed Church of Lebanon, Iowa, was recognized as an official congregation. Prior to this time, a small group of worshipers had been meeting in the schoolhouse east of Lebanon for their divine services. These worshipers were originally members of Sioux Center and Rock Valley churches. However, because of the distance to travel to church and the poor road conditions, they decided to locate their church in a more centralized site, closer to their farms.

---

[93] Oral history from Aunt Jennie Haverhals.

One of this group of organizers was the Remko Kooi family. Mr. Kooi performed many beneficial services for the church, although he never became a member of the Lebanon Christian Reformed Church. The church totaled approximately fifteen families at its organization...

On Christmas Day, 1903, the congregation decided to build a church, which would have the dimensions of 32 feet by 32 feet, on an acre of land that Mr. Remko Kooi donated for that specific purpose. Construction of the church was begun immediately, and by the summer of 1904, the church was finished and dedicated. Two years later, the congregation decided it was time to call a minister. Benefits offered to the first minister were a salary of $650 and feed for one horse.[94]

The town was named Lebanon because it was set on a hill, and in the Old Testament of the Bible, the cedars of Lebanon came from hilltops. In 1912 the congregation had grown large enough to build a three-room Christian elementary school, and, because of the steady influx of immigrants from the Netherlands, thirty feet were added to the church. Lebanon now consisted of a store, church, school, two houses, and a blacksmith shop.

The time between 1890 and 1920 was prosperous for Iowa farmers. Remko Kooi invested in all the new types of farm machinery, homeware, and so forth that came out. He liked to buy each new car that came out. A 1915 photo, recently reprinted in the *Sioux Center News*, shows Remko and Grada Kooi standing in front of a Regal car. They also owned a Carter Car, bought in 1913, which had cloth sides. It is believed that they were among the first residents of the area to buy a car. Pa remembers his first ride, in 1907, was in a one-seated car without a top. His parents sat in the one seat in front while the children stood in back. The driver put on the motor uphill, then turned it off and let it coast downhill.

The second son in the family, Peter, drowned in the Rock River at age twenty-two. The details of that tragedy were told and retold to succes-

[94] *Our 75th Year: Lead on, O King Eternal*, 1903-1978, Seventy-fifth Anniversary of the Lebanon Christian Reformed Church, November 15, 1978, pp. 2-3.

sive generations, no doubt as warning. His photograph is familiar to us all. Jennie was three-and-a-half years at the time he drowned on July 12, 1914.

> On a Sunday in the early evening, a group of Lebanon Church young people were at the Cannegieter farm three miles north. Cannegieter's daughter had married Mike Harmsen; both families were from Lebanon Church. The Rock River flowed to the southwest, a short distance away. A few of the young men went to the water to wade. Two boys got in trouble as there were deep holes from the swift movement of water. Neal Cannegieter and Peter Kooi went to their aid but were the ones who sank in the holes. Someone must have told the Kooi parents, for we were standing on our open porch waiting. When Bertha, age 16, came home to tell, "The two bodies had been found," I have a "mind" picture of my parents clasped in one another's arms in their grief.[95]

At school the next day, George could see Peter's name carved into the wood in the hall by a hook that was where Peter hung his coat. At that time, at busy times of the year, farm boys stayed home from school to help with farm work. George remembered himself and Peter being in the cow milking area in the big barn, across the road. A calf was to be moved out to pasture and the mother cow pushed George (age eight) down in the wet yard south of the barn. Peter got George out from under the cow.

From what I have been able to learn about the personality and style of Remko Kooi, I surmise that he was the kind of person I would have liked, as long as I respected his dominance and opinions. It appeared that he was an easy talker, quick to make decisions, a wheeler-dealer who rarely forgot how someone had treated him; genial, a family man who felt comfortable with himself. He worked hard and was willing to take risks, a deal maker with an instinct for the give and take of business, proud of his holdings, and generally happy with life. I like to imagine that Grada was a kindred spirit, someone he took pride in being married to, someone special, seemingly in the background, but, in fact, a self-made woman. The grandparents are spoken of by the grandchildren who knew them as being

---

[95] Jennie Haverhals, in the "Kooi Book."

strict, dominating, serious, and severe. The switch came out when grandson Ray, my oldest brother, broke a new well gadget, but only as a threat, no whipping. The few photos that still exist show both the serious and the playful sides of Remko and Grada Kooi.

Aunt Jennie's funeral was in March of 2000, at the Lebanon Christian Reformed Church. The pastor read an entire chapter of begats from Genesis: so-and-so begat so-and-so, on and on and on, begats I had not heard since Pa read them decades earlier. The chapter of begats were a fitting preface to his message about Aunt Jennie's love of family history and genealogy. In the cemetery behind the church, Aunt Jennie is buried next to her late husband, Adrian Haverhals. (At the funeral, it so happened that I was seated next to Barry Haverhals, who, with his wife, Jodi, now lives on the homeplace. After the funeral, burial, reception, and lunch at the church, my brothers, sisters, and I went to see the homeplace.)

Aunt Jennie's oldest son, John Haverhals, gave the eulogy, telling of the events in his mother's life, and conveying her love of genealogy, part of which was about her parents' and grandparents' connection with the Church:

> Even though Grandpa Kooi was never a member of the Lebanon Christian Reformed Church, he donated the land for the church and cemetery. He attended church regularly, and Grandma Kooi and their children became active members. [Author's Note: Grandpa Kooi never made Public Confession of Faith, which he would have had to do to become a church member.] Where the present church parsonage now stands was once the location of the Kooi store. Grandpa Kooi's father-in-law, Benart, did not approve of his daughter Grada's marriage to Remko. Grada was the oldest of six consecutive daughters. For all practical purposes, Grada was a farm hand for her father and he did not want to lose her. This disapproval of the marriage seemed to have lasted for a lifetime and profoundly affected Remko. Great-grandfather Kastein was a member of the Christian Reformed Church in Sioux Center. Remko said that he did not belong to a church because there were too many hypocrites in church. Without doubt, this was meant to mean his father-in-law.

The main diversions from the hard work of farming were the social activities and musical programs that took place at church and at home.

> The pioneers loved home organs. In the early 1900s Sears Roebuck sent thousands of organs to homes in Sioux County. Later came pianos, then phonographs. In the Remko Kooi home, music was central: Edison cylinder phonograph records, a piano, and an organ. In Wyoming, all of Uncle Peter's girls played. Brother Ben sang. My father made musical sounds with spoons. I recall him singing "Life is Like a Mountain Railway." Also, that was sung at Uncle Ben's funeral. The Kooi brothers liked music and singing. Fred played the accordion. We had a pump organ. John's piano from 1904 is still in use. The three brothers, John, George, and Ellis, still love to sing. Ben and Fred tried playing also. Uncle Ben and Aunt Lura moved their home organ to Pella with them when they left Sioux County. Much later, he had their home organ with him in the nursing home in Pella. Some talented piano and organ players came from the Koois: Fred of Earl, Ray of Fred, and many in the fourth and fifth generations of Kooi descendants.[96]

Peter Kooi, living in Wyoming, sent two pianos to his brother's family at the homeplace when Jennie was a little girl. She took piano lessons from the Schirmer School of Music, and then taught piano and organ to the children on neighboring farms. Since she could drive, she would take her mother along when she went to these farms to give lessons. One of the nephews she gave music lessons to was Ray, my oldest brother.

> For twenty-five cents an hour, Aunt Jennie, at age nineteen, taught me, at age nine, to play the Reed pump organ in our farmhouse. Each week Jennie would give me an hour's lesson while Mother visited with Grandma Kooi and they drank coffee. Then Grandma and Aunt Jennie would go to Uncle Ben and Aunt Lura's to give their son, Lewis, a lesson, but that lasted only a month. Aunt Jennie had other farm-

---

[96] Conversations with Jennie Haverhals. At the funeral services for the oldest Kooi brother, Ben, in 1981, Mr. and Mrs. Fred Kooi (Ben's grandson and his wife), sang "When the Roll is Called Up Yonder." Fred Kooi was the organist. Ben (Benart) Kooi is buried in the Graceland Cemetery, Pella, Iowa.

ers' children whom she taught to play the organ and piano.[97]

While Aunt Jennie gave a piano lesson to Ray, Grandma could see how her grandchildren were getting along. In the kitchen, around Mother's skirts, were five or six little ones. Sometimes, Aunt Jennie took snapshots of her nephews and nieces. These are the few snapshots we have of life on the Lebanon farm before 1935. That is the year that Ray got a Brownie Box camera. Now Mother could stop taking each new baby into town for a studio portrait. Most likely she breathed a sigh of relief. Think how much work it must have been to dress the baby in a starched white dress with its matching slip, booties, and cap, then travel to the studio to have a photograph made of the squirming infant propped up against pillows, especially by the time Mother had her seventh baby. She had to nurse and dress the baby as well as get the other six children ready before she could start out on the rough dirt roads to town with Pa driving the car. What a job! So, no studio portraits exist of the last four of the eleven babies in our family, or of the baby who didn't survive. What remains is a composite of the oval photographs of the seven oldest as babies. Snapshots of the four youngest were put on the thin black pages of a photo album, each snapshot bracketed into place at its corners.

From time to time, Jennie was the church organist in the Lebanon Christian Reformed Church. From 1904 when the church was built, to 1918, all of the services were in Dutch. For the next forty years, 1918-1949, most of the services were in Dutch. Some Dutch services did not end until 1949.[98] During World War I, people were not supposed to speak the Dutch language. After the War, church services were supposed to be conducted in English only. However, Pa said, "I wonder about that. No minister, or very few, could preach in English, and after the War, I'm sure that law changed quickly, since very few people could understand English

---

[97] Conversation with Raymond Kooi.

[98] G. Nelson Nieuwenhuis, *Siouxland: A History of Sioux County, Iowa* (Orange City, IA: Sioux County Historical Society, 1983), p. 226.

except the kids." As late as World War II, when Gladys was in the W.A.V.E.S. (1944-1946), there was still one monthly church service in the Dutch language in the Hospers Christian Reformed Church. Perhaps, what happened in Sioux County was similar to what had happened in Friesland when Napoleon decreed that the Dutch would take a surname. They resisted. In Sioux County churches, the Dutch Christian Reformed people, after each war, simply resumed doing what they had always done. They spoke the language that was customary and comfortable until their children changed, and then their own ways changed.

One Sunday in the Lebanon Christian Reformed Church, a substitute organist was needed, so the Dominie asked Mother if Ray could play the organ for church services. The organ was a pump organ that depended on someone behind it, hidden by a curtain or something, to pump the air into the organ. Without the "pumper," there would be no sound when Ray pressed down a key. He was only twelve or thirteen, and his feet could barely reach the floor keyboard of the organ to play the bass and tenor keys. Mother hesitated, "Well, yes, perhaps he can." And so, before the service started, the Dominie would write the page numbers in English of the Dutch hymns listed in the church bulletin. This way, Ray could find the number in the Dutch Psalter Hymnal and know what hymn to play. Once, the Dominie forgot to write down the English numbers. The congregation was ready to sing, but not a sound came from the organ. The Dominie looked at Ray and waited, then he saw what the problem was, and came down from the pulpit to the organ to whisper the page number to Ray.

The Lebanon Christian Reformed Church is part of the Christian Reformed Church in the USA, which was founded by Calvinists from Holland in Western Michigan in 1857, not far from Lake Michigan and in an area riddled with lakes and rivers. The Indian name, "Mich-igama," means big water. The water all around and rolling sand dunes gave new Dutch immigrants a feeling of home since they were recently from The Netherlands, which is below sea level. Authors writing about Holland around 1900 tell about the dominance of the Dutch Reformed Church:

The people in many of the smaller towns and villages of Holland practice a severe Calvinism. The pastor's word is paramount: he holds a tight rein over the flock in his charge. There are long services in the Dutch churches.... All the population went to church ... and from all over the town, in snow or sleet, in rain or sunshine, there rose the sound of psalm singing on the eternal Sabbath air.[99]

The shepherd (dominie, minister, pastor, preacher) wielded great influence over his flock. Attendance at the two services on Sunday was mandatory. Tithing was "right." The rule for daily life was more than the Ten Commandments, it was every word of the Bible. Settling an argument with, "Well, according to the Bible," was tantamount to saying, "This is the truth."

In the 1880s the Dutch stuck together, solidly maintained their homogeneity, shunned secret groups such as the Grange, and carried on their traditions and religion through the generations. Our life on the farm was church and school, ruled by the Ten Commandments. We believed in the Apostles Creed, Heidelberg Catechism, and the other doctrinal standards learned in weekly catechism classes where we were asked questions (Question School) to which we had to memorize answers. Each creed, church ruling, and belief was in the back of the Psalter Hymnal that we sung from on Sundays. A public "Confession of Faith" during a church service was the rite of passage for a teenager to become a church member and begin to take communion. Everything in life was orderly, governed by rules, predestined—snugly wrapped in a life-to-death security blanket. The church provided ceremony and substance for all the way-stops between birth and death: baptism, communion, confession of faith, the Bonds of Holy Matrimony, education of the young, celebration of holidays, burial rites. Excommunication was a rite like extreme unction, used only as a last resort to ostracize an unrepentant sinner from the flock of faithful.

Calvinist fatalism seems to act, paradoxically, as a spur to enter-

[99] Op. cit. Jungman, p. 10, 37.

prise; surely one of the curious features of New World development is that a Protestant nation dominated by believers in an inflexible and inscrutable predestination should have proved so dynamic.[100]

This Calvinist fatalism did, indeed, spur us on to work. We were God's chosen people, special, inscrutably predestined, commanded to "be ye perfect." Ray, the oldest, showed exceptional initiative, with a determined pursuit of reading and learning, making certain his departure from farm labor. Clarence followed along the same path, as did the rest of the eleven children in our family.

Social life revolved around the church, home, and school, church being dominant. Sunday would dawn into a hushed atmosphere uncommon in a household of thirteen people. Pa and Mother set the tone of reverence for the Lord's Day. Breakfast over, everyone went to their bedrooms to put on their Sunday clothes: starched and ironed dresses for girls, suits and ties for boys, hats for Mother and Pa. When I came down to the kitchen all dressed up, someone would comb my hair and braid it into two pigtails tied with ribbons. The rubber bands holding the ends of the pigtails would pull my hair and I would squeal. Sometimes my hair would have been done up with rags on Saturday night to make pipe curls. Before church, someone would unwind the rags, comb out each corkscrew into pipe curls and say, "There, now, don't you look cute?"

Church at the Hospers Christian Reformed Church began at 9:30. By 9:15 we would gather in the vestibule to get ready to file in: a last-minute hair comb, ties straightened, then a finger went up to Mother's lips: "Shhhh, shhhh." The door to the sanctuary was opened by Pa, and he went in first. Silently, we eleven went down the aisle after him, oldest to youngest. Mother came last. At the head of our pew, Pa would turn around and stand to watch each one of us march up the aisle and file into the pew, the youngest was the last one in order before Mother, sitting next to her. The look in Pa's eyes exhorted: Behave yourself or else. After everyone was

[100] John Updike, "Such a Sucker as Me," as quoted by David Donald in a book review in *The New Yorker*, October 30, 1995, p. 104.

seated, Pa would sit down next to the aisle, where the head of house always sat. The church bulletins in our hands that had been handed out at the door would rustle open. It told us who had a new baby, who was sick, who had died, who was publishing the bans of marriage for the first or second time, or who had gotten married. Everyone would study it for the first few minutes and then look around to see who else had come to church. There were always the same families. If strangers happened to be present, they were stared at until an older sibling or Mother nudged. If a nudge did not stop the staring, she whispered, "Don't stare."

The order of the service was always the same, beginning with silent prayer and ending with the doxology. The long sermon was hard to sit through and was endured with much fidgeting and fussing, folding and refolding of the bulletin, poking the next person, looking at the hymns in the red-covered *Psalter Hymnal*, reaching into Mother's pocket and eyeing her purse, hoping for candy or gum or maybe a peppermint. About half way through the sermon, I would lay my head on Mother's lap to take a nap. When I woke up, the pipe curls on that side of my head would be gone. Toward the end of a long sermon, Mother might hand me her handkerchief, always white, perhaps embroidered with some design, the edges crocheted. I grabbed it to see if she had tied peppermints into one corner of the handkerchief. Peppermints were separated by two or three knots, which required some time to undo. Each peppermint was a taste treat. This kept me busy and quiet while the Dominie droned on and on. Waiting, I studied the colors, designs, and the texture of the sticky hankie, waiting for the doxology.

After filing out, everyone stood around and talked a while. Small groups always formed in the vestibule, as well as outdoors, after church services. People stood around to talk for as long as twenty minutes before dispersing, and then three or four couples might go to have coffee and cake at someone's home to continue talking. This practice continues today: same-age groups of women with women, men with men, girls with girls, and boys with boys. Mother might invite another mother's family to come over for cake and coffee. That was more likely to happen for the people who lived in town than for the farmers. Farms were too far to go to for coffee and still get back for the afternoon service at 1:30. Social life was either at church, or with the relatives whom we also saw at church and after the second service in the afternoon.

Staying in Sunday clothes through Sunday dinner meant no spilling on good clothes, so that we could pile back into the car before one o'clock, to once again take the long ride into town and hear another long sermon. Being dressed up came to mean using good manners and behaving. But, by five o'clock we were home free! Free to hang our Sunday clothes in the closet until next Sunday, free to read *The Banner*, or other religious literature and play quietly. We might sing around the piano. Sunday supper was light: leftovers from the big, special Sunday dinner and Jell-O or cake for dessert. If relatives came to visit, they often came on Sunday afternoon after church, before the evening chore of milking cows.

Sundays by Grandma

We went there—on Sundays after church.
Pa would say—in his off-handed manner
"Ja, I guess we'll go to Ma's for a while."
Grandma had cake
        and a gramophone with a low booming sound
        only Aunt Jennie might wind it.
We cousins fought for a place
on the four-seated swing
And after too much lemonade
        found our way down the too narrow path
        to the privy in a dark scary grove.
The rules were firm
        no going into the parlour
            nor the barns
        share the pedal-car
        don't push each other off the porch
        And stay out of the flower bed.
Grandma—with her hair in a bun
and her print cover-all apron
        made good cake.

Beneath Gladys' poem is an accolade scrawled in Uncle George's hand-

242

writing under her signature, Gladys I. Gritter, "I will give you 100 on that, Gladys, by George Kooi."[101]

Remko Kooi died in the farmhouse that he and Grada had built. At the time of his death, on Friday, October 31, 1924, at 11:15 a.m., he had lived on the homeplace for thirty-four years. In the Lebanon Church Cemetery, his gravestone looks back toward the gently sloping fields that fold up and around The Homeplace. The program printed for his funeral has a tombstone, descendents' names, and this verse:

Death's but a path
That must be trod
If man would ever
Pass to God

Scrawled around the verse in the margins are these details, written by the oldest of his ten children, Gertie Kooi Haverhals:

Remko Kooi born July 4, 1864, Chicago, Illinois. He had hay fever for nearly thirty years. Otherwise strong and well. Last illness began September 28. Pleurisy lung tapped Sunday, September 28, by Dr. Runipan from Sioux City. On Monday pus was removed from his left lung by Dr. McLaughlin of Sioux City. His lungs filled up. Nurse Bernice Virtue came to care for him. On October 2 Uncle John Kooi came from Chicago. Uncle Pete came Saturday, October 4, from Sheridan, Wyoming. Monday, October 6, very low. Crisis passed, it seems, gaining October 9. Two Kooi brothers left for their respective homes. Sat in chair October 10. Up a little every day. October 29 complaining of swollen legs. October 30 not very good. No nourishment taken, uncomfortable. Passed away suddenly when Miss Virtue had just helped him back in bed from chair on October 31, 1924, at 11:15 a.m. Funeral services at house Monday, 12, at church 2 p.m. Rev. Wm. Kok. Burial in Lebanon cemetery.[102]

When his father died, Fred was thirty and married to Ida Sybesma.

[101] "Sundays by Grandma," by Gladys I. Gritter, *The Banner*, weekly magazine of the Christian Reformed Church, June 18, 2001.

[102] Handwritten by Mrs. Gertie (P.J.) Haverhals, born August 9, 1889, west of the homeplace.

They had two babies, Ray and Gladys, named after his father and mother. Ray was three and his earliest memory is of Grandpa laid out on a bed too high to see into, and of Pa lifting him up to see into it. The custom then was to have home visitation after a death. Each of Remko's nine children and their spouses would have come with their children, lining up outside the bedroom, and then filing past the bed where Remko was laid out, each person pausing to say goodbye.

Eleven years after Remko's death, Grada fell ill. Each of her many grandchildren were allowed into Grandma's sick room, one at a time. She said each name, and shook each one's hands. Grada died of a brain tumor on The Homeplace on February 13, 1935. When his mother died, Fred was age 41, and Ida was eight months' pregnant with her ninth child. Jennie was newly married and settled on a nearby farm. Grada was buried alongside Remko in the cemetery of the Lebanon Christian Reformed Church. Their married life had spanned 36 years: from September 25, 1888, to Remko's death in 1924. Their ten babies had grown up; nine had married and settled on nearby farms, and were raising large families: six, eight, ten, or twelve children. The Lebanon Christian Reformed Church remained at the center of the lives of their children and grandchildren. In this church, eleven of us twelve children, born to Frederick Kooi and Ida Sybesma, were baptized.

Within two years after both grandparents had died, the will was settled. The estate was to be equally divided between the nine children. A lengthy legal abstract describes the farms and tells the story of how they were to be given to the intertwined, intermarried families of Koois and Haverhals. Peter Haverhals had married the oldest Kooi daughter, Gertie. Adrian Haverhals had married the youngest daughter, Jennie Kooi. Another daughter, Dreaka, had married Case (Cornelius) Haverhals, and died young, leaving two minor children. These children were to inherit their part of the estate. Peter Haverhals was the executor for the will.

The oldest son, Ben, inherited The Homeplace. Uncle Ben and Aunt Lura lived on the farm for a short time and then sold The Homeplace to the Haverhals family. Apparently this caused some hard feelings among the Kooi heirs. For many years (1935–1950), The Homeplace was owned by

244   Mr. and Mrs. John H. Haverhals who lived there with their five children. Then from 1950 to 1980 their son, John, Jr., and his wife, Artie, owned it. Barry Haverhals, one of their five children and a nephew of Jennie Marie Kooi Haverhals, now rents part of the farm from his mother, Artie, and lives on The Homeplace. One wing has become a garage. Artie Haverhals Bonnema continues to hold title to The Homeplace.[103]

In 1976 the State of Iowa, in conjunction with the Iowa Farm Bureau Federation, established its Century Farms Program, and designated any farm owned by the same family for one hundred years or more as a "Century Farm." The Homeplace would have qualified. Despite the depressed economic situation of the surrounding farms today, the town of Lebanon continues to exist. From the rolling land of the church and cemetery, The Homeplace is easily visible, a landmark in the history of Sioux County, Iowa. In Lebanon, Hofwegan's Store no longer exists.

On Saturday Afternoon

Pa gave each of us a penny
            that was six pennies
            a lot of money in 1932
and while we waited for Question School to start
        I spent my penny in Hofwegan's Store
                ...past the Dominie's house
                        halfway down the hill
my nose pressed against the glass
        it took a long time deciding
        a 1¢ Baby Ruth or a 1¢ Butterfinger
                or a sucker (2 of them)
                        but suckers were for little kids
one time I thought...all through those years
        I looked forward to Saturday
                and 1¢
                and deciding
                between a 1¢ Baby Ruth
                and a 1¢ Butterfinger [104]

[103] Legal abstract, Artie Haverhals Bonnema, Sioux Center, Iowa, 2000.

[104] Gladys Gritter, "On Saturday Afternoon," *The Banner*, January 12, 1981.

Blue Grass Stock Farm of Remko and Grada Kooi in Garfield Township, 1995.

Garfield Township District No. 8, near Lebanon, Iowa. School children
include Fred, Bertha, Peter, and John Kooi, 1905.
Next generation went to same school.

Kooi Homeplace at Lebanon, Iowa, 1908.

Remko Kooi stands between team of horses with sons Ben, Fred, George, and
Peter. No Smoking signs are on the barns, 1910.

Remko Kooi at home in Morris recliner with Jennie, 1912.

Ben, Fred, and Peter Kooi on a postcard given to family and friends.
Lebanon, 1912.

Remko and Grada Kooi at Homeplace with 1915 Regal car.
Reprinted by the *Sioux Center News* in 1994.

Church cleaners spent the day cleaning the Lebanon Christian Reformed Church.
Ida Sybesma is kneeling fourth from right. Lebanon, 1918.

Grandparents Remko and Grada Kooi and Bertha with Lebanon Christian
Reformed Church pastor and wife, the Reverend and Mrs. Jonker,
at the Homeplace, Lebanon, 1918-19.

At Kooi reunion are five Kooi brothers with four brothers-in-laws, three Haverhals, and one Vander Lugt. Fred Kooi is the one in overalls 1936.

Kooi Homeplace on Dry Creek. Lebanon, 1995.

22

Double Wedding

Ida clearly loved her oldest sister, Gertie Bierma, like a mother, and Gertie was, in fact, old enough to be her mother; and "Ja, Watse was such a gentle man." Ida became best-friends with their oldest child, Bertha, who was seven years younger than herself. They grew up together, and were more like sisters than aunt and niece. Before Bertha was old enough for school, Ida and Sam took the horse and buggy to school in Sioux Center. After school they often waited for Mattie, who was then a hired girl in the Sioux Center area. As she got bigger, young Ida learned to hitch Old Sam to the buggy and drive them to school or to "help out." The harness on Old Sam had blinders on either side of his eyes. One afternoon after school, she had to wait for her older sister, Mattie, outside the home where Mattie was working. In the winter evening, as they were going home in the buggy, it grew dark.

> "We came over a short hill, and I said in Dutch, 'Oh! What a bright star!' All of a sudden the horse jumped right into the ditch, and swift past us went this thing. The buggy tipped over, but Old Sam just stood there. The men got out of that old Ford and asked if we were hurt. We were all right, but the buggy was broken. The men helped turn the buggy upright."

Mother chuckled as she recalled seeing her first car, "I thought cars were crazy things! Almost no one thought they were there to stay." Pa remembered that the roads were too narrow for cars, and horses just ran away when a car came along.[105]

Ida lived with the Biermas until she finished seventh grade at age fourteen. Then, Ida "worked out" on the farms of relatives or friends, just as her

---

[105] Tape recording made by Nanette Chadwick of her grandparents memories of Iowa, during Nanette's visit to Denver, Colorado, 1976.

sister, Mattie, had done before her marriage. By the time Ida was sixteen, her brother, Syne and his wife, Christina, had been married six years, had babies, and needed the help of Ida. She also worked at the Fiekema farm, milking all of their cows. Working all day, she earned one dollar.

At the end of this chapter, a snapshot of Ida Sybesma shows her standing in front of what appears to be the wall of a farmhouse made of horizontal white clapboards. Under her feet, the fuzzy grass appears in spotty billows, scorched by the heat of summer past. If it is mid-September, she has just turned sixteen. Behind her is one window that has a double sash. During summer days, she would have lifted the bottom half up or pulled the top half down to cool the room we dimly see behind her. A slab of concrete appears to be the foundation for the house, and a dark space is visible underneath it. Her dress is long and simple, belted with a tie of the same plain fabric, probably made from flour sacks. Where her right arm curves around to clasp her other arm in back, another shirt appears below her sleeve, perhaps an undershirt. Sun falls across her bodice. Her hair is softly pulled back, probably to the bun that she nearly always wore later in her life. Her chin is lifted, and a smile creases her cheeks. Her face is fresh and eager, as though she is facing the world with a blithe spirit and indomitable attitude. The wind is blowing the skirt of her homespun dress against her legs and whips it into deep folds that move away from her. She looks like a young member of a homesteading family on the Great Plains, confident and happy, like a girl going places.

During 1917 Ida was working on the farm of her oldest brother, Syne. No doubt she had already noticed the Kooi boys at church, particularly Fred. On Sunday nights during 1917-1918 in the Highland Church, there would have been some kind of young people's gathering, probably a Hymn Sing. When it was over, Ida was already in the buggy, ready to ride home with her older brother, Sam, when Fred came up to ask her if she would ride home with him in his buggy. She turned to Sam and hesitantly asked his advice. Sam urged her on, "Go ahead, he's a good boy." So, off they went on a dirt road in a horse-drawn buggy, out together for the first time.[106]

Today, there is no town of Highland and no church there, but once there were two churches, one on each side of the road. There also was a shopping center on the northeast corner. According to my sister, Bernice Afman:

> The town of Highland, near Lebanon, became a ghost town. In a recent issue of *The Banner*, there was a great picture taken from the hill where Highland once stood, of what used to be our land, and in the distance, our farm. You may not remember Highland Church, but we kids used to go in that church—it always stood open—and wonder about the story behind it. It was as if one Sunday everybody walked out and never came back. There were hymn books in the pews and a Bible in the pulpit. If I remember correctly, Ray used to play the organ. I think there were birds flying around in the abandoned church.

The courtship of Fred and Ida lasted four years, but their "going out" together was interrupted by World War I. Fred was twenty-four when he left to join the Army. Most likely he had never been out of Iowa. He was sent to France. At the end of this chapter, a snapshot dated July 25, 1918, shows him leaving home for Camp Pike in the East. He is dressed in a suit and tie, carrying a valise, standing with four of his siblings. Flowers go around the hat that Bertha is wearing. George and Ellis have on knickers and boots. Jennie is a slight six-year-old.

When Pa was ninety-one, he told me about marching with Army troops under cover of darkness from a forwarding camp somewhere near the American East Coast to a large harbor. In the dead of night, his platoon marched aboard a military transport ship to the muffled beat of marches played by a military band. After years of hearing Pa play his accordion on the farm in the evenings, I still hum some of those tunes and sing the

---

[106] Gladys Gritter in letter, dated March 29, 1985: It was the Highland Church, because in that day, they never had church services at night in Lebanon.

words. In imagination, I stand on that same eastern shore and hear the band play:

> When Johnny comes marching home again, Hurrah, hurrah!
> We'll give him a hearty welcome then, Hurrah, hurrah!
> The men will cheer, the boys will shout,
> The ladies, they will all turn out,
> And we'll all feel gay,
> When Johnny comes marching home.

Another favorite song of Pa's was:

> Keep the home fires burning
> While your hearts are yearning
> Tho' your lads are far away,
> They dream of home.
> Keep the home fires burning,
> Till the boys come home.[107]

In the vest pocket over his heart, Fred carried a small Dutch Bible, hard-covered in grainy black leather, snapped shut to protect the 1,020 tissue-thin pages edged in gold—as well as to protect his heart. He was ready to go forth into battle wearing the breastplate of righteousness. "Stand therefore, having your loins girt about with truth, and having on the breastplate of righteousness" (Ephesians 6:14). His Bible, published in Leeuwarden, contains the New Testament (*Nieuwen Testaments*), the Psalms, and a lengthy *"Catechismus in de Nederlandsche Gereformeerde Kerken"* (Catechism of the Dutch Reformed Church). The book of Psalms, (*Het Boek Der Psalmen*) has all 150 psalms set to music. It contains selections from Exodus, Deuteronomy, Matthew, and Luke. Pa liked to sing the Psalms of David, humming the tunes he liked best and skipping over words or lines forgotten. A ribbon marker was left in the thin leaves between Psalms 80 and 81.[108]

[107] *Golden Book of Favorite Songs* (Chicago: Hall & McCreary Company, 1915).

[108] The Bible remains with his daughter, Bernice Afman, in Denver.

Although World War I raged in Europe from 1914-1918, sweeping around the world at the same time was an even deadlier enemy. The influenza pandemic of 1918 and 1919 killed as many as 40 million people. The *Sioux Center News* reported: "Among the 107 Sioux Center men that saw military service during World War I were Fred Kooi, Ben Kooi, and Gerrit Vander Lugt. Only one (of the one hundred-seven men) lost his life and that was due to flu, not war."

> In October of 1918 a strain of Spanish influenza, which killed thousands, hit this country. The unnerving thing about this flu was that it struck strong young men and women in their twenties and thirties most severely. In Sioux Center all the churches and schools were closed and no meeting of any kind was allowed except in the open. By Armistice Day, November 11, the threat of the disease had passed. During this time (1915-19) in Lebanon, Reverend Jonker was ministering to the eighty families who were members of the Lebanon Christian Reformed Church. He shall long be remembered for the sacrifices he made in behalf of the congregation during the flu epidemic. When he couldn't ride, he would walk. And he lost many a night's sleep sitting up with those whom the doctors had given up.[109]

During the weeks on the troop ship going over the ocean to France, Fred got sicker and sicker. When they docked at St. Lazare, he was put on a stretcher and carried off the ship to a waiting ambulance. At the hospital he recovered, but apparently not completely. In the spring of 1919 he was recuperating in a forwarding camp sixty miles south of Paris when he got a two-week furlough. He joined a group of recuperating soldiers taking a bus south to the top of the Pyrennes Mountains. On the way, they went through Lourdes, the Catholic shrine where the faithful come to be healed by taking the waters. Fred bought a tinted photograph that he carried home, titled *"Lourdes–La Basilique–Vue Plonegeante–L.L."* He framed and hung this picture on his bedroom wall where it remained until he died. In 1985, as he told me where he was, where next, in which part of France, how the

---

[109] Mike Vanden Bosch, ed., *A Pocket of Civility, A History of Sioux Center* (Sioux Falls, SD: Modern Press, Inc., 1976), pp. 101, 121, 229.

shot-out train looked, the buildings and towns shot-up, during the two-week furlough, it was apparent that his memories were clouded. Apparently he had been very ill in France. Fred turned twenty-five during the year he was in the Army. Aunt Jennie describes his homecoming:

> I was seven years old when Fred sent postcards to me from France. Ben wrote to me too, in 1918. My mother wore a Service pin for her sons in service: red, white, and blue with one or two stars, 1918. We knew the day when Fred was supposed to come home but not the exact time. When Ma could see him coming on foot from a distance, she ran out to the front porch and was so excited she jumped right off the porch onto the sidewalk—not using the cement steps—quite a distance for her to leap. It surprised me. It was the only time I ever saw her do that, and I never forgot how she looked, leaping into the air, rushing out to meet her son, unusual for her.[110]

On a "Carte Postale" dated May 13, 1919, that Fred sent from France to Jennie, he has a scared look, sober countenance, and serious eyes staring straight. "Pvt. Fred Kooi, Army Service Corps, Le Mars France" is scrawled on the back of the post card. His uniform is made of scratchy, heavy wool, in Army "olive drab" khaki. To me as a child, Pa appeared to be strange, different from his brothers and sisters, distant from me, even when I got up the nerve to approach him. Sometimes he talked to me on the farm but only when I pulled it out of him; otherwise, there was a silence. Was he left affected by that severe bout of flu in addition to his childhood illnesses, or was it something genetic, or a combination of both of these? One can only conjecture. In any event, what the children and grandchildren remember is the World War I gas mask Pa kept in an attic or closet. He occasionally got out this dusty old mask to show it off and sometimes would let his grandchildren play with it. His khaki uniform still exists, as does Mother's wedding dress.

Ida Sybesma had become friends with Fred's sisters—Bertha and Dreaka Kooi. Later in her life, Bertha spoke about that time. "Well, ja, I felt sorry for your mother. Being as she didn't have any family, we kind of took her in, you might

---

[110] Oral history from Aunt Jennie.

say." Readily apparent to us as children was the fact that the Koois and Sybesmas were quite different kinds of people. The Sybesmas were of a musical nature, intuitive, easier socially, and more interested in education for their children, while the Koois were more practical minded, straight shooters, incisive, with a get-the-job-done and get-to-the-point kind of nature. The Koois, as a body, were dominant, hale, and hearty, while the Sybesmas were of a softer, gentler constitution. Sister Bernice says that "The Kooi family was considerably better off financially than the Sybesmas. Bertha Bierma talked about the Kooi Mansion. There weren't many farmhouses like that, and Grandpa owned many farms."

> Many Dutch farmers were able to buy not one but several farms. Their economical habits more than anything enabled the Dutch to buy land, often buying farms from under their neighbors. One non-Dutch old-timer recalled that the Dutch "didn't drink beer, didn't go out on Saturday night, and spent so little on entertainment in general that when a farm came up for sale, the Dutchman could afford to outbid anyone else for the land. Furthermore, the Dutch had large families, and although this might be considered an economic drawback today, kids were assets on the farm because they represented cheap help. And if they weren't needed, they worked out, returning the money to Pa until they were 21 years old.[111]

At that time, a girl prepared for marriage by sewing things for her "hope chest" years before marriage, an old custom carried on in Holland and commented on by Jungman: "She spent all her time knitting hideously bright wool mats and antimacassars. She had piled all these obnoxious articles in a vast oaken chest, in expectation, she coyly informed me, of her marriage."[112] But many things that went into the hope chest were not hideous. Between 1915 and 1922 Ida wore a crocheted, creamy-colored chemise under her dress instead of a bra. Perhaps Ida had crocheted the chemise for her hope chest. Little sisters pester big sisters. I would see Gladys or Bernice mak-

[111] Op. cit., Vanden Bosch, p. 77.

[112] Op. cit., Jungman, p. 65.

ing something and taunt them, "Is that thing for your hopeless chest?"

Shivarees were in vogue before I was born. Probably a shivaree sounded like an army marching off to battle: tin pans rattling, boys whistling, heavy banging, and marching. Gladys remembers the shivaree:

> Usually at a wedding reception a group of young people, invited or not (probably both) would come sometime during the evening. They would be outdoors and would be banging on tin cans, using loud whistles, etc. The shivareeing would go on until the bride and groom went to the door; they usually invited them in and gave them money to go away. I did it a few times but have only vague recollections of it. I think sometimes shivareers were kids who weren't invited but wanted to be.

Shivaree comes from the French word "charivari," originally a form of hazing. It was a gathering of persons armed with noise makers to express derision or disapproval. The newly-married couple would have to "purchase" peace with a ransom of food or drink, or the money to buy same. The French in Louisiana and Canada introduced the custom to America, especially in the rural areas, for any newly-married couple. In the middle west, the "shivaree" money would be used for the party, sometimes a supper or a dance for the neighbors who participated. If the bridegroom hid on shivaree night, or refused to give any money or promise of a party—the fact was held against him all the rest of his life. He might as well move out of the neighborhood. By the late thirties, the practice had dwindled almost entirely. Couples just went ahead and had a wedding dance.

Although the Dutch didn't dance, the program that followed a wedding was fun. Held in the church basement, it was the part of a wedding that little kids really looked forward to—especially while sitting through the ceremony on hard church benches, trying to keep quiet. The master of ceremonies for the program was usually jovial as he introduced each skit, recitation, story, or musical number. We would sing, and afterwards, there was wedding cake, nuts, candies, and good things to drink.

> Culture apart from religion interested very few. Some did travel to Sioux City, but then it was to shop, do business, and not to take in

any culture. People's religion encompassed so much of their lives that it ministered not only to their spiritual lives but every aspect of their lives.[113]

Wall art on the farm was a calendar, plaques with Bible texts, and pictures of pastoral scenes. In 1999, the national media noted that a movie theater was kept out of Sioux Center, which it called "the Dutchest town in all of the USA." This kind of battle was and still is waged to keep movies out. The vital question is: For Christ or against Christ: those for were anti-movies; those against were pro-movies. Parents substituted bands, choirs, and ball games for going to the movies, preferring to see their kids perform in these activities. At any rate, economics (not enough business to keep the one theater open) and ethics joined hands to keep the devil out of Sioux Center in the early fifties.

As recently as 1996, the *Sioux Center News* reported that the City Council ruled, "no beer license for bike race vendors, even if they locate outside the town's border." The single spire of the Lebanon Christian Reformed Church in rural northwestern Iowa looked down on the places where the tight-knit Dutch were hatched, matched, and dispatched. Outside of the farm, their world centered around the church and the Christian school.

Moving day for farmers generally was agreed to be March 1, before planting began. For this reason, many marriages took place in January or February. Farm implements or necessities might be given for wedding gifts—even a manure fork or pitch fork. The couple in Grant Wood's painting, "American Gothic," shows the deeply-felt, serious nature of Iowa farmers: the man holding the upright pitchfork and the woman's hair pulled back severely into a tight bun. This upright seriousness is what I knew as a child. Pa and Mother were steadfast in purpose, raising up their brood of kids in the "way of the Lord." Make no bones about it. Although Grant Wood's painting has been poked fun of and satirized on everything from postcards to T shirts, it honestly depicts Iowa, and the images in "American Gothic" tickle my funny bone.

[113] Op. cit., Vanden Bosch.

The wedding day of Frederick Kooi and Ida Sybesma was set for Thursday afternoon, January 27, 1921, at the Lebanon Christian Reformed Church, Lebanon, Iowa. They were to marry in a double wedding ceremony, the other couple being Fred's younger sister (and Ida's good friend), Bertha Kooi, and Gerrit Vander Lugt. Ida and Bertha Kooi would have handed out wedding invitations to friends and relatives after Sunday church. One of Ida's handwritten envelopes is shown at the end of this chapter. Bertha Kooi recorded in her diary: The brides wore identical dresses made by Sioux Center seamstress, Lizzie Vander Ziel. The dresses were fitted on January 20 and delivered by mail to Lebanon on the day before the wedding. Gerrit Vander Lugt and the brides bought ice cream in Sioux Center, while family members baked the cake on the day before the wedding.

At the Lebanon church, previously, the eighty families had endured nineteen months of no minister. But then, in 1920, the Reverend Sweiringa (J.J. Steigenga, according to Bertha's diary) answered "the call." He was said to be a man of intent purpose. He performed the double wedding ceremony at one-thirty in the afternoon. Afterward, about sixty relatives and friends went to the homeplace for the wedding reception. All of the Kooi and the Sybesma relatives were there. Most likely there was a program. Syne Sybesma Bierma told Aunt Jennie of being at the Kooi home after the church ceremony. He described kitchen details, whose lap he sat on, and "The Cake!"

Three days later, Sunday services in the church were held as usual, but on that Sunday night of January 30, 1921, calamity struck. The church, and the school which was meeting there, burned to the ground. The pulpit Bible was the only thing rescued from the flames. The parsonage and the barn next to the church remained, and during the building of the new church, the congregation met in the barn. The school met in the Lebanon store. The young people collected money for a pipe organ.

Light fixtures went into the new church powered by the new Delco light plant. On occasion it became necessary to wait for the batteries to be charged before the lights could be turned on, causing some delay and embarrassment.[114]

Besides the fire, the only other catastrophe was the tornado of June 16, 1944, that completely destroyed the church. Since the foundation remained following the fire, a basement was built on that and used for services during the re-building. Nothing could stop church services, but the next wedding planned for the Kooi family had to be moved to a different church. Aunt Jennie Haverhals recalls:

> Fourteen days after the fire that destroyed the church, Uncle John and Aunt Gertie married in the Hawarden church. I was ten and rode with the newly married Fred and Ida in their horse and buggy. Those thirteen miles over dirt roads were rutted, but it must have been mild weather or the wheels would have bogged down in mud. The Sioux Center newspaper gave accounts of teams getting stuck in the mud.

Fred was twenty-six and Ida was twenty-one when they were married. She had saved $500. In later years, both Fred and Ida spoke with awe in their voices about this large sum of money. Two months later, when Ida's brother, Sam, married Carolina Faber at the Faber Farm, the newlyweds were there.

In June, Ida wrote a letter and sent wedding pictures to her relatives in Friesland, "I have a big family now."

> Hawarden Iowa. June 6. 1921
> Beloved Uncle, Aunt, Nephew & Nieces,
>   There is a letter from us. Everyone is in good health and we hope you're healthy too. We are married four months already and we thought it's about time to send you the photos. (Time goes fast.) We took the pictures the 19th of February. We are very busy working in the fields (if it doesn't rain.) The garden looks very nice because of all the rain we had. We had terrible frost at night especially between the 13th and the 19th May.
>   The potatoes and beans were frozen otherwise we had an early spring. We have 15 acres of Alfalfa. We live on a 200-acre farm,

---

[114] G. Nelson Nieuwenhuis, Siouxland: *A History of Sioux County, Iowa* (Orange City, IA: Sioux County Historical Society, 1983), p. 229.

it is in good condition. We have six rooms, three upstairs and three downstairs and a basement. Also we have sixteen apple trees and some plum trees. Water is near by the house. We have two lilac bushes in front of the house. Also there are two big barns, a pig-pen and a chicken coop and a corncrib, 50 pigs, six cows and six calves.

Yesterday we visited brother Sybe (Sam). He lives 5 miles away from us. They belong to a different church, therefore we don't see much of each other. Our church is in Lebanon, but it burned down the 30th of January. We have our Sunday service in one of the big barns. They are building a new church, and if all goes well, it will be ready in September. It was a terrible loss especially during bad times. Although produce is cheap, eggs are 17¢ a dozen and butter is 25¢. Lard and corn are 40¢ a bushel. Wheat is cheap too.

Land does not sell. Syne bought an 80-acre farm near Sioux Center. We would like very much a visit from all of you, Aunt. Is Ynschje married? Does Geertje have a baby? How are Ytje, Cornelius and Sientje doing? We met. I hope, Aunt, you will write me a long letter. I wrote to you before, but I didn't receive an answer. We love to hear from you. I have a big family now. My husband has 8 brothers and sisters. Two brothers and two sisters are married. Mother and Dad live four miles away from where we live. We visit them every Sunday right after church. The "baby" in the family is a girl; she is ten years old. Our best wishes to you all from us, and please write us a long letter soon.

With friendly regards from
Fred Kooi, Ida Kooi Sybesma

Remko Kooi is described in various histories and by his several children as a man who led the way. Both Remko and Grada enjoyed seeing their children grow up, marry, and begin farming on the Sioux County farms that Remko had acquired. Their two oldest, Gertie and Benart, were already on nearby farms by the year 1921. Their third, Peter, drowned when he was twenty-two. By 1921, when the fourth, fifth, and sixth—Fred, Bertha, and John—had married, they started farming in the Lebanon area. The last four, Dreaka, George, Ellis, and Jennie, would follow suit within the next few years. Of the ten children, only two, Peter and Dreaka, died as young adults, she, after a ruptured appendix in 1927, leaving two small children with her husband, Case Haverhals.

Mother had an uncommon amount of common sense, called horse sense on the farm. For example, she never read the scientific studies showing that it is better to hold back a shy five-year-old boy from first grade that first important year of school if he isn't ready to go, but she did just that. She talked with the neighboring farmer's wife, who also had a five-year-old son, and they both decided to keep their small sons home from first grade for one more year. The year after Mother's shy first-born son started school, her outgoing, first-born daughter was ready to go, and Mother told her son, "You take good care of your sister and watch out for her. Remember, she's your sister." Much later she would confide, "But it was really the other way around." Mother admonished all of us to watch out for each other at school, and there usually was a goodly number of us in the one-room country school and weekly catechism classes to see to it.

Occasionally, Mother sacrificed one of her chickens for Sunday dinner. One Saturday, I asked her how she killed the chicken. "*Och heiden, kind*, it's a dirty business. You don't want to see *that*." But I did, so I lurked below the front stoop one Saturday morning to watch.

In a wild flurry of feathers beating the ground and dirt flying up, Stanley caught the chicken that Mother had pointed out. He quickly handed it to Mother, standing on the stoop three steps above the ground, and he disappeared. Feathers were bristling, and the chicken was screeching to high heaven. Keeping the chicken's head down, Mother grasped its feet together tightly with one hand while her other hand was wringing its neck as quick as a wink. Her own neck stiffened and turned away. The dying chicken struggled, then wrenched out of her grasp and flopped along the ground, flaying feathers and whip-lashing the dirt in a final frenzy. She waited for it to stop, then lifted it up by its feet. The head was twisting and falling away from the neck. Holding it away from her body, she stepped past the screen door into the washroom off the kitchen and doused the dead chicken in a round tin washtub half full of boiling water.

"How long does it stay here?"

"Maybe an hour or so."

"Oou, it smells awful."

By the end of Saturday morning, I have absorbed her disgust for the screeching, the flying feathers, and the terrible odor of scalding feathers being plucked from singed skin. Stanley and Verna Mae got the disagreeable job of plucking feathers. I did not stick around to see that, or any other chicken being killed ever again. Decades later, a cousin recalled that "to kill a dozen chickens, the women would hang them on the clothesline, then chop off each head. That way the blood and feathers all stayed in one place." Her eyes rolled back as she reflected on this scene. She slowly added, "And they did stay alive quite awhile after their heads came off."

Snapshot of Ida Sybesma at sixteen, Sioux Center, 1916.

Ida Sybesma made friends with Fred Kooi's sisters; Bertha and Dreaka.
Lebanon 1918-1920.

Fred Kooi leaves siblings, Bertha, George, Ellis and
Jennie, at Homeplace for Camp Pike, 1918.

Photograph on Carte Postale by Pvt. Fred Kooi in
Le Mars, France, to Lebanon, Iowa, 1919.

Photograph on postcard sent by Ida Sybesma to Fred Kooi in France.
December, 1919.

Ida Sybesma and Fred Kooi on left, at Vander Lugt farmhouse.
Decoration Day, 1920.

Mr. and Mrs. Birma and children
Bertha also for the evening.
Reception at the home.

Mr. and Mrs. R. Kooi
request the honor of your presence
at the marriage of their son
Fred
to
Miss Ida Sybesma
and their daughter
Bertha Jeannette
to
Mr. Gerrit vander Lugt
on Thursday, January the twenty-seventh
nineteen hundred and twenty-one
at 1:30 P. M.
at the Christian Reformed church
Lebanon, Iowa

Invitation for double wedding ceremony of
Fred and Ida, Bertha and Gerrit, 1921.

Wedding picture of Fred Kooi and Ida Sybesma, 1921.

Faber Farm wedding guests hold apples.
Newlyweds Ida and Fred are on right. March 1921.

Part III

THE OUTSIDE WORLD

23

Aunt Mattie

Her breasts roll down like loaves of white bread rising under damp dish towels made of flour sacks on the sunlit table at home. Aunt Mattie's front feels like a substantial bolster of down pillows above an airy quilted comforter, comforting to me, a small child, skinny-legged and freckle-faced. Frightening too, this big lady; but she smells good, like bread dough rising—so different from Mother, who has the faint scent of breast milk and sweat coming through her housedress. Above Aunt Mattie's housedress are eyes lit by love, framed by rimless spectacles. Above her broad, pale forehead rises hair piled into a bun. Perspiration flecks a faint moustache above her lips. Doughy cheeks lapse toward her neck where her housedress comes up. Her upper arms prolapse toward dimpled elbows. A plain gold band indents one finger on hands at rest or in motion. Kindness kindles her coming and going. A large personage who does not need to bustle is the Aunt Mattie I know as Mother's beloved older sister.

I have just arrived to stay with Aunt Mattie and Uncle John on their farm. Pa has left. I am settling in and barely out of sight when I overhear Aunt Mattie tell Uncle John, "Well, ja, I told Ida on the phone, 'Sure, it's fine with me to have your little girl here a week or two...'" Her kindly voice pauses, and now there is the tone of uncertainty, "...if she doesn't get homesick. There's nobody for her to play with here, you know, that's the only thing." Again she pauses and then resumes and now she is apparently speaking to Uncle John alone. "I don't like it if she gets homesick. We're so far away, you know. It's not like we can just bring her home, and Ida says Fred's too busy to come get her during plowing." But apparently Mother and Aunt Mattie had come to an agreement during their phone conversation because, for two weeks during the summer of 1942, I stay on the farm of Uncle John and Aunt Mattie near Renner, South Dakota. Their farm is located north of Sioux Falls, only about sixty miles from our farm near Hospers. However, since I never have been in another state—and, in any case, never have been more than twenty miles away from home—this is another world, faraway, strange, and feared.

Like any five-year-old faced with something brand new, I closely watch for clues to gauge the situation, to see if this place is safe. Will I be liked here? Will I have to work hard? Was Mother right when she said that Aunt Mattie liked children? There are not any children here, only cousin Frank, who is twenty-six and out plowing every day.

> I recall bits and pieces of family stories and conclude that Aunt Mattie, "knows about little girls my age." I comfort myself with Mother's last words before I got into the car and the door banged shut. Kissing me goodbye she assured me, "Sure you'll have a good time there. Aunt Mattie likes little girls." She was twenty when both of her parents died in Friesland, leaving her to support her eleven-year-old brother, Sam, and seven-year-old sister, Ida. Mattie's mission was to get them onto a boat bound for America where their two older siblings, Geertje and Syne, had already gone and were working on farms, sending as much money as they could to help pay for their siblings' fares. Metje had been their "mother" and sole support for the year of waiting to leave Friesland. Three years after she succeeded in getting them to America, she married John Feikema and had nine children, four of them girls.

Now Aunt Mattie is saying, "We'll bake cookies." Seeing no response, she begins mixing up the cookie dough as she keeps on mentioning things we could do that might appeal to me. I remain tongue-tied, closely watching her. While Aunt Mattie is putting sheets of cookies into the oven, I hear Mother's "Watch out for that oven door—it's very hot." I remember that I have always liked Aunt Mattie, and that Uncle John seems kindly, quiet and old, in the distance somehow. Next to Aunt Mattie and Cousin Frank, Uncle John feels small—not like his son, Frank, whose glowing cheeks match his large body and outgoing good humor. Frank has a receding hairline and an easygoing manner.

The cookies are coming out of the oven. Some are cooling near the window, and I am waiting to taste one, eager to run outside, when Aunt Mattie asks, "What do you like to do at home?" Nobody ever asked me that before. Now I feel really strange and more tongue-tied than ever. Shrinking back from her friendly gaze and growing anxious, I take a cookie and run out the door to wander around the outside walls of the house, to look around at everything on the farm, to see where I am.

Cousin Frank is bigger than I remember, big with bulging ruddy cheeks and laughing blue eyes that look right into you. He wears the regular dark-blue striped overalls over the long-sleeved blue work shirt that all farmers wear; a wide-brimmed straw hat in the fields and a cotton-billed hat when he works around the farmyard, milking cows, slopping the hogs, pitching hay to the cattle.

At nine o'clock the next morning, Aunt Mattie gets out Frank's black metal dinner pail, and since I am here, a little pail for some lunch for me too. Into the cover of Frank's pail she slides a thermos of coffee. A metal guard holds it inside the lid to keep it from falling down and smashing the sandwiches and cookies in the main compartment below. She turns to me and asks what I want to eat. I am still tongue-tied. "Cookies?" Nobody at home asks me what I want to eat. Food simply appears on the table or in the lunch pails, then disappears just about as quickly. My brothers and sisters seem to know how to take what they need but not more than they can eat. At the table, bowls of food come around once, usually. Although we do not expect a second helping, neither do we worry about getting enough. There is always enough. Now I look at Aunt Mattie, blurt out a yes, and try to make myself smaller, invisible if possible. I am sure she can read my thoughts.

"See now, Ida's little girl, if I show you the way, can you take lunch to Frank in the field, and carry back the lunch pails after he's had his lunch?" Remembering Frank's friendly wink at supper last night, I have a cocky, quick-as-a-wink answer. "Sure, I know how to do that." Carrying the midmorning and afternoon lunches to men in the fields is a familiar chore. And now Aunt Mattie is saying, "And then I'll show you how to crochet." I smile. It isn't going to be bad here. Aunt Mattie isn't going to make me work all day picking strawberries in a hot field because she doesn't know what else to do with me. I'm not going to have to play with a bossy, older cousin who owns lots of store-bought toys but hoards them all to herself. Her cheeks are as prickly-red as the chipped polish on her stubby bitten fingernails. She brags about how much richer her father is than mine, while whirling past Milly and me on her own merry-go-round. It isn't as big as the merry-go-round in the park that everyone else has to use, but it is her very own, as is the slide and teeter-totter. Milly and I just pretend we don't care as she taunts, "Just try to get on." We then taunt her. "Fatty pants, fatty pants, we don't care!" and walk off, wishing we really could walk home.

Here, Frank is the only cousin, and he is big and nice, with a friendly smile stretching from one red-round cheek to the other. Gradually I am beginning to feel as though I might like this place. These two weeks might go all right.

Frank is plowing corn in the second field behind the barn. I kick at the overturned black earth, pick my way between rows, then try to walk on the top of a row of humped-up, soft-plowed clods. But with each step I take, my small feet slip down from the top of the pyramid along with the dirt into the deep furrow, unbalancing me. The cow pasture is easier to cross, but I must sidestep cow pies and I must be careful to avoid the far fence where a red-eyed bull waits, pawing the ground. After the pasture, I must cross the part of the stubble field that Frank's plow has not yet come to. Trying to avoid the scratchy stubble on tender soles, I kick dirt clods and test the needles of a thistle.

Frank sees me coming. I wait in the shade of the only tree. We sit on the ground and open our pails. First he asks me about my folks. "Well, how are Uncle Fred and Aunt Ida doing?" Then he asks about each older brother and sister, each one by name. After a few days, I begin to ask him lots of questions: hog prices, politics, why this, why that? Pretty soon I am talking nonstop, testing his limits. "Well, are you Democrats then, or what?" When we discuss politics, it is apparent that our feelings about some things are quite different. After arguing for a while, I get mad, determined to stick to my opinion, especially when backed into a comer. "Hey now, you just won't give up, will ya!" he gently teases as he hoists his large, sweating body back up into the metal seat of the John Deere tractor with its umbrella overhead. I try to stop him from leaving by yelling, "Hey, how come ya got that umbrella over you?"

"Keep off the sun." He pauses. With a reflective look, he adds, "Surely your brothers sit under one too." The way his "one too" rises up into the cloudless sky raises a question I don't entirely understand. Maybe he means that Pa should have put an umbrella over the tractor seat to protect my brothers from the sun. Maybe Frank's a sissy—but no, that can't be it. Here in this place it is so different. Here I am, for the first time in my life in another state, a long way from home for two whole weeks, and I can't get back home until the time is up. Here people do things differently. The way they live is different, yet they are farmers like us. In my mind, I go back and forth, arguing for them (they are our relatives) and conclude the matter (Mother loves Aunt Mattie).

Each night on my way to bed, I pass wedding portraits standing in gray cardboard frames on top of the organ in the parlor. All five of Frank's siblings are married, three of them younger than he is. Once I had asked Mother, "Why isn't Frank married? Is he too old to get married?" But she shooed me out the door and dismissed the concern on my upturned face with a fleeting smile and pensive look. "Oh, maybe he's just taking his time."

As the days pass, my questions to Frank in the field become increasingly bolder. "How come you aren't married?" Frank's eyes gaze into the distance as I wait, pursuing his stare into the next field. "Don't you want children?" Briefly his eyes grow nostalgic, but then suddenly his body turns and something clouds his naturally sunny face, and he issues a gentle warning, "Hey, little cousin, you don't ask such things." I am being put in my place. Blood rushes into my face. Seeing how hurt I am he tries to divert my attention by teasing me. "Say ... uh ... where'd you get those freckles on your nose?" No answer. He tries again. "Better stay out of the sun, it's pretty hot today." When that elicits no response, he tries to get rid of me. "You know ... the bright sun will give you too many freckles. You better start walking home now." As a last resort he simply ends lunchtime by standing up and saying, "Well, gotta get back to work. Now you watch out for that bull as you go across the pasture." Suddenly alarmed, I glance at the far fence and see that the bull is still behind it. Mad and red-faced from the sun, I pick up our empty pails, turn toward the farmyard and walk off, shouting over my shoulder, "Hey, there's no bull!" Roaring with laughter, he grabs the top of the tractor's huge tire with his big hands and easily swings his large body upward and into the metal seat in a single smooth motion.

Walking barefoot through a field of stubble only hurts until the soles harden, but now that I am mad at Frank for laughing at me, both my soles and feelings are wounded. To top it off, I stub a toe.

The Puzzle Stitch

One morning Aunt Mattie says, "Do you like to sew?" I try to think of a way to wiggle out of sitting still and doing that kind of work. I often have watched my mother and older sisters sew. Needles and stubble fields feel the same as stinging nettles. Backing away, I answer, "I've never held a needle." Seeing me balk, her eyes light up from some faraway memory. With a kindly look, she holds up her handiwork to let me admire the crocheted edges of a soft white hankie. She takes me into her bedroom, opens the hankie drawer in the tall dresser, and tells me to pick out any hankie I'd like to have for myself. I imagine Mother's pink and white peppermints tied into the corners of each pretty handkerchief. I see myself sitting next to Mother in church, working out the knots around each peppermint, happily occupied, quietly unraveling each sweet reward while sitting through the long Sunday sermons on the hard pews. I pick up the prettiest hankie in the drawer, look at its two inches of lacy edging, and say, "That must have been very hard to do."

"Here, this is easy," she says, handing me a hankie with a single row of loops crocheted around it. "Would you like to try to do this? I'll show you how." Seeing no way out—if I want the hankie I have picked out for myself—I nod okay, imagining a pink peppermint melting on my tongue.

She starts me on the most basic crochet stitch, a series of loop d' loops running around the four sides of a white hankie. "When you get all the way around the hankie, bring it to me so I can see it," she says as she goes through the door to the kitchen. I sit in the front parlor on the fancy chair that she offered and look around at the lacy doilies on the back and arms of the sofa. I wander over to the highboy, then go look at the family pictures on top of the pump organ. These studio photographs hold familiar faces in their gray cardboard frames folded back to make them stand up. I study them, picking out my favorites: Uncle Sam and Aunt Carolina with their twelve children, all in their best clothes, are arranged oldest to youngest. The four little girls have pipe curls tied with ribbons and the four big girls have pompadours.

Wedding photos of Aunt Mattie's children show: Bernard and Mary Lou, Gladys and Dewey, Clarence and Ann, Catherine and Hank (the only two who live in faraway California), and Betty and Steve. I study the white trains of the brides' white dresses swirling around in front of them in a perfect circle. I sigh. There is no way out.

I sit down and make my fingers go as fast as I can. Finishing in a jiffy, I run into the kitchen to show Aunt Mattie. She holds the hankie up to the light of the window and exclaims, "Perfect! Why, not a single dropped stitch!" She asks me to go around the hankie again, to add a second row of loops. Quickly bored with the monotony of doing the same stitch over and over, I snarl it up this time, jump out of the chair to ask her for help, and risk asking if I may go outside. "Sure honey, you run and play now. *Ach heiden, kind*, what a snarl! I'll see if I can straighten it out."

The next several mornings she patiently shows me how to add increasingly more complicated stitches to the hankie's edge, one on top of the other. Finally, it is time to choose a design. I fix my sights on crocheting the fancy edge she says is the puzzle stitch. "Sure, you can do that," her eyes moisten, "after you learn a few more stitches, sure." I jump up, ready to run and play outside, but she stops me. "What color thread would you like to use?" So many choices at this place—so many here, at home so few. After many hesitations, I settle on a long loop of variegated pastels, rainbow colors like some of the broken crayons in the tin can on the windowsill at home. The loop of crochet thread she finds is new, held by a shiny band of paper, much like the gold band that girdles the cigar that Uncle Pete lights up after dinner, his large frame sinking into his favorite easy chair and the smoke rising.

At first it is easy. I simply crochet around all four sides of the hankie three times, each time making a different stitch. But then the design requires crocheting separate pineapple shapes from the thin thread and holding these half-dozen slender loops of pineapple shapes away from the crocheted edge of the hankie with one finger, before reconnecting these lacy loops to the hankie's three-tiered edge. This must be done at measured, counted intervals. Each time I snarl up the loops into knots, I run to the kitchen to find Aunt Mattie. She is kneading the bread dough. Her heaving breasts emit warmth. She stops, looks at the knobby mess, and says, "*Ach heiden, kinderen, ach.*" She can see that I am going to stick with it and finish the project. "Ja," she says, over and over. Back to the front parlor I go again, to the appointed chair. I hold up my work to see how far I have to go before I can stop, and then the crocheted edges of Mother's Sunday-best hankie hook me. I gaze out the window. Through the lace curtain I see myself in another place. Dressed up, bent forward, pipe curls almost covering my face, intent on something, sitting quietly next to Mother, my perspiration-soaked dress sticks to the hard pew. I am working away at tight knots in the corner of a white hankie trying to get a peppermint untied.

The Puzzle Stitch stretches the agility of my short fingers and stretches my patience to its limits, but the pineapples grow, a precious few each day. At the end of my two-week stay, I proudly hold up the rainbow-colored pineapples to admire, ready to go home to Mother. Aunt Mattie beams. She has baked cookies; I have eaten them and have crocheted around a hankie. Frank and I have solved world problems while eating lunch in the field. He winks at me as I climb into Pa's gray Chevrolet. Clutching the door handle with one hand, my other hand waves as we drive away in a cloud of dust up the driveway to the highway. All three continue to stand there, watching and waving until we are out of sight. In my eagerness to see Mother, I almost wet my pants.

Six years later Frank married Irene Schaap and told her, "I waited so long because I was looking for the best." They settled into farming near Leota, Minnesota, where they went to the Ebenezer Christian Reformed Church. Forty-eight years later, Frank was harvesting soybeans on a son's farm east of Leota when another son, working in another part of the field, noticed that his dad had come to the end of a row, stopped, and not turned into the next row. The son went to see why and found his dad slumped forward in the tractor seat. Frank was dead at age eighty. His passing was grieved by his wife, three sons, a daughter, thirteen grandchildren, two brothers, two sisters, and a host of other relatives.

Uncle John and Aunt Mattie Feikema seated,
among standing children is Frank on the left, 1942.

Aunt Mattie holding Frank, Uncle John Feikema, and three more children, 1918.

284

Sybesma boy cousins at Sybesma reunion.
Ray is third from right in front row, 1930.

Sam Sybesma Family. Platte, South Dakota.1944-45
Top row: Sam, Carolina, Carolyn, Stanley, Mary Jean, Sam Jr.
Middle row: Bertha, Clara, Clarence, Marion.
Front row: Anna Mae, Gertrude, Mildred, Darlene.

24

One-Room School

Uncle John and Aunt Mattie's second daughter, Catherine, was born in 1915 and experienced the Great Depression first-hand. She recalled that, "In the spring of 1925, the state mandated that all herds of milk cows had to be tested for tuberculosis. I remember seeing anguish, tears, and, yes, even terror on my father's face as the trucks left the yard with the supposedly stricken cows, robbing him of his means of livelihood. The whole area was outraged as farmer after farmer lost all! Later it was established that the test was defective, flawed, and lacked sufficient evidence. Then came the Great Depression. This caused unbelievable hardship for the townspeople who were laid off. In addition, the farmers suffered because of a severe drought and no saleable products on hand."

Catherine began high school not knowing how her parents could pay for her to stay at her uncle's house for two dollars a week. She heard her mother say, "If I have two dollars and a half to three dollars a week, I can feed my family." The next two years Catherine stayed at home and walked the six miles to school, then home again. Farmers would give her a ride—and was she ever thankful for every lift. She never had a single fear about riding with strangers. Nevertheless, she was cold, wet, windblown, and frozen by turns. The most comforting sight or sound was the one of a brother coming to meet her on horseback. In her senior year (1932-33), farmers were still deep in depression. Now she had an upstairs room at the home of church friends, but she furnished her own food, heat, and other necessities. In return, her family paid the friends two to three gallons of milk per week. She graduated with a Normal Training Certificate for country-school teaching. She married Henry DeBie in 1939 and they moved to Artesia, California. In the spring of 1995 Catherine was still teaching part time in Artesia.[115]

---

[115] Catherine Feikema DeBie, "The Life and Times of Catherine Feikema DeBie," n.d. Excerpts used here were carefully edited with author's permission.

286   Mother's niece, Bertha Bierma, recalls that, "The 1929-41 events of the depression were lasting. On February 18, 1932, in the middle of the depression, Jim Geels and I were married. We would liked to have gotten married before, but we had to wait because there was no farm available."[116]

My father talked about the economy before the depression. "There was the money wash and price drop, and half of the farms were taken over by large insurance companies. In the twenties, things seemed to get better, then The Depression! In 1932, I switched to Democrat. My father had always voted Republican, but I did not think much of Herbert Hoover."

President Roosevelt's REA (Rural Electrification Administration) put men to work during the Depression. In 1934, Ray was twelve when gasoline replaced kerosene in the lanterns. For Ray, this meant better light for reading around the kitchen table after supper. And then, in 1936 electricity came onto the Lebanon farmyard when the REA strung a line from pole to pole along the dirt road from town. The men ran posts into the ground from farm to farm. At each farm, the men would string a line from the road to a tall post in the farmyard. The coming of electricity provided jobs and improved the lot of the rural people. The wire coming into our yard sang. The swaying wires hummed from pole to pole along the road to town. At dusk, two tiers of blackbirds would perch side by side on the lines, their silhouettes an echo against the blushing sky and darkening rows of corn with their golden tassels waving as we drove along the road going to town.

Phone lines were always separate from the electrical lines, and were already there when the folks married and Ray was born in 1921:

> The party line meant one phone line for everyone, but Mother and Pa would not listen in unless there was some emergency like a barn burning down. We were taught never to touch the phone. To call Sioux Center meant a long distance call—15 cents—and we would call Uncle Watse in Sioux Center only if someone was sick or there was some emergency.[117]

[116] Bertha Geels, op cit.

[117] Oral history from brother Ray Kooi.

The children from the farms around Lebanon walked to a one-room, public school-house. The oldest seven in our family (Ray, Gladys, Clarence, Bernice, Peter, Stan, Verna Mae) went to this school (Eagle Township District Number Six) until 1939, as recalled by Bernice:

On August 28, 1931, I was five years old. The next day school began, and I was in the first grade. Monday started the school week. The period of time between getting out of bed and entering school was always a mad rush. Each of us had our duties to perform. Finally we would take out dinner pails and start off to school. The year when I had my own dinner pail, and no longer had to share it, was a milestone in my life. School was a half-mile from our home, a pleasant walk in the summer and a bitter one in sub-zero weather. There were two hills to climb, the little hill and the big hill. In the spring I used to walk in the ditch and pick violets and pink roses. Sometimes I would take the long way home, following the creek through our pasture.

The new teacher that first year was Marie Sinkey, a slender, brown-eyed, young woman with a bad complexion, who took her teaching very seriously. She was an excellent teacher, and I felt fortunate. She was conscientious but also imaginative. She once gave me an assignment to observe a small baby for an hour and then write about it. We had no home economics courses, but she taught us to embroider. Neither did we have physical education courses, but she had us stand next to our desks and do stretches and jumping jacks. It was a public school, but she said a prayer every day and read the Bible. When she got married, she stopped teaching, of course. We were all invited to her wedding during the Sunday evening service in the Ireton Christian Reformed Church.

The first few years of school were challenging. After that, I was sometimes bored. With eight grades in one room, you learned a lot about the material you would have the following year by listening to the older kids as they sat on the recitation bench and recited. To pass the time when I was finished with my assignments, I read library books—but it was a small library and how many times can you read *Reynolds the Fox* and the *Bobbsey Twins*? I would place my colors beside me on my seat and arrange them into families. The long, darker colors were the fathers, and the long, lighter colors were the grown women, the shorter colors the teenagers and the children. I made up elaborate games for all these people to play, but when the teacher looked my way or came marching down the aisle, I quickly shoved them into my desk. During seven-and-a-half of my eight school years, I had but one classmate and never any other. We always provided good competition for each other.

When Gladys, and then Bernice, reached age twelve and finished eighth grade, each one stayed home to help Mother in the kitchen. Gladys says, "I gave up my teen years to help take care of the family. I loved school but stayed home to work side by side with Mother. I missed out on girlfriends and high school, that time of life when girls usually get initiated into the mysteries of womanhood by their peers."

Like the one-room school, the annual visit from the Dominie was part of farm life. Bernice describes House Visitation on the Lebanon farm.

Huis Bezoek

Once a year the Dominie and an elder come to the Lebanon farm. They are dressed in dark suits. The house is clean, our faces are washed, our clothes clean, our shoes on. The living room is lined with chairs, and after each of us shakes hands with the dignitaries, we quietly take our seats. There is no laughter. Smiles are rationed. The Dominie stands next to the oval oak table in the bay window, which today is covered with Mama's best embroidered cloth. He places his large black Bible on the table, then opens the hour with prayer and scripture reading. He questions us: Do you love God? (such an intensely personal question). But the answer is easy and I shyly whisper: Yes. Other questions to other members of the family. Do you like church? Again, only one acceptable answer: Yes. Has your faith grown? Do you read your Bible? Yes. Yes. Are there any problems in your spiritual life? This time the right answer is: No. My parents, I think, are a little embarrassed. They would never think of asking such personal questions, but they play the game. The hour is finally over. All is well here. Everybody loves God. Everybody loves to go to church. No one has a problem. We smile a little, shake hands. Till next year. Same place, same scenario.

By the time I was old enough to remember House Visitation, we had moved from the Lebanon farm to the Hospers farm, where the front parlor did not have a bay window, and the Dominie was called minister or pastor. We got ready early for visitation: dishes washed, dried, and put away right after supper. Spiffed up, hair combed, clean behind the ears, we endured warnings. Mother was calm. Pa was nervous. Visitation was one of the times we clearly got the word from the older ones on how to act, what to say, and what not to say. "Now then, you know what you are supposed to say."

"Well, when are they coming?" Pretty soon now.

"Stand still so I can tie your sash, again. Stop picking your nose."

"Don't talk unless you are asked a question; then answer right away."

"Sit up straight and keep your hands to home," which meant that we four little kids sitting close together on the davenport must stop playing tic-tac-toe on each other's knees. Sitting still and waiting is one of the worst things a little kid has to do. Finally, there is the sound of tires crunching down the driveway and we get a final warning.

"You behave yourself while they're here, *you hear?*"

Either the Pastor or Elder asked each one of us a question, going around the room. When it was my turn, he asked me to recite a Bible verse. I fell silent. In acute embarrassment, I stared at the floor. Next day, Milly taught me the shortest Bible verse to know by heart in case that ever happened again: "Jesus wept." She also taught me to say where it is found in the Bible: book, chapter, verse; and she reminded me, that we all knew, 'For God so loved the world that he gave His only begotten Son, that whosoever believeth in Him should not perish but have everlasting life."

Right after reciting, be sure to say where it's found: John 3:16.

Mother's teaching had taken root. "Look good, act good, be good. Behave your best when you are dressed up." Her teaching reflected her ancestry. Throughout their history, the Dutch people had taken a keen interest in art and the artifice of clothes. The importance of appearance in costumes, caps, and jewelry was repeatedly described by writers, and continues to be noticed by observers of the Dutch people and culture.

Have you ever gone abroad only to find yourself back home—at your beginnings? Biblical Israel was part of the Friesland culture that Mother knew, and both of these placed influenced her life in Iowa. Currently, in Israel, another *Intifada* rages on, similar to the *Intifada* that occurred when I was there in 1989. Cycling forward, history repeats itself. We imagine ourselves to be in a completely different place than we were the last time we were there, but are we really?

25

Where Babies Come From

The children's bedrooms were upstairs in both the Lebanon and Hospers farmhouses. "When I was a child we slept three in a bed—two beds in the room—I called that a private room!" writes Gladys. "Ray and I would bet on who could stay upstairs and wait the longest to see the new baby, this one being Stanley. To bet money was a sin, so it was simply a verbal bet. Ray won. All births but the last one were downstairs in the same farmhouse bedroom.

"There is a big difference between the generations as to how they went about explaining where babies came from. In 1913 my mother was thirteen years old and lived with her oldest sister, Gertie Bierma, who was expecting a baby. Mother didn't know anything about that, when one day Aunt Gertie said, Do you know where babies come from? Mother said, No. Aunt Gertie said, "Read the Bible and you'll find out." Mother didn't ask any more.

"In 1936 I was twelve years old, and Mother was expecting a baby. Although we had a new baby in our house every other year, I did not know where they came from. That September I was out of school, finished with my eight years of grammar school education. We housecleaned each spring and fall. That fall, Mother and I cleaned the trunk in which was stored all the off-season, or too-small, or too-big clothes. We sat on the floor, and as she took out baby bands, small shirties and diapers, she said, "Lay them over there, Gladys. We'll need them pretty soon." I looked at her furtively, looked at her stomach, noticed that it was big, and I made my own deductions. I didn't ask any questions either.

"In 1955 when my Bob and Ken were eight and six years old, I was expecting Cindy. When I was about seven months pregnant, I told the boys, "We're going to have a new baby." They asked a few questions and I answered honestly, careful not to tell any more than was asked. In 1983 Cindy's little girl, Rachael, was almost four when she told me, her grandmother, the story of her birth. "I was in Mama's tummy and one morning Mama had a pain in her tummy. You came, Grandma. Pretty soon you and Mama went to the hospital, and pretty soon Mama pushed me right out of her tummy, right down here, with a big puff—and there I was."[118]

In 1936, there was a total crop failure, an experience that Sioux County never had before. Even the grasshoppers died of starvation. It was the hottest summer on record in the state of Iowa. In July, the country was in the middle of the worst heat wave ever recorded. Temperatures as far north as North Dakota climbed to 120 degrees. Sixteen states set their all-time record highs during this heat wave. On July 16, the afternoon highs at 113 locations in Iowa averaged 109 degrees. Extreme heat and extreme cold marked the year 1936 for the entire country. The temperature swing of 181 degrees in the same year was unprecedented in the United States and has not been duplicated since.[119] The drought and high winds that came are remembered by Bernice Kooi Afman:

> My parents stare at the sky. I feel their anxiety. The rains do not come. All winter and spring they have made preparations. Seed was stored through the winter and then, at the right time, the fields were plowed, the seeds planted. They sprouted and the fields were harrowed and disced. And the rains stopped coming. Now the corn and wheat droops, turns brown. My parents stand helpless, looking at the sky. The winds blow hot. Gritty dust is on the window sills, on the furniture. On Sunday the farmers sit stolidly in church. Shoulders sag a little, but there is no bitterness. The Dominie prays for rains. He reads from the Word, "I pour out my soul in me, for I have gone with the multitude ... to the house of God ... Oh, my God, my soul is cast down within me ..." He goes on, "Hope thou in God, for I shall yet praise him. Many are the afflictions of the righteous, but the Lord delivereth them out of all their troubles." And more promises: "He waterest the hills from his chambers, the earth is satisfied with the fruit of thy work. He causeth the grass to grow for the cattle, and herbs for the service of man, that he may bring forth food out of the earth. Thou visiteth the earth and waterest it, thou preparest them corn, thou settlest the furrows thereof; thou makest it soft with showers. Thou crownest

[118] Gladys Gritter, "Where Babies Come From," in Journals of Gladys Gritter, November 16, 1983.

[119] Craig James, "Weather News," in the Grand Rapids Press, July 14, 2001.

the year with thy goodness. The valleys are also covered over with corn; they shout for joy, they also sing." The service is over. It will rain again, if not this year then next. The valleys will shout for joy again and also sing![120]

The winter of 1936 was severe as well. Snowstorms closed roads. In the freezing cold, white snowdrifts piled up and draped the clothesline poles, turning them into ghosts, scarecrows, slouching snowmen. The children pressed their noses against the kitchen windows to peer out through storm windows iced with magical scenes in Jack Frost tracery. Icicles hung from eaves troughs. The wet clothes hanging outside on the clothesline to dry, froze. Overalls and dresses stood out with stiff limbs, chests and stomachs, and looked like headless people. The little kids peering out the windows called them "dead stiffs."

At the end of 1936 I was born on December three. At that time, Ray was boarding in Hull, Iowa, in tenth grade at the Hull Christian High School. He was fourteen, about to turn fifteen. Curious about the circumstances around my birth, I recently asked Ray, "Since I was the tenth baby born, what did you think?"

On the fourth of December in 1936, 1 heard that I had a baby sister, told to me by a cousin, Chris Sybesma, as I was walking down the hall to Latin I. The Sioux Center doctor's name was William Maris. He was our family doctor for several years. I especially remember that when he came out to our farm over the dirt roads (often muddy), his 1935 model car was driven by a chauffeur. I was fascinated by all this. Outside of books, I'd never seen a chauffeur. He was an "old" man (probably 40-50) who drove Dr. Maris all over; he was a handy person to have for changing flat tires. No fancy uniforms for the chauffeur–just "old man's" clothes. The chauffeur waited outside in the car until someone called him in to wait beside the wood and cob box next to the stove in the kitchen. I wasn't home the day you were born, but you probably had a chauffeur-attended birth.[121]

[120] Bernice Afman, "The Drought."

[121] Letter from Ray Kooi, dated September 29, 1993.

The last baby born to Mother on December three had died on December 23, in 1933. Now, three years later, on the same date, Mother gave birth to me. No doubt Mother remembered her own mother, and the six babies who had died at their home in Friesland. No doubt the turbulent weather that marked 1936 as a bad year for farmers added to her worries. When Mother's milk came in a couple of days after my birth she noticed that I fed poorly. She telephoned the doctor in town. He said that he didn't know what was wrong, to keep trying to get me to suck. She tried to coax me to eat but that did not work. I sucked less and less over the next several days. And then, some days later, I did not even try to suck.

Another snowstorm covered the farm and the dirt roads leading to town. She and Pa discussed what to do. He could, he said, hitch horses to a wagon and get through the drifts that way, to fetch the doctor in Sioux Center. So, he and one of the older boys hitched up and started out, but snowdrifts came over the fences and completely covered the road. The horses struggled forward only to sink deeper into the snow with each step, then struggled to go another step. They got only as far as the top of the first hill before it grew dark. Snow continued to swirl down. Pa had to make a decision: go on and try to make it to the next farm and stay there overnight, or go back home. Either way was about the same distance. If they made it to the next farm and slept there, by the next morning the sky might clear and then he would need to go home anyway to do chores at dawn. Might as well go home and wait. Besides, maybe the baby would eat.

When Pa got home I was still not sucking, but Mother had talked to Doctor Maris on the phone again. Again, he had offered to come to see the sick baby if someone could get through the snow to get him. No one could. She decided to try steaming open my airways, just in case a clogged nose or sinus was preventing me from sucking. Over the baby buggy she draped a large piece of white cheesecloth. Water was kept boiling in the big iron teakettle on the cookstove. Then the kettle was carried to the buggy. From the spout, steam poured inside the cheesecloth. Breathing the steam, I seemed to stir. She coaxed me to eat by dropping sugar water from a tiny spoon onto my lips. She waited and tried again. Gladys and Bernice helped by keeping the wood stove going and taking care of the others. Again, night closed in. Mother and Gladys took turns staying up all night, steaming me in the buggy, trying to get me to swallow a few drops of warm milk. I kept breathing. The next morning, Doctor Maris phoned. Mother told him that I seemed a little better. Four days before Christmas the crisis passed. Much later, I asked Mother, "What was wrong with me?"

"Well, I never knew. The doctor didn't either."

By the age of eight, I wanted to know where babies came from, and since most things came hand-me-down, I naturally asked my next older sister. She promised to tell me later, "Outside in the toilet when you're old enough—next year." At age nine I asked her again and got the same answer. By the time I was ten, we had moved to the city where pre-adolescents gathered in neighborhood basements, turned out the lights, snickered, and told jokes such as, "I want to drive my car into your garage." I figured it out.

Within the nineteen years between 1921 and 1940 Mother gave birth twelve times, just as her mother had done. All twelve babies were born at home in the bedroom and all were nursed, just as her mother's twelve babies had been. Mother's first eleven babies were born on the farm near Lebanon, where she and Pa had gone to live after their wedding in 1921. Ray, the oldest, says, "It was not unusual to come downstairs in the morning and find a new baby."

In 1939 the estate of Remko and Grada Kooi was finally settled. Their property was divided among their ten children, with Uncle John and Aunt Gertie getting our Lebanon farm in Eagle Township. Some people thought the Hospers area had better land, but moving to a farm twenty miles away from Lebanon was a major move for our family. This was particularly so because we were moving away from the area where the farms of all the other Kooi families were clustered around the homeplace— where two generations had been born, grown up and continued to live. Also, we were leaving the Lebanon Christian Reformed Church, the one-room Ireton school within walking distance of our farm, and the town of Lebanon with its family history and nexus of trading.

The Ireton School neighbors gave a Surprise Farewell Party before we moved in February of 1939. Pa stayed home with the three little ones,

Elmer, Irene and Milly while the others went to the party. At the party Ray played the piano. Mother gave an acceptance speech for the going away gift of two pictures. The families of the Browns, Nettens, Meullers, Bonnemas and Ten Napels were at the party.[122]

Early in March of 1939 came the big move to the Hospers-area farm. It took several days to move all the livestock, farm machinery, and tools, and household goods. Ray, the oldest, was seventeen. Elmer, the youngest, was ten months old. I was two years and three months. One year after the move, Mother gave birth again. The twelfth—and last—baby was named Harold Glenn.

---

[122] Mother's words written on the back of one of the two gift pictures, currently hanging in Glenn and Patricia Kooi's home in Denver, Colorado.

Frederick Kooi, born 1894,
Lebanon, Iowa, 1895.

Milk pails draining next to Ray in dress, Lebanon farm, July, 1922.

Raymond and Gladys Kooi,
Lebanon, 1924.

Mother holding Clarence, in wagon is
Gladys with cousin Margaret Vander Lugt,
Lebanon, 1925.

Katherine Bierma visits cousin Gladys Kooi on Lebanon farm, 1938.

Irene and Milly Kooi on Lebanon farm, 1938.

Red sunsuit made by Gladys for Irene in 1938 ...

... and handed down to Glenn in 1941.

26

The Prize

Sixty years after the 1939 move from the Lebanon farm to the Hospers farm, I lie in an Israeli campground, cradled in sand dunes hung with the green draperies of the Tree of Heaven. Yahweh feels near tonight. In this verdant oasis next to the Dead Sea, evening comes. Gazing at a distant kibbutz cut into the pink sandstone hillside, I drift into mists and mystery: Yahweh, Jehovah, God, Christ, Lord, Jesus. "God said to Moses, I am who I am" (Exodus 3:14). Before sleeping, I read some of the Old Testament stories I heard as a child: How Absalom's sister, Tamar, was forced by Annon and how Absalom killed him for it (2 Samuel 13). Stories about King David and his beloved son, Absalom. How, racing on horseback, Absalom's long hair got caught in the low branches of a tree. David's deep mourning. Finally a line from a hymn carries me off, "Cradled in his everlasting arms." Shortly I am in "The Sweet Bye and Bye," in the Sunday School class inside the Hospers Christian Reformed Church. I am five or six and we are singing:

	When Israel was in Egypt-land
Refrain:	*Let My People Go...Oh!*
	Oppressed so hard they could not stand
Refrain:	*Let My People Go!*
	Go down, Moses, way down to Egypt-land
	Tell old Phar-aoh
Refrain:	*Let My People Go!* (Exodus 5:1)

Shouting the refrain, I wake up hoarse, years away from Sunday School.

While living in Israel during 1989, we traveled to Egypt-land where Moses grew up and dwelt in the house of Pharaoh during the first forty years of his life. After killing an Egyptian overlord who was beating an Israelite worker, Moses escaped into Midian (Arabia). He returned to lead the Israelites from their bondage in Egypt. During the next forty years, he led the Israelites on their journeys toward the Promised Land, through the wilderness, criss-crossing the deserts of Sinai, Midian, and the Negev. The stories of Moses with the Israelites during this time period are rewarding reading: the burning bush, the ten plagues, the parting of the Red Sea, God giving Moses the ten commandments on tablets of stone, the fittings of the tabernacle, and so forth (Exodus 3:2, 7:14, 12:30, 12:37, 20:2, 25:10, 27:20).

For the last forty years of Moses' long life he led the Israelites on journeys to capture the Transjordan, but he never got his people into the Promised Land. On Mount Nebo, in the wilderness, God permitted him to view this promised land before he died. In Deuteronomy 34:7, we read, "Moses was one hundred and twenty years old when he died. His eyes were not dim nor his natural vigor diminished." His chosen successor, Joshua, led God's chosen people into the Promised Land (Deuteronomy 31:7). As tourists, we cross the Sinai Desert twice, climb Mount Sinai, and dwell upon the Plain of Elijah.

Old Testament stories about Elijah were sermon topics in Iowa. After the long church service came Sunday School. Our class of five-year-olds would stand up to sing a Bible story, patterned into a simple, rhythmic ditty. Our restless little bodies would mimic the teacher's motions. Little arms reached high, stretched higher, then swung down toward the floor to Fish! Fish! Fish! before voices launched louder and stronger into:

> I will make you fishers of men
> Fishers of men, fishers of men,
> I will make you fishers of men
> If you follow me.

After each verse we would repeat the chorus, our voices going faster and higher until we were squealing:

> If you follow me
> If you follow me.
> I will make you fishers of men
> If you follow me.

On our way to the school picnic, we are packed into the gray Chevrolet as tightly as sardines in a tin can. Pa, as always, is at the wheel, and we are careening down the dirt road, kicking up a cloud of dust on the way to Hospers. If it was the Fourth of July or Decoration Day (Memorial Day), we would be on our way to the park in Sheldon.

On Decoration Day in Sheldon, Pa buys red paper poppies from the "Veterans of Foreign Wars" and wears one in the buttonhole of his suit jacket. In his shirtsleeves, he pitches horseshoes with the men. Mother sits at the picnic tables with the women and talks. Some of us go swimming in the community pool. Scared, I hang back and hold onto Mother's skirts until she shoos me off by asking, "Did you see the swings yet?" We go down long slides and land on our bottoms in a basin of dirt. We balance and wobble on the teeter-totters. We pump ourselves higher and higher on the swings to see if we can get high enough to go over the top of the bar. We whirl around on the merry-go-round until we are dizzy. Sometimes we roller skate in the indoor roller rink. At the end of the day, we are almost too tired to get into the car to go home.

On Labor Day, we are on our way to the church yard in Hospers where the school picnic will be held. Pa is steering the Chevy down the dirt roads and cornering the sections of soil so fast that we must lean into each other as we go around each corner. His Sunday straw hat sits straight across his forehead. In the back seat I am squeezed next to the left door handle. My butt is jammed onto the front end of the seat, into what is left over from Peter, Stanley, and Verna Mae. Milly is jammed in at the other end of the seat, next to the right rear window. I hang onto the back of the front seat as I listen to Pa.

"No doubt about it," Pa is droning on and on, talking as much to himself as to the rest of us in the car, "those labor unions are a good thing. Maybe they went too far sometimes, but still..." His voice drifts off. "Now, some of those big bosses like John D., like John Lewis, maybe he went a little too far but, no doubt about it, they needed the union, a good thing. Ja, then there's those strike busters. Now I don't say I agree with all that some of them did, but..." The back of Pa's neck between the wheat-colored straw hat and the collar of his long-sleeved white shirt is red. I study the deep creases in the skin of his red neck. Today, his tie is a little brighter than the one he wears to church on Sunday. It will come off before he begins to pitch horseshoes. He has on his dress pants. His shoes shine. Crunched between him and Mother in the front seat is Elmer. Glenny straddles Mother's lap. The window is half-way down, and I can see down each row of corn as the rows whiz by. Even though I have memorized each farm we pass, I study each one again: the shape of each house, grove, barn, and other buildings; the haystacks, pigs, and horses; the driveways that go between lines of elm or cottonwood to the farmhouse; the fields of corn, wheat, and alfalfa; the cow pastures. We have plenty of time during the long car ride to think about what will happen at picnic: the food, fun, and games.

During the thirty-minute car ride through the steamy Iowa sunshine to the School Picnic, my anticipation runs high. There will be foods to eat that we never get at home. My favorites are the ham buns and the half muskmelon filled with one round scoop of vanilla ice cream. The ham buns will have a slab of ham, mustard, and butter on a potato bun. The top of the bun will be dusted with flour, baked by a real baker in a real bakery, not the usual homemade bread. The buns will be free, but the muskmelon— for which I'll have to wait until nearly the end of the afternoon—will cost one whole quarter. The ham buns will be piled high, like a pyramid, on giant round platters placed on the board of a booth higher than my head. They will be there next to other sandwiches and next to huge, speckled graniteware pots of coffee made by the Ladies Aid Society. The school picnic is held at the church because the two-room Hospers Christian School has no kitchen in which to make coffee. During the long, hot afternoon, Mother will sit on a folding chair in a circle with other women and drink coffee.

Everyone is dressed up. Milly and I are wearing matching red-and-white-striped pinafores with stiff ruffles running down from the tops of our shoulders to our waists. A week ago, Mother picked out the pattern and material for these pinafores at the dime store in Sheldon. Gladys cut out the pinafores, laid and pieced them together on the dining room table, then sewed each piece together on the Singer sewing machine, both of her feet pumping the wrought-iron treadle back and forth, over and over. Playing paper dolls on the floor, Milly and I heard the whirring wheels and the humming Singer's song. Enough material was left over to make bows for the ends of our pigtails today, and there were enough scraps for doll clothes. Only last Saturday we got these new, brown leather school shoes with brown laces from the store in Hospers. Intended for the start of school tomorrow, they pinch feet that are used to being bare except for the necessity of squeezing into the hated, weekly-polished, Sunday shoes.

As Pa pulls into the parking lot, I strain at the door, my hand already on the handle, ready to burst out of the car as soon as it comes to a stop. I race for the food. Such picnics are the only time I ever recall not having to wait for the long prayer before being allowed to eat. Mother goes to sit with the women. Pa stands around with the men folk, all farmers. Each one of us goes to find kids our own age. I heap up potato salad on my paper plate and try to take two sweet pickles and two ham buns before one of the ladies in the booth smiles, "No. You can come back, you know." There is real lemonade with real ice cubes in a heavy glass pitcher. Impatiently, I wait for one of the ladies to pour some into a paper cup. I must remember to keep the cup if I want more. I know I will want a lot so I make sure to keep it.

Knowing the games could start any time I eat fast. Although I want to be in on every single game I have to wait on the sidelines until I hear the call for my class. In order, I am allowed to compete in the one-legged gunny-sack races, the high jump, low jump, broadjump, wheel-barrow races, and other events. Every ten minutes, I beg Mother for "Just one more nickel, please, please." When I think my stomach can hold just one more thing, I beg her for "Just one whole quarter. If you give me one, I promise I won't ask for another thing." She looks into my eyes and gently asks, "What for?"

"For the muskmelon filled with ice cream. It's the best thing here."

She says, "Well I guess so, but that's all, now." I get so full that I feel sick all the way home, and somebody chides, as we whiz along the dirt roads in the car with the sun going down, "Well, ya shouldn't of ate so much then. Next time you'll know better." But I won't know better. At every school picnic I eat too much, compete too hard, play too long, then sit on the edge allotted me in the crowded back seat of the Chevy and hold my hurting tummy all the way home, moaning until I know I better stop—or else.

When the games are about to begin, the men stop talking about haying, threshing machines, combines, and hog prices. They stop pitching horseshoes. The women stop talking about canning and who is doing what, stop wiping the little kids' noses with handkerchiefs, and stop putting Band Aides onto skinned knees. The kids stop stuffing themselves. Everyone quiets down and crowds around to watch. The school principal announces the start of the one-legged sack race. "First, the first graders."

"Choose your partner!"

The way to win is to get your partner to run the same speed you do, with your one leg in the gunny sack next to her one leg. Usually you get a partner who stumbles, pulls sideways, or, even worse, falls down. The best thing, of course, is to choose a partner beforehand who is well coordinated, fast, and wants to win as much as you do. First graders, however, are unlikely to know whom to choose unless they have the help and experience of older brothers or sisters. While other families might have as many as three siblings at the picnic, we probably have as many as seven—far more brothers and sisters to coach us, far more to cheer us from the sidelines, far more to help us choose a partner. There is strength in numbers.

"Line up on the starting line!" The right leg of one contestant and the left leg of the other one go into a scratchy, brown gunny sack, held up around our waists—or higher—by sticky, sweaty hands. For first graders, the finish line of white chalk is not very far away. "Get Readyyyy ..." yells the principal, drawing out the "y" to a long "e" and holding it as long as he can while he assesses how unready the line of little kids really is. "Get Set ..."

Someone always steps over the line before he yells "GO!"

"Everybody back behind the starting line." He waits until all the kids in the gunny sacks are where they are supposed to be. "Now, this time wait to start until you hear the Go! Get Readyyyy ... Get Set... GO!"

Early in the day prizes are something to look forward to when you are squeezed between your sister and the door handle, half-sitting on the front few inches of the back seat, hanging on, and sliding down toward the floor around each curve.

At the end of the day, our family carries home more than its share of first, second, and third prizes.

Profile of Mother in front yard of farm at Hospers, 1944.

27

Two-Story School

The Hospers Christian School is set in the middle of a pie-shaped field at the edge of the town. Grades one through four are in the downstairs room, and grades five through eight are upstairs. Each room holds thirty to forty students. Like our farmhouse, the schoolhouse is a two-story, square, white clapboard building. We leave the farm at eight. School starts at nine. Since Pa usually drives fast, we have time for outdoor games when we get there. School lasts until four, with lunch at noon and fifteen-minute recesses in the morning and afternoon. We get home at four-thirty. Girls and women teachers are not allowed to wear pants, slacks, or shorts, even to school picnics. Wearing dresses discourages unladylike activities like hanging upside down on playground equipment. Under our dresses are thick brown stockings. The tight elastic of the bulky, scratchy, homemade bloomers leaves red marks around our legs and waists.

I am five that cold September morning when Mother hands me a dinner pail and buttons up my coat. The others are in the gray Chevy, its back door open. I know I have to go, as I stand there sucking my thumb. Mother hugs me close and whispers into my ear. "You won't want to do that at school. The other kids will tease you." It takes more self-control than I can muster to keep my thumb out of my mouth, but I succeed the whole first day until four when I again am safely in the gray Chevy for the seven-mile ride home. The next day, though, by 11:30 the comforting thumb finds its way back in. During the noon-hour recess, I understand how right Mother is. The teasing is merciless.

The school day begins with folded hands and closed eyes while the teacher says a prayer. Standing with hands over our hearts, we pledge our allegiance to a little flag on a stick above the blackboard. The teacher then goes to the piano, and we sing a hymn or a patriotic song such as, "Our country 'tis of thee, sweet land of liberty, of thee I sing." The lessons for all four grades have been written on the blackboard before the school day begins. First, the first grade gets a lesson. "Children, open your primer to the first page."

312   "Rodney, will you stand up, go to the front, and read?" He plods up to the front of the room, his head hanging, and shuffles through the words. "See Dick. See Jane. See Dick run. See Jane run." I am fidgeting with the ink jar in the inkwell on my desk while the boy behind me, Henry, is testing the point of his pencil on the middle of my back. I give him a mean look, but he continues. I lean forward, but he presses harder. I raise my hand as the teacher wearily nods in my direction, then calls on me with a questioning tone, "Yes, Irene, what is it?"

"Henry is poking me with his pencil." Of course he is not now. He is paying perfect attention to the written page, his pencil quietly resting in the slot at the top of his desk. "Henry, go stand in the comer," she orders. He shuffles off loudly. Rodney plops down in the desk in front of mine and sneaks a torn scrap of paper back to me that hisses, "Tattletale! Tattletale!"

Since the Christian school functions as an arm of the church, weekly catechism or question school is either at the church or school on Wednesdays or Saturdays. We learn that evolution didn't happen. Since Adam, all boys have twenty-three ribs, all girls twenty-four; God having taken a rib from Adam to make Eve. The teacher knows church doctrine: "Christian instruction implies that secular subjects are taught according to the Word of God in every possible manner. God in all instruction as well as in school—life and discipline—that is what is meant by Christian instruction in distinction from public instruction." Our classmates have Dutch names such as Gesink, Toering, or Woudstra. We all go to the same church.

Occasionally, Verna Mae carries a thermos jug to school that is filled with soup. She leaves it behind the screen in the comer of the room. At lunchtime she goes in back of the screen and pours the soup into containers and brings soup to each one of us five. Pete and Stan are upstairs, and three of us are downstairs: Verna Mae, Milly, and me. Peter will graduate from eighth grade in 1942. The previous year he won the county spelling contest and went to Des Moines for the State contest. Stan will graduate Valedictorian in 1943, the same year he will go to the County spelling contest. Verna Mae will graduate in 1945. In age she is the middle child, not only at home but also at school, and in this position in the family, she remembers having to do some dirty work:

I recall having to clean Elmer's dirty pants when I was in school upstairs and he had an "accident" downstairs. I took him down to the basement where there was a sink with water, found an old rag, and did the best I could, then hung his underpants on a pipe.

Rubber overshoes are left in the hall below the hooks for hats, coats, and mittens. The blackboard that stretches all the way across the front of the room is interrupted by the only door into the room. On the sill under the blackboard are erasers and chalk. The "teacher's pet" is chosen to stay after school to clean the blackboard. Since the car to take us home will be waiting, we never get this dubious honor. Calling someone "teacher's pet" means retaliation on the playground. There is safety in numbers. A sister or brother will yell at me if I'm late to come in when the bell rings to signal that recess is over. "Hurry up, hurry up! Didn't you HEAR the bell ring?"

The upstairs teacher is also the principal and custodian. State law requires fire drills and so we are marched down to the Catholic School for semi-annual fire drills since our school doesn't have a fire escape. Up their stairs we march single file; we go out a door, sit down at the top of a long, enclosed, metal chute, and slide down to land on the ground. What fun!

During recess we play tag, hide and seek, drop the handkerchief, pump-pump pull away, and other team games. Sides are chosen. "Red Rover, Red Rover, Send Janice right over!" Then we race out to tag Janice before she can run over. Chase games are favorite pastimes. A bamboo pole held between two tall poles with measured intervals marked on it, is lowered for the low jump and raised for the high jump. Once, while playing chase during recess, I got mad at the boy who tagged me too hard. I raced around the corner of the schoolhouse, determined to get him. Instead, I hit the blunt end of a long bamboo pole that he held out in front of him like a spear as he came running from the opposite direction around the same corner. What happened to him I will never know. What happened to me became a permanent dimple just below one eye. If the pole had hit a half-inch higher, it would have taken out an eye. Hospers had no doctor, so the teacher marched me—pressing a hankie to my cheek to stop the bleeding—to the parsonage where the minister's wife applied a cold washcloth, then a piece of gauze with white adhesive tape. Their talk about stitches went over my head. The bandage was clean and white, just like Ivory Snow. This greatly impressed me, along with the kindness of the teacher and the plush interior of the parsonage. Tears disappeared. For three more days, I got to wear the snowy-white bandage like a badge of honor.

The excitement of leaving the farm each day to go to school along with the bigger kids soon faded. Within the first week, I found out how easy it was to read: "See Dick. See Jane. See Dick run after the ball." Life on the farm was so much more than running after a ball. Things happened. Once, Pa hung a dog from a tree in the grove. I was playing in the front yard next to the pump when I heard a terrible screeching. When I looked to see where it was coming from, I saw a dog writhing and twisting at the end of a rope tied to the limb of a tree. I stood stunned, frozen. Suddenly someone older grabbed me and said, "Get in the house!" Then someone else yelled, "For Pete's sake get that dog down!" The terribly painful noise stopped. Milly couldn't eat supper that night. Still scared, I tried to forget what I'd seen. What did school have to do with anything?

Stilts were made from old boards, using the big and little vices on the workbench and the hammers and nails in the tool shed. A hazy snapshot of Stan shows him on tall stilts three feet above the ground, tottering forward, wobbling above the trees on the dirt road in front of the house. On warm nights we played outside until dark, and sometimes after dark, in the yellow circle of the yard light until called in to bed: tag, kick the can, IT, hitting up fly balls, home base, or hide and seek. Softball in the cow pasture took ten of us for two teams. One of the rules was: Don't step on a cow pie; but if you do, clean it off on the grass before you go into the house. After supper in the winter, we played games in the parlor or the kitchen, made fudge or popcorn. We played tick-tack-toe or played the piano, embroidered, or whittled objects from sticks. The older kids taught the little ones how to make paper planes and fly them. Many different kinds of ball games were invented to suit the mood or the situation. Jacks, pickup sticks, dominoes, toothpicks, or old buttons littered the bare linoleum floor during long winter evenings. Checkers was a favorite board game. Someone bigger and smarter always won.

Farm life was interesting: school lessons were not, neither was the idea of becoming a teacher. What it took to teach grade school was to go through high school. What it took to teach college was to go through college, and the same for graduate school. To be a teacher, all anyone had to do was outlast this terribly boring preparatory work. Anybody could do it! I certainly didn't want to, not ever. Why would anyone want to be stuck inside all day long? In school, how boring to copy from the blackboard the same old A-B-Cs over and over. Impatient to see what came after Dick and Jane, I would listen to what the teacher said to the upper grades or sneak quick looks at blackboard lessons meant for second, third, or fourth graders. On the upper-class blackboard were fractions. Hey! Interesting! The teacher put a stop to this. She would walk down a row of desks from behind us to monitor us, and slap fingers with a ruler if a pupil's eyes did not stay on the work on her own desk. Soon I learned how to keep track of where the teacher was so that I could entertain myself when she wasn't looking. Soon I was teasing or whispering to pupils at neighboring desks, stabbing them in the back with a sharp pencil, and passing notes. Clearly, I was at odds with the teacher.

To escape from the prison of my desk, I learned to use the rules: One trip only to the pencil sharpener before each recess. Raise high your hand with one finger if you must go number one, with two fingers if you must go number two. Permission to go number one or two meant going alone down steep stairs to the toilet in the basement. Only one square of paper was allowed for number one, two squares for number two. The toilet seat was not warm like the wooden one on the farm.

Whenever I glanced up to see that the teacher wasn't looking my way, my thumb crept back into my mouth. I yawned with boredom. The trick was to keep from openly yawning. Yawning turned out to be my undoing.

The room was evenly divided in half down the middle by a long, shiny, empty table, by the black stove with its stove pipe going up through the ceiling, and by the teacher's desk in front. Grades one and two were on one side of the room; grades three and four were on the other side. After noon recess we would stand in straight rows beside the upright piano in the back corner to sing. The teacher would direct, while an older girl from upstairs played the piano.

Sneaking sucks on my thumb, I used the other hand to cover up

316   yawns. When I yawned one time too many, the teacher called me out of the lineup. "If you're that tired, you better lay down," she said, pointing to the table in the middle of the room. I turned red and stalled. She glared at me. I did what she said. She walked to her desk and opened the top drawer. "I've got just what you need," she said, thrusting a baby bottle into my unwilling hands. "You just lay there and suck on this until you go home." I had no choice. I closed my eyes and laid there, embarrassed, sick, scared, mad, quiet, the bottle in my mouth. When the bell rang, I got up and walked out. I hated the teacher. I hated school. Never again did I suck my thumb.

The forbidden-to-look-at blackboard grew into the forbidden everything. Do not race ahead and find something more challenging. You will be made to do what is required, like it or not. In memory, the teacher wears a pinched, black wool coat buttoned up to her chin. After the deaths of Mother in 1984 and Pa in 1986, some of what happened in school during the first four grades gradually came into focus. I clearly see the white-frame schoolhouse on the outskirts of Hospers with its two stories of windows. Inside, I ascend the wide, wooden stairway and go up to the one large room for fifth, sixth, seventh, and eighth graders. I see the teacher, his steady gray eyes and kindly manner and his suit and tie, but I remember nothing about actually being in fifth grade, not even noon hour or going out to play during recess.

Before sixth grade started, our family moved away. The new teacher was soft eyed. Every curve of her hair and face was beautiful. The report cards from the first five grades had As on all the lines (Reading, Penmanship, Arithmetic, Recitation, Spelling). Although many checks appeared in the deportment boxes, there were zeros in all the absent and tardy boxes. At the new school, the teacher, and then the principal, looked at these report cards and questioned what I had learned. Apparently, I was one year behind the other sixth graders. Certainly, I was in a much different place in both language and life experience. The only way to keep from being put back a year was to stay after school each day to catch up. I agreed to do this. Fractions were fun—they were easy to learn. The teacher lived around the block from where we lived, so, after staying after school each afternoon, the teacher and I walked home together, holding hands. As we walked, she smiled. I fell in love with her.

Going to school carrying dinner pails, wearing homemade clothes:
Milly, Stan, Verna Mae, and Irene, 1942.

Fourth graders at Hospers Christian School, include Irene Kooi, 1946.

28

Strong Boxes

Pa kept his valuables in a green metal box on the top shelf of the one small closet in their bedroom. Into this strong box went anything of importance: the bank book, savings bonds, title to the farm, birth certificates, his honorable discharge from the Army. The box was too small to hold much else. Their marriage certificate was a large, framed document, embellished with flowing graphics in the romantic colors and style of the twenties. It hung from two wires that came down from a nail pounded into the picture molding rail above the wallpaper in their bedroom.

Before Pa went to town on Wednesday afternoons, he took down his strongbox, unlocked it, removed what he wanted, re-locked it, and put it back on the high shelf in their closet. On this narrow shelf next to the strongbox were their Sunday hats. Pa's was made of felt and had a band around the crown, the brim turned up just so, in the right places. I seem to see a little feather sticking out of the band. His eyes appeared to be a little nervous when he put on his felt hat, perhaps because the hat meant he now would have to deal with townspeople. When he wore his felt hat to church on Sundays, his eyes were simply his ordinary in-a-hurry, going-places eyes. During the summer he wore his dress-up straw hat to church.

Their small closet held very few clothes. On one hook was Mother's long flannel nightgown, its scent the distillation of warm milk, sweet and comfortable, resting like drapery until dark. At night that same hook held Mother's housedress and apron. Pa's long-Johns and overalls were on another hook. On two hangers over another hook were their Sunday clothes: Pa's suit, shirt, and tie and Mother's dress and coat. Underneath the hooks sat their Sunday shoes: Pa's shiny oxbloods and Mother's high, black laceups. At that time, closets, valuables, and snapshots were smaller and fewer. What people have less of they might value more, or perhaps people who have fewer things to care for have more time to spend with others. In any event, that closet held many a mystery for us little kids. Children love what is forbidden or out of reach! Pa's strong box—small, locked, and always up high on a closet shelf. We were forbidden to go into that closet in their bedroom. So we watched. Usually, a rule was not broken until we were old enough to get away with it or old enough to run faster than the others. Although we may have borrowed shoes to play dress-up or searched closets for hidden presents, I don't think we ever got into Pa's strong box.

Sometimes I watched Pa open his strong box on the dining room table after supper. If Mother, Gladys, or Bernice had been sewing that afternoon, and a dress, curtain, bloomer, or what-have-you had been cut and was laid out in pieces on the table, Pa would first clear off a little space for the box. This took some doing. The pieces must be carefully laid aside so that they could be returned to their same positions when he was done. Then Pa could put down his strong box and take out the checkbook or bank book, remove something, put it into his back pocket, write on something and put it back into the strong box, lock the box, and lift it back up onto the high shelf. Seeing me watch him, he would grunt, settle himself on the couch in the front parlor, and stretch out his body along its length. After a while one arm would fall to the floor, and he would start to snore.

Pretty soon Mother would come in from the kitchen and say, "Now, you little kids go upstairs to bed." Hearing her voice, Pa would turn over, snort, and look at us strangely, as though he was coming to after being knocked out. One foot would fall to the floor, then the other foot would fall with a bang. He would pull his body up off the couch and head for the bedroom door. By now, Mother would have shooed us through the swinging door that led into the kitchen. There, we would pass between the wood stove and table to get to the door that led up the stairs. Out the windows it would have turned completely dark.

On their closet shelf, Mother kept Christmas in a brown box: red tissue-paper bells in accordion pleats that hung from the ceiling light. Green-tissue swags that made graceful loops from corner to corner, following the molding rail around the room. Alternate ropes of green and red tissue-paper were draped from the center bells to the corners. Presents were dolls and trucks, sox and bloomers, Sunday clothes, but never candy. Christmas candy always came in a little brown bag after the Sunday School program at church, where we were the program, reciting poems and singing songs. A printed church bulletin was handed out at the door as each family entered the church, listing the title and performer of each recitation, song, chorus, or piano piece. After the last song was sung we filed out, one by one, orderly and good, past the smiling deacon standing at the back door, until he handed each one of us the coveted bag of hard candies, with maybe a piece or two of soft candy in it. I would thrust my hand inside to feel the candy before the smile left his face, pull out whatever I found, and bite into it so hard that my back teeth had to work on it all the way out to the car in the parking lot. There, Pa and Mother would be waiting, eager to get into the Chevrolet and start for home. Mother would   pat me on the head as my sticky fingers pulled at the piece of hard candy stuck to my teeth.

I would climb into the back seat—or the front if that's where she motioned me to go—and examine each piece of candy, each the same as last year's: small, red-striped, green-striped, or yellow, nearly all hard. Picking out the candies I liked best, I would place those on the top—the soft chocolate-covered ones. Vicki recalls that "We kids would barter and exchange, 'three pieces of hard candy for one chocolate ...' always ending up in some kind of fight. Mother would get irritated at hearing us quarrel and say, "Why do you do that then? Just keep your own candy." Sometimes there was an orange at the bottom of the bag. Mother seemed to breathe a sigh of relief when the car finally stopped in the driveway and we tumbled out, clutching our little brown bags with sticky fingers, dragging our feet up the stairs to go to bed.

"What was Christmas like in Holland?"

"Oh, I don't know." But we would press her.

"Saint Nick comes in early December, the fifth, I believe. Before the little children go to bed ... real early so they can get up real early ... they are supposed to leave their wooden shoes at the front door. St. Nick, dressed something like Santa Claus comes and leaves fruit and sweets in their shoes, sometimes an orange. Presents get hidden around the house to be found on Saint Nick's Day. Lots of sweets, gingerbread men and women, made with old-fashioned wooden moulds." Her description was vague, but since our knowledge of Santa Claus was hearsay, we could not press for more. To us, Christmas was Jesus in the manger, the Star in the East, the wise men bringing gold, frankincense, and myrrh. Joseph leading Mary on a donkey. Snow drifts and icicles. Runny noses. Vicki Peterson titles her Christmas story, "Green Is A Color."

I never had a doll of my own. Mother, if she were alive, would probably question this—but it's true. Except for Bitsy, and she really didn't count. When I was about five years of age, I inherited a doll from my older sister, Bernice. The doll had a cloth body, arms and legs; its head was made of rubber or plastic. One leg was missing. I dressed her, wrapped her in a blanket, and played house with her. I named her Bertha. She was okay, but it wasn't like having a doll of my own. She was a castoff from an older sister—a hand-me-down. In second grade we had a Christmas present exchange at school, and I received a small doll. She was all rubber, about ten inches long—very small. I played with her, but it was not the doll I had dreamed of. She was just too small. I named her Bitsy.

When I was eleven, Bernice went to work in a large city. She came home at Christmas time, telling of magical things: lights, big buildings, rich people, fancy houses. Also, she brought presents. She wrapped them in bright Christmas paper and laid them carefully on the small oval table in the living room. I examined the packages. A square box. A rectangular one. And oblong ... could it possibly be? A doll? A box just the right size for a real life-sized doll.

Christmas came. I held my breath. Elmer and Glenny, my two younger brothers, got to open their presents first. What they got I forget. Then Irene, the next in line, age-wise; then Milly who was two years younger than I. Milly was given the oblong package. My heart stopped. She unwrapped it and there it lay. The most beautiful doll I had ever seen, as big as a real baby. All-plastic body, arms, legs and head, she had on a blue-checked, ruffled dress, with bonnet to match. No hair, but the most gorgeous eyelashes, with eyes that opened and closed. The eyelashes were long, dark, and thick. We all took turns holding the baby doll in an upright position, and then down again, just to see those eyelashes open and close, open and close.

My gift was a housecoat. Blue chenille and long, with a wraparound belt. "That's a nice gift, too," Mother said, looking straight at me. I ran upstairs. A housecoat! It wasn't fair. I was the oldest of the three little girls. I should have gotten the doll. I flung the housecoat on the bed. Afterwards, I heard snatches of conversation from behind closed doors. "But, a doll ... and Verna's the oldest," from Mother. An irritating voice from Bernice, "I never can seem to do anything right."

On Wednesday afternoons Pa went into town. This particular

Wednesday, almost the whole family went with him. I was home alone, with only two older brothers. (With six siblings older than me, and four younger, our house was seldom without some member of the family.) Stan and Pete were upstairs taking a nap. I eyed Milly's doll. It lay on the living-room couch. Milly had wrapped it in a blanket. I lifted it up. The eyelashes opened. I lay her down. The eyelashes closed. Automatically, I got a small scissors from the kitchen. Even more automatically I picked up the doll, held it carefully, and beginning on one side and going to the other, cut off all those long, beautiful eyelashes. It wasn't until I was done that the full impact of what I had actually accomplished hit me. I had ruined Milly's doll! I laid it down. It looked strangely naked without its eyelashes. I hid it underneath some clothes in a downstairs closet.

Milly found it, of course. She was heart-broken. "My doll! My beautiful doll!" When I saw her sitting in a chair in the kitchen, crying, I felt a sense of remorse. But, even then, a small part of me cherished a feeling of triumph. Mother—would she punish me? She raised her hand to slap me. "Why did you do it?" she said, but as she was talking, her hand fell to her side. She knew, of course, and let the matter drop. But to this day, I still look at dolls with long eyelashes with a special kind of yearning.

Five little kids with dolls on Hospers farmhouse porch, 1945.

29

Runaways

School was thought to be a privilege, not a necessity. It let out in early May and did not start again until after the crops were in so that farmers could have their sons work in the fields. Also, at any other time that extra help was needed, young boys were taken out of school. During these times and the hot summer months, Pa was a hard taskmaster. Farmers' sons learned to drive in the fields by the age of eleven or twelve so they could go to get a wrench, or whatever, from the yard when a plough or harrow broke down. Learning to drive this way was good practice. There was the creek to ford, gentle inclines to negotiate, and rough fields to turn around in and get across. Learning permits did not exist, nor did driver's education at school. The day Ray turned fourteen, he could legally drive on the roads. Pa took him to Orange City to take the test and get his driver's license. Now Ray could drive to town on errands for Pa.

In 1937, at the beginning of their fifth summer of working as field hands for Pa, Ray and one of the other older brothers decided to run away. For weeks they carefully, secretly planned how to manage every detail. They had to save enough money for gasoline and food, bundle up clothes to take, and choose which direction to go. Success meant making sure the plan was foolproof. On the night of their escape they went upstairs to bed as usual. After they were certain the folks were asleep, they sneaked down the wooden stairs, silently let themselves out the screen door, and gingerly walked through the yard to the shed where Pa kept a second-hand 1929 Chevrolet. The main family car was a 1936 model. They topped the tank with gasoline the day before, using gas from the common gas supply on the farm.

Carefully now, slowly, they opened the two slanting old doors of the shed, knowing that Pa's alert ears were tuned to hear any unusual sound in the farmyard. Noiselessly, they pushed the car out, then down the dirt drive-way past the dark windows of the house. They pushed the car out onto the graded road and down the road a good ways before jumping in and then, soundlessly holding the doors closed, they started the car.

Windows down, leaning forward into the wind of freedom, they drove all night, straight east, not stopping once. For nearly one hundred fifty miles, Ray drove. As dawn broke they came into Waterloo, stopped at the City Park, lay down on the grass, and slept. When they awoke the sun was high, and they were hungry. They dug into the sack of food they had brought. Satisfied, they walked to Main Street, saw a theater, and bought tickets with part of the five dollars they had in their pockets. To see "The Virginian" cost thirty-five cents each. They sat through it twice. Then, movies started at ten in the morning and ran continuously without intermission. For two Christian Reformed farm boys who had only read about movies and dreamed of seeing one, this was a big thrill—heady stuff.

At home that next morning, when the two boys did not come downstairs to tramp across the kitchen, go out the gate, across the road, and into the barn to milk cows before breakfast, Pa hollered up the stairs, hollered again, then waited. Hearing nothing, he went up and discovered they were not there. He ran out of the house to the shed and saw that the second car was gone. Surprised, he went back into the house, his rage barely under control. He went into the bedroom and told Mother what had happened. Her heart was heavy. "Well, guess you will have to go to town and tell the sheriff."

She went into the kitchen to start breakfast and saw the note Ray had left on the stove. As they read it, Pa nodded. He would do what Mother said after the chores and breakfast. Gladys recalls that "There were tears in Pa's eyes as he prayed at breakfast."

After the day in the movie theater, the boys counted their change, got in the car, and, recalls Ray, "We rode out into the country and stopped at the first farm we saw. The farmer hired me. Since we both needed a place and this farmer had enough work and room for only one of us, the farmer looked at my brother's youth and strength and said, 'I know a farmer who needs someone.' So Ray took his brother to that farm, and he got a job there. The farm family that Ray was with was good to him. His salary was a dollar a day. They had a nine-year-old girl and a thirteen-year-old boy who did not have to work in the fields. On Sundays Ray went with the family to church in Cedar Falls. On Saturday afternoons and evenings, Ray was free to do as he pleased.

He often drove around Waterloo and looked at the high school; he was impressed with it and wished he could go there. Ray did not see his brother for a whole month.

Then, one evening on the drive going to Waterloo, Ray saw the State Patrol following him and thought, "Oh Boy, they're going to pull me over." Sure enough, they did. One of the troopers rode with Ray into Waterloo. They put him in a cell with ten older men, prisoners who were kind to him. Pathetic- looking food was shoved through a hole. Ray could eat only a little of it, but the others were only too happy to eat the rest. "I learned that night that I didn't want to spend any more time in jail." In the morning, Pa and Mother were there to get Ray. Driving to the other farm to get their other son, Pa was taking no chances. He drove alone, and Mother rode with Ray. When they found their other son, Pa drove him the many miles back home to the farm. With Mother along, Ray drove the other car and, along the way, they stopped at Clear Lake. It was hot. Mother sat on the bank and watched Ray cool off in the water. At home no one uttered a word about what had happened. A few days later, the hired man, cousin Frank Feikema, asked Ray about it in the barn, and Ray more or less shrugged.[123]

[123] Oral history from Raymond Kooi.

30

The Outside World

In the early 1930s the first radio came into the farmhouse. It was a bulky floor console made of varnished wood with a crocheted doily on top. Heavy brown fabric covered the speaker that often sent dense static through the scuffle and ruckus of us little kids playing around a potbellied stove on the cold linoleum floor. We were fascinated with this link to the outside world. Most especially, the oldest, Raymond Kenneth Kooi, was eager to tune in. Our parents, however, would not let him listen very often and not at all to some programs, such as "Fibber McGee & Molly," the "Jack Benny Show," and the "Charlie McCarthy Show." After dinner or after supper, Pa would draw the wooden rocker up close to the radio, lower his head to the speaker, and turn the dial back and forth, trying to tune in the Sioux City station. Frequent static on the airwaves meant that tuning in took awhile. Some nights, Pa could barely hear a faint voice weaving in and out. Then he would turn the battery-operated radio off and either go to bed or read the *Sioux Center News*.

Pa liked to listen to market reports, hog prices, news, and weather reports—also to some of the political programs. Mother, however, was pretty much apolitical. Her realm encompassed the traditional role of Dutch, Christian Reformed women: *kinderen, keuken, kirk*. Besides, American women had not been allowed to vote until only recently. Women's suffrage had a long struggle. The Nineteenth Amendment to the Constitution was introduced in 1878 but not ratified until August 1920. When questioned about voting, Mother would tell us that she did not care to vote. When pressed, she coyly replied, "Oh, I think Pa can do that for me."

Pa tuned in to President Franklin Delano Roosevelt's fireside chats. Usually, all of us children went to bed early because the day started at dawn when the oldest boys milked cows and the oldest girls lit the fire in the cookstove. However, at night, without being seen, Ray often sneaked into the front room, found a place that was out of the way, and listened. In this way he had been able to hear parts of the 1936 Democratic and Re-

330   publican Conventions and then something really special—FDR's stirring
1936 acceptance speech. As he grew bolder, Ray would listen to the radio
anytime he could get away with it, so that eventually he heard all kinds of
programs aired at anytime. He became entranced and decided that he would
become a radio announcer.

"Clearly only someone who was Dutch could pronounce, or spell,
the name 'Kooi,'" reasoned Ray. "No announcer could be expected to say
'Good Evening, this is Raymond Kooi with the eight o'clock news.'" So,
he decided to change his name from Raymond Kenneth Kooi to Kenneth
Raymond. At night, in the boys' bedroom upstairs, he would practice on
his next-older brothers to get the hang of how it was going to be when he
auditioned to be a radio announcer. For newscasts he started with "Good
evening, this is Kenneth Raymond with the latest developments in the
world. Tonight in Washington..." Then he would make up news stories.
His brothers listened raptly. When they grew tired of the news, he would
air "The Magic Show" or invent other programs to hold the attention of
his live audience. Pete asked Ray, "Do you want to be an entertainer?"

"Oh no," said Ray, "I want to do the interviews of the man on the
street." For him, radio was serious; it must inform people. Raised by a strict,
no-nonsense father, he was all business. When the radio programs in the
upstairs bedrooms grew too loud, and the ruckus shook the house, Mother
would call up the stairs, "Quiet down now. Time to sleep."

SUMMER OF 1941

Tell me of summer mornings
        the rooster's wake-up call
        children rising from their beds
        Pa and boys in the barn
        milking cows, feeding pigs
        Mama in the kitchen
        baby on her hip
        oatmeal cooking on the stove.
            Lord Bless This Food

Tell me of summer afternoons
        rain-smell of earth
        fields of growing corn and wheat
        brown-limbed children
        straw hats, bare feet
        trapping gophers
        bringing lunch with lemonade
        in old gallon syrup pails
        to hired men and Pa
        girls hanging clothes on sun-hot lines
        Mama in the garden
        ripe cherries and green beans
                Lord We Thank Thee For This Food

Tell me of summer nights
        canopy of endless stars
        children playing in the yard
        hide and seek, kick the can
        Pa reading the Sioux City Journal
        head tilted high to see the print
        Mama nursing the baby
        hair falling down her back
        in one long braid
        the animals, land, and family
        slowly settling into night.
                Now I Lay Me Down To Sleep

Was that the last summer
        we were children, safe, a family
        an island on an Iowa farm
        before the war closed in and Mama's sickness came
        before the children grew too tall?
                I Pray Thee, Lord, My Soul To Keep[124]

News of the Japanese attack on Pearl Harbor came on the radio after
Sunday dinner on December 7, 1941, the day after Ray turned twenty. He

[124] Bernice Kooi Afman, "Summer of 1941," Denver, Colorado, April, 1994.

was taking the second car to Sheldon Junior College to take classes, and without telling the folks he bought a radio, plus a second-hand typewriter, for his bedroom. The impact of the bombing of Pearl Harbor changed our country overnight, but no immediate changes were made on the farm, except for our becoming more aware of what was happening in the outside world. The usual "News on the Hour" coming from the radio now focused on the war starting with news from the front. Names such as Walter Winchell and Lowell Thomas were in the air, as were World War II songs such as, "You'd Be So Nice to Come Home To," "I'll Never Smile Again Until I Smile at You," and "Don't Get Around Much Anymore." The fall after the December bombing of Pearl Harbor, I started first grade in Hospers where my sisters, Milly and Verna Mae, also were in school. Stan was twelve and starting high school in Hull.

When Ray's draft number came up in the spring of 1943, he researched the various options available to him. He was qualified to apply for the Navy V-12 Officer's Training Program because he was an unmarried male willing to stay unmarried until commissioning, between age 17 and 20, and could show evidence of potential officer qualifications, including appearance and scholarship. So he applied to take the two-hour written exam, which was given to 315,952 pre-qualified young men on April 2, 1943, at the same time in various locations across the continental United States. This examination was a milestone in American education, the largest test of its kind, and the first one ever offered to every (any) male student, regardless of income level or educational background. It offered a doorway to college. When Ray passed the exam, the next step was the physical examination, then an interview. He was one of 70,000 men accepted into the V-12 Program. On July 1, 1943, they reported to 131 V-12 under-graduate schools in 43 different states.[125]

Ray finished his first year at the Sheldon Junior College and took a train across the state of Iowa, bound for St. Ambrose College in Davenport, Iowa, one of many colleges across the country that supported the Navy's V-12 Program. When Ray left home to begin "Officer Candidate Training" at the

---

[125] James G. Schneider, *The Navy V-12 Program*, 2nd ed. (1993), pp. 70, 104.

end of June, 1943, he was the first one of our family to leave the farm.

He is eager to go, and is the only one of us who does not notice that everything is unnaturally quiet. Even the chickens are not scratching in the farmyard. Not a single farm machine is leaving the yard. In the house no fire crackles in the cookstove; no radio is on; no kid is running lickety-split across the linoleum, trying to get out the front porch and through the screen door before the spring bangs it back, shut tight. At the kitchen door, Mother embraces Ray goodbye and says something too soft for us to hear. Pa is already sitting in the gray Chevy outside the wrought-iron gate, anxious to get Ray to the train in Sheldon on time, nervous about the war. We watch a cloud of dust spiral up behind the car as they leave the driveway and go down the center of the dirt road toward Sheldon, seven miles away.

St. Ambrose College had many new experiences with its V-12 unit. Previously, nearly all of its students had been Catholic, but now, of the 296 trainees the college received, only 20 percent were Catholic. To make room for the V-12s, the college moved faculty and civilian students out of two residence halls. The dorms were now considered "ships." Floors and walls became decks and bulkheads; windows became ports; restrooms, heads. Letters went from commanding officers and college presidents to parents, congratulating them on the selection of their sons for officer training. "He was chosen for this honor on the basis of outstanding aptitude and ability. You have every reason to be proud of him. The Navy is expecting great things from him. Let him know that you are, too."[126]

As in other cities during the war, Davenport's civilian population helped young men in uniform who often were away from home for the first time. The USO, American Legion, Masonic orders, and other civic groups organized dances, parties, open houses, and concerts for the V-12s, besides the dances the V-12s held on their own. Citizens gave servicemen on the streets rides here and there. When the boys in uniform appeared at church on Sunday, they often were invited into homes for Sunday dinner.

Between 1942 and 1945, Christian Reformed Service Homes were lo-

[126] Ibid., pp. 107, 476.

cated near training camps all over the country. These homes were modeled on *the Christelijk Militaire Tehuizen* established by Dutch *Kuyperians* and were very popular. Families with young people in the service would encourage them to go to a nearby Christian Reformed Church on Sundays and then to spend the day in a service home. This provided the continuance of familiar family traditions and religious ways, with the benefit of meeting their own kind of young people, and, in the due course of time, marry in the church.

"Is there a Christian Reformed Church there?" Mother would have asked Ray, expecting him, of course, to go to our own church. Perhaps there was not one in Davenport. In any event, Ray visited a community church one Sunday and afterwards was asked by the Van Walterops to go to their home. They invited him back, which he did when he was free, on weekends. Together, they went to concerts. Norman, the boy in the family, was fourteen and played a bassoon. His two older sisters were about Ray's age. The younger of the two sisters, Vera, played an oboe. Ray played the piano. As time went on, the two of them often played together and he accompanied her when she played the oboe for various groups. Ray had found a music teacher at St. Ambrose College and was taking lessons. He practiced George Gershwin's "Rhapsody in Blue," then performed it with an orchestra.

The family life he experienced at the Van Walterop home was easy going, friendly, and casual, an atmosphere he most likely welcomed after the strict, religious tone of the farm life he had known. In this open climate, it seems as though his natural expansiveness and curiosity flourished. The Van Walterops became his new friends, and when he went on leave from later postings, he returned to Davenport to visit them. He met their relatives, and shared snapshots of his own family. He wrote home about them, giving us views of another world other than the farm.

Since the outside world we were getting a glimpse of seemed far away and foreign to us, our inside world held onto the familiar neat squares of farm land and the crocheted edges around dresser scarves and the hankies we used. Although Mother's crochet hook connected the fine threads of variegated colors with ironed squares, our understandings increasingly ran into loops, frills, and snags. My Aunt Mattie's face and voice frequently came into view. Gently she took the hankie and crochet hook I held out to her. "*Ach Heiden, kleine kind*, what a mess!" Frown lines appeared between her eyes.

Weary, we little kids trudge up the stairs to bed. Even with the windows open, it is hot. To get some air we drag our mattresses out the window to the roof over the front porch, even though Mother's warnings ring in our ears. "You could fall through that roof, you know, it's so thin." As I jump up and down trying to keep the soles of my bare feet from sticking to the hot tar roof, one of the older kids taunts me with "Scaredy cat! C'mon, don't be such a cry baby."

"But Mother *said...*"

"Shuddup or she'll hear you." And then placating, "See? It's already cooler. Just lay down and go to sleep." I lie down and huddle into a ball, expecting to fall through the roof any minute. After a while, I uncoil and look at the sky blazing with a billion stars. Not even one cricket is singing. Not a single bullfrog is croaking out deep, sonorous, territorial grunts. No ripe apple falls—kerplunk—into Mother's fenced garden across the dirt driveway.

"Where's Davenport?" I demand of Mother. Her eyes are wistful and distant. "Oh, across the state, a little below Des Moines, to the south, and then east some."

"How far?"

"Maybe a couple hundred miles or a little more, I'm not real sure, honey. Now you go run outside. Go play."

"When will he come back?"

"I don't know."

"Is he going to fight?"

"Well," says one of the other little kids, "He's only going to a school for officers, not off to the war."

"What's that?"

"Dummy, it's a college," is the swift comeback.

"He's at this place, training to be an officer in the Navy," adds a bigger kid.

"What's that mean?"

Our chatter holds challenge and bravado as we try to ward off fear, hold up our spirits, and buy assurance that the oldest of us will not be in danger. We're feeling the scary unknown in a way we can't ignore. Back and forth we go, questioning, trying to understand what's happening to our small world uninhabited by toy guns, destroyers, submarines, or plastic armies.

I was in second grade at the Hospers Christian School when the next brother joined the Army Air Force in October of 1943. He was sent to Amarillo, Texas, for three months of training and then to Drake University in Des Moines for three more months of training as an Aviation Cadet. One day an officer walked into the classroom and said, "You're finished. This class will be gunners."

At home, on the roof at night, I let myself slowly count the stars in the Big Dipper, then the Little Dipper and remember the metal dipper that hangs on the pump. Water runs off the lip of the dipper in an arc into the mouth of a big brother as he lifts the dipper high above himself. His face is streaming with sweat. From the fields come other brothers, hired men, and Pa to take turns drinking from the dipper.

Elmer whispers in my ear, "See that? You see that? Look!" He points at the Milky Way.

"Where? I don't see anything."

"Look quick! There goes a shooting star!" Sure enough, I do see one falling, diving, a spear of blood blazing into the earth ... or an airplane diving ... "How do you know that isn't an airplane?"

"Ah, c'mon, don't be silly."

My eyelids tighten as my head pivots into the pillow and I fall into sleep. The nightmare that jolts me awake is a bomber flaming toward earth. Shivering, I tiptoe inside.

From the mailbox on the corner came letters from the sons away from home. When the letter from Ray comes, Mother is in the kitchen. She wipes off her glasses with a corner of her apron and slowly opens the envelope. Her voice carries an edge of expectation mixed with apprehension. "Well, I think I'll sit down to read this." We wait while she reads. Looking up, she says, "Well, he's going home for Sunday dinner with a family that has a Dutch name, but they don't go to our church. They have a boy and a girl, an older girl too." She turns toward a window and her eyes catch the light. Something sparkles. "Well, well, Ray says that all parents are invited to a review of the naval cadets on the parade ground, and the Van Walterop family has a room where I could stay." Her eyes fix on some distant object. "Well, I don't know."

The idea of Mother going away feels like a heavy bag of flour settling slowly. Rays of sunlight sift through her hair, down through her slight body seated in the wooden rocker. Fine flour settles onto the linoleum under her black shoes. Gravity surrounds her like an aura; its halo sparks, its earthiness solid and irrefutable.

"Will you go?"

"Well, maybe." She pauses. "We'll have to see about that." She gets up to do something. We run off to play.

When the day comes for Mother to take the train to Davenport, she puts on her Sunday dress, straightens the seams on the back of her legs, and ties the laces of her black shoes. She lays the camel hair coat with the black velvet collar across the back of a chair. I watch her take down from the closet shelf her two-handled black purse held together by a shiny clasp. She brushes off her hat and settles it firmly above the bun that brushes the nape of her neck. I love watching her position the long hatpin just so, pushing it deeply into the hat, through her hair, and out the other side again. "How do you know where to push the pin so it won't go through your head?" She smiles and pats me on the head. "It's pretty easy, Snooky. Here, look, you see?" She stops, hands me a hatpin to hold, pushes a hatpin through the hat into her hair, and then looks down at me. "I'll be back in a couple of days." I hand the other hatpin to her and remember the unnatural quiet in the kitchen when she embraced Ray goodbye while Pa waited, anxious to get Ray to the train. Ray has not come back. Mother is busy now and doesn't notice me standing there, waiting, hoping she will not go.

Mother took the train to Davenport and stayed at the home of the Van Walterops. She brought back snapshots of the parade ground at St. Ambrose College that showed square platoons of V-12 Navy cadets in white uniforms. In another snapshot, Mother is smiling as she stands dressed in a Sunday summer dress and straw hat between her two tall sons, one resplendent in Navy whites and the other one dapper in a suit. Their relaxed poses and Mother's short-sleeved dress suggest summer.

While playing on the front porch, I watch long clouds of dust spiraling behind a car coming from some distance away. I race to the gate, swing on its hinge, then run out into the driveway. Pa spins the Chevy off the road into the narrow driveway. The car stops. Mother lets herself out the door. She looks different, but I can't figure out how. We little kids crowd around, hugging her knees, stopping her from moving toward the front porch. Our questions come tumbling out all at once.

"What about the train ride? What did you do? What are THEY like? What does Ray do there? When is he coming home?" As she makes her way toward the house we step back. In turn, she hugs each one of us.

"Sure nice to be home again. Let's go inside first, then I'll tell you all about it."

In the front room she puts her bag down on the dining room table, removes her gloves, and smiles. She reaches up and slowly pulls out the hatpins, one by one. She takes off her hat and places it on the table. She pauses, then looks up. "Well, they aren't like us, but they are good people. The mother is such a kind of..." In the pause, her eyes go far away. "... Well, a jolly sort of woman, nice and round. The boy plays a ... well ... it's like a horn, and the girl plays an oboe."

"What's that?"

"Well, you know, a pipe that sounds like a bird."

"Does Ray like her?"

"Oh," Mother demurs, her voice growing softer, "I don't know about that."

"The father is a nice man. He works in town somewhere, I believe, and they have a nice house. The church was so strange, not at all like what we're used to."

"What kind of church?"

"It's called Community Christian Church or something like that. Nothing like ours at all, but it's good Ray has a place to go to church on Sundays. You know, we don't have a Christian Reformed Church in Davenport."

"What's Davenport like?"

"Something like Sheldon, maybe bigger, and Ray lives in a big dormitory at the college." Her voice grows anxious, "He's in training for something secret. He couldn't say what. You know we must not talk about what our boys in the service are doing." Her tone of voice changes gears. "My, you should have seen how good those boys look in their uniforms, especially on the parade ground. My, THAT was really something to see, something special."

"What did you do on the train?"

"Oh, look out the window," she smiles. "It was so nice and green, so nice and quiet." Her voice has grown soft and wistful, but it quickly switches. "Run outdoors and play now."

Our oldest sister, Gladys, enlisted in the WAVES the next February, in 1944, when she was twenty. For many years, the older sisters had mothered, dressed, fed, changed, bathed, undressed, and put us to bed, as though we were their own live dolls. Unlike real dolls, we often were in their way, nuisances, pests to be endured. Even after each one of us entered school at age five, the work of caring for us continued. From Gladys and Bernice we learned that the WACS were the women's branch of the Army Air Corps, and the WAVES were the women's branch of the Navy.

I was six and in the second grade when Gladys was sent to New York City for six weeks of boot camp at Hunter College in the Bronx, and then to Bethesda Hospital in Maryland for nurses training. In May of 1944 she was sent to San Diego where she cared for wounded servicemen in a military hospital. In July of 1944 Ray left Davenport and continued his Naval training at Columbia University in New York City, prior to spending six weeks in Asbury Park, New Jersey. In August, Midshipman School was at St. Simon's Island Naval Station off the coast of Georgia. His next posting was to Newport, Rhode Island, to prepare a new ship for its shakedown cruise.

Mother kept ration coupons in her purse, but some of the rationing did not make an impact on our lives as much as others did. The limit of three pairs of shoes a year was not that important. We were used to getting two new pairs of shoes a year—one pair for school and the other for Sunday—in late August before another school year started. By the next June we could go barefoot except on Sundays, when a pair of hand-me-down shoes might fit. Thrift had been a way of life on the farm, and we were used to making do. As the war wore on, more things were rationed, including gasoline and sugar. At the beginning of each week, Mother would measure out the half-cup ration of sugar for each one of us, put it into a screw-top jar, and write each name on each lid. On Saturday, what was left in the jars was combined and used to make a cake or cookies or maybe fudge. We'd compete to see whose jar had the most sugar left in it at week's end. First silk, then nylon stockings for women were gone. As time went on, many common things could not be found anywhere. Posters everywhere exhorted us to buy U.S. Savings Bonds. Pa kept ours in his strong box, reminding us that we each owned a five dollar war bond: "Now, isn't that something?"

Along the road to town was a billboard. Uncle Sam pointed a long finger down at us. His furrowed face was over-shadowed by a tall hat in stripes and stars. He shouted, "Uncle Sam Wants You." The oldest three of our family had answered his summons. No longer were thirteen of us seated around the kitchen table, impatiently waiting for Pa's opening prayer at breakfast, dinner, and supper.

In January of 1945, Bernice was eighteen when she boarded a train in Sheldon to cross the State of Iowa to Davenport to visit Ray and the Van Walterop family. Ensign Ray was on leave from the East Coast and visiting the Van Walterops. At midnight the train was due to arrive in the only train station near Davenport, either De Witt or Marysville. Bernice was to get picked up at the station by Ray and his friends That evening Ray waited up with the Van Walterops for her phone call so they could go to get her. Probably it was Bernice's first trip on a train. The train might have been crowded with servicemen looking for the company of pretty girls to pass the time. In any event, the train stopped briefly at the last and only station in the vicinity of Davenport, Iowa, before crossing the Mississippi River into Illinois. When Bernice realized that the train was moving out of the station, she found the conductor and told him what had happened. But now the train was crossing the wide river, bound for the next small town that had a station, either Fulton or Hillsdale, in Illinois. As time went by, Ray and the Van Walterops wondered what had happened. Sometime after midnight, the phone call came, and off they went, across the river into Illinois, to get Bernice. A snapshot shows Bernice and Ray standing together in the snow on the steps of the front porch of the Van Walterop home. Both are wearing white shirts and thick dark coats. Ray wears a Naval officer's visored hat and somber expression. Bernice sports a big grin.

At the time Gladys was stationed in San Diego, the Navy was a huge presence there—a staging area for the war in the Pacific. Gladys missed sewing dresses for her little sisters, so she sent dresses as well as letters. She regularly attended services and events at the Christian Reformed Service Home in San Diego, where she met a sailor and fell in love.

Our second oldest brother was sent to Las Vegas for three months of gunner training, then sent to Florida for more training. In December of 1944, the Eighth Army Air Force, known as the Mighty Eighth, sent him to Sudbury, England. B-17 Flying Fortresses were America's main strategic weapon in Europe during World War 11. From numerous airfields in the south and east of England, Boeing B-17's carried the air war to Germany, bombing heavily defended targets while dodging flak and enemy fighters. For thirty-three months, Eighth Air Force planes pounded Germany's great industrial web with strategic bombing strikes. Able to withstand severe damage, the "Fort" (Flying Fortress) commanded great respect. It was on its way to becoming an American legend."[127]

Assigned to fly weekly missions over Germany in a B-17 bomber, our brother was a ball-turret gunner, suspended in a plastic bubble under the belly of the bomber where he could shoot at enemy planes. In this vulnerable position, curled into a transparent ball that hung below the plane, he flew twenty-eight missions over Germany. Pitted against some of the most experienced fighter pilots in the world, B-17 crewmen sustained heavy losses. More than 47,000 crew members either died or were taken as prisoners in daylight raids over Germany. Most of the men were barely into their twenties.

On hot summer afternoons we little kids would walk the half mile on the dirt road to the mailbox on the corner, hoping to find a letter from a sister or brother. Then, Mother would read it while we hung around her skirts, waiting.

In the kitchen, Mother wipes her hands on her homemade apron and then wipes the dirt from her glasses, using the apron's less soiled underside. She pauses a moment, maybe to pray, before taking the letter handed to

---

[127] Edward Jablonski, *The Illustrated Biography of the B-17s and the Men Who Flew Them*, (Garden City, NY: Doubleday & Company, 1965).

342 her. The unsettled silence in that pause makes us want to run, but we are as quiet as barn mice, whose habits of evasion we know so well. She stands still, riveted to the thin piece of paper she holds. Waiting in unaccustomed quiet, we read her face and are rewarded when her eyes glance up with a smile. Relieved, we dance out the screen door, letting it bang behind us as we run to playhouses in the grove. In a tumble of emotions, we are happy, afraid, proud little kids, The front window of our farmhouse frames a red white and blue, gold-fringed, service banner with three blue stars.

Gold-fringed, shiny-white banners with stars hang in nearly every front window of the farmhouses that we pass on our drive to church on Sundays. Mother explains that a gold star means that a son has been killed in action; a silver star means he is missing in action. The number of blue stars tells how many sons and daughters in this farm family are serving our country. When we drive by a window that has a blue star replaced with a gold star, Mother's somber eyes convey awe as she confides how fortunate our congregation is to have lost only one serviceman. "And you know, in our church, only one Gold Star Mother."

While Ray was still in Newport, Rhode Island, there was much waiting for the heavy cruiser, the "USS Columbus," to be commissioned. This involved months and months of going to sea to test every single facet of the cruiser, then coming back into the nearest port to correct anything wrong. While the ship was in dry dock he had long shore leaves. He spent his free time building a radio with a friend.

At first, in England, any airman in the Army Air Corps who completed 25 combat missions was sent home on leave and then got a ground assignment, but in 1944, the mission ante was raised to 30 and later to 35. After our brother's twenty-eighth combat mission over Germany, he was sent home on a troop ship to New York. Over the next couple months, he was sent to California twice before being mustered out. He arrived home on Mother's birthday, September 6, 1945, but she was no longer there.

The war in Europe came to an end, and V-E Day was May 8, 1945. Then Japan surrendered on August 15, 1945, and VJ Day was September 2, 1945. The war in the Pacific ended. Finally, the "USS Columbus" was ready with Ensign Raymond Kooi as Combat Information Officer in charge of a large crew. They sailed through the Panama Canal bound for China and ports in Japan and Hawaii. Ray was discharged on July 1, 1946, after they sailed back to San Diego. "I had a good time in the Navy. The only bad food was during the time in Asbury Park, New Jersey, and then only for six weeks. I had lots of free time and went to lots of interesting places."

Gladys had been corresponding with the pen pal she had met while she was in boot camp in New York City. On September 19, 1945, her pen pal, Abbey Hengeveld in New York, sent this letter to Gladys in San Diego:

> Can you imagine the excitement and dither on V-J Day! The crowds, the bits of paper flying here, there, everywhere! Car and taxis scooting past, decorated with red white and blue flags! A big pasteboard box tumbled out of a window above, nearly knockin' out my permanent wave! And we had a circus, too, no less. One especially excitable gentleman mounted a window ledge, held on with one hand, and with the other, adjusted his Hitlerian moustache. Then, gravely, amidst the excited cheers of the throngs, he stretched forth his hand in stiff "Heil!" fashion. We craned our necks to read the news atop the Time building. It was all too good to be true. Strangers thumped strangers on the back, and oh---everyone was so happy! Why you couldn't have torn me away from the city that night! New York surely goes for things in a big way.

344

Home on leave,
Clarence and Gladys Kooi,
November, 1944.

After Gladys left home,
Bernice took care of Glenn, 1944.

Ray home on leave
from V-12 program.
Cornhusks litter yard.
Hospers, 1944.

Bernice took train across Iowa to visit Ray
in Davenport, January, 1945.

31

Dutch Letters

Three of the émigrés—Mattie, Sam, and Ida—carried on a correspondence with their Friesian cousins, Brandt and Ytje, between 1921 and 1968. The letters are written in Dutch, and the three Americans shared each letter that came to any one of them; probably their Dutch cousins did the same. The tone of the letters is friendly, courteous, optimistic, and compassionate. The émigrés recall their feelings about events in Friesland during 1907 and emigrating through Ellis Island in 1908. They discuss World War II rationing, war criminals, and negotiate the business of sending goods to war-ravaged Friesland after the war. The Americans write to their Dutch cousins about big and little events: births and deaths, weight, age, health, numbers of acres, cows, pigs, and chickens; the severity of winter weather on the Great Plains. Mail service was interrupted for five years by the war. This meant that family news that happened at the beginning of the war did not reach the Dutch cousins until after the war was over. For example, the news of Uncle Watse's death in 1939 did not get to Cousin Ytje Van der Laan until 1946, when Aunt Mattie writes:

> Geertje's husband, Watse, died suddenly. In the afternoon he still attended a meeting and in the evening he died. Heart problems. Back to Geertje. Well, she looks just like Mom. I doubt that she's a hundred pounds. She's not strong but always very gentle and calm. She is living with her youngest daughter in Sioux Center.

Similarly, the news of Syne's death, in January of 1942, did not reach Ytje until four years later in an undated letter by Aunt Mattie, postmarked 1946:

> Siene (ie = y) died from the same illness as our Dad—bladder cancer. He had that long before anybody knew about it. I don't need to tell you how shocked I was, because it's a nasty, painful disease. In the beginning of 1942 the pain was severe and kept him day and night without much rest. He was hospitalized in Sioux City where he had surgery and after a week he died. We visited him there, but he couldn't

348

talk anymore. He still knew me, though. Ida happened to be there too. The next morning he passed away. He left a wife and children. When he died, Siene had about 800 acres of land, so they're well off.

The weather was a topic in Uncle Sam's letter, dated December 18, 1945, from Platte, South Dakota: "This morning, 15 below zero. Fortunately, the kids' walk to school is only 15 minutes. But the washing is hard. It freezes before you can get it outside on the line. But they say Dakota has a healthy climate, so a cold nose isn't so serious." In Aunt Mattie's January 1946 letter, from Renner, South Dakota; "Lots of snow here this year and very cold, 10 below for about 4-5 weeks, but that doesn't mean much here. There's no ice skating; my husband used to try, but the ice isn't very good quality."

For two years, Uncle John and Aunt Mattie lived on a two-hundred-acre farm just north of the present-day Oak Grove Park near Sioux Center. In 1941 they sold half their farm to the State of Iowa for a park because the farm became too small to pasture their forty-five head of cattle. They rented a three-hundred-acre farm near Renner, South Dakota, using a third of it for pasture and the rest for crops. Aunt Mattie adds, "We have about 65-70 head of cattle, a few horses, 65 pigs and 400 chickens." About herself, Mattie writes:

> I'll soon be 59, and Geertje is going to be 62, my husband soon 68, so we're getting to be old people, right? My leg bothers me some (I'm maybe 70 pounds overweight), but I've always been heavy. Otherwise, we're healthy. My husband is still very quick and energetic, gray of course, but healthy. Ida is 46, I won't write about Sam; I think he'll do that himself. Sam has a wonderful family, 12 children, a great wife. Larger families than you have, but it's really too busy when you have such a large family, an awful lot of work.

The war was a major topic: details of shortages, rationing, and other hardships. Uncle Sam writes from Platte, South Dakota, on a one-cent post-card dated September 8, 1945, to C. J. v/d Laan, Roptaxyl outer Wynaldem, Friesland, Nederland:

> We would like to hear how you all are doing. Did you experience hardship? Is there poverty? We long to hear something from Friesland now that the mail service works again.

When Uncle Sam again heard from his cousin, he replied on November 26, 1945:

> Ytje, my sister, we call her Ida, has a son, Clarence, who was top gunner at a Forbess [sic] airplane. They flew 30 [sic] times over the European mainland and flew three times over Leeuwarden and Franeker which was not too far away from you. A few times he realized that he was near some relatives. Fortunately he returned from the war safely.

The tone of the letter conveys a kindly spirit of concern, and even though some facts are inaccurate (Fortress and 28), they were probably as good as were available at that time.

The Americans sent not only letters but also goods to their Dutch cousins. From the distance of fifty years, I recall the semblance of conflict in Mother's voice when, once, she implied that the relatives in Holland were asking for too much. Apparently she meant they were unrealistic to expect to be sent items like bicycle tires which were too expensive, too large to send, unavailable, or all of these. The Dutch cousins, on the other hand, may have felt encouraged to ask for such items after reading American braggadocio into the letters from their cousins. They may have assumed that items not available in Friesland because of the war could readily be bought in America and sent to them.

The Americans, on the other hand, questioned whether the Dutch people really were desperate. "We often heard that in the Netherlands, people in the cities, as well as in the country, had much money. Is this really true? We thought the Germans had stolen every penny?" Later in the same letter, Sam asks, "How are things at your place? Did the war destroy anything? Did it cause severe damages in Franeker? We read about the liberation of prisoners in Leeuwarden and about the derailment of a munitions train near Workum. Yes, those are inspiring heroic deeds. But it will probably take a generation or two before the Netherlands is where it was prior to the war." He goes on to say, "We cannot send the bike tires since they cannot be folded due to the iron wires in its fabric. Here many goods are scarce too, like underwear, clothing, and other household articles, as well as machines. It all involves money." However, by the end of the long letter, Sam writes, "Now we will try to mail to you that which you requested, although for us civilians it is hard to come by, whereas for soldiers in the military it is available abundantly. There they do not know what to do with it all. Well, dear ones, God's indispensable blessings are what we wish to you. Be greeted by all of us. S. Sybesma, wife and the twelve."

Uncle Sam did not send this letter, however, until Aunt Caroline added her own letter two weeks later. On December 6, 1945, she explains: "In our town we weren't able to buy underwear last winter, and still not now. Last week we went to a large city, 75 miles from here, and even there we couldn't get underwear. I've ordered these articles out of Chicago." She lists the eight articles of clothing they hope to send, and adds a regret: "P.S. It's too bad, that when the first call of need came from Holland, that we had already sent off through the churches all the blankets and clothes we could get. It would probably have been better to send that to family. But it's too late. I can't promise for sure that we'll get the clothes because we keep getting the money back that we sent for orders. But we'll do our best."

Then, just before Christmas, 1945, they did send women's clothes, listing items that added up to $9.07, and added a PS. "If you're not able to pay, that's all right with us too. We're not allowed to send bike tires." On January 21, 1946, they sent a second package. In the letter Aunt Carolina writes: "This week I was in an old store with the owner, an 85-year-old man. He still had new but somewhat soiled underwear available, which is almost impossible to get. So I bought it for you and your girl at once. We hope it fits. We can't get men's underwear. We still had a coat we no longer need, which I included too. Also hose and mittens. If you have no use for it just give it away."

Three days later, she sent a postcard with regrets: "We offer our apologies for the black hose. We thought that they were OK, but when I prepared another package I saw the moth damage. I'd been so happy about the 20 pairs, they're so hard to get, and now it's worth nothing. I hope the other stuff fits."

Also, in January of 1946 Aunt Mattie wrote; "Everything is non-rationed again now, except sugar and car tires. We can only get 5 pounds of sugar per person every 4 months. We've been without for two weeks now. But meat and lard we can get again too."

Bike tires came up again in Aunt Mattie's letter to Ytje in February of

1946: "About the bike tires. Well, it's impossible to send them. In the first place, we have no bike, so we can't get them. Besides, it's forbidden. Gladys (her daughter) was able to buy 2 yards of elastic, but we hadn't been able to get that for the last four years. (Elastic was important because it held up homemade bloomers worn under dresses.) There are other things like that too. So we can easily imagine that it must be even worse there for you. Along with this letter we'll send some anklets and socks, but we don't know your size. We hope there'll be something that will fit somebody. We can't get silk here now either. It seems to be even worse now than during the war. But I think so much is being sent overseas, and that's good too. We can easily get along without for a while. This month they're going to have another drive here for the Netherlands. We hope a lot will be contributed. We had one last summer too. I sent Tante Ytje a very small package with coffee and tea, but I never heard from them whether they got it."

On the subject of war criminals, Uncle Sam wrote on November 26, 1945, "The government is too lenient in its actions. Things are not proceeding with speed. Why not punish the guilty? Our sons had to give their lives and now the government is so weak in its dealings that the murderers there in Germany keep their lives." Two months later Aunt Mattie wrote, "What a terrible war it's been, heh? How cruel Germany has been. You must be very grateful that your son's life was spared among those barbarians." Also, "Yes, Ytje, I can still remember so clearly those last few days we spent with you. I thought it was so quiet by the sea. But when I first came here, I thought it was even more quiet. I didn't like that at all, but one gets used to everything, for later on I often thought of how nicely you people lived there, even though I thought at the time that it was too quiet."

In 1945 Uncle Sam wrote to his Dutch cousin, "It is 38 years since we emigrated. Those beginning days are days we will never forget in our lifetime." In one of his later letters to cousin Ytje, in 1968, he wrote, "Franeker is and will always be my place of birth, and I still remember the 'sugarland,' but at that time it was not a sugartime for us. We're a lot better off now, and all our children too." Certainly, it was no sugartime for Metje, Syne, or Ietje, during the years between their births in Friesland and their immigration to America. Certainly, America was a better place for all five émigrés to live and

352   raise their large families, where only five of their fifty children died young, whereas in Friesland, seven of the twelve children born to Klaas and Bregtje Sybesma died in childhood. Today, in America, there are nearly a thousand descendants of the five Sybesma émigrés.

Sam's correspondent, Brant Sybesma with wife,
in Harlingen, Friesland, c. 1965.

32

Leaving

Runny noses and coughs during the winter were part of life on the farm. So much so that I always thought that the coming of cold weather in the fall caused a runny nose, and that the coming of warm weather in the spring caused my nose to stop running. Each winter Mother would get a chest cold and cough. When spring came again, she would be fine. At first Mother appeared to have the usual winter cold. However, the next winter, Mother's coughing was worse and lasted longer, but then, toward spring she was fine again. One winter she coughed until she was exhausted and had to lie down in the bedroom. At first, she was in bed for only a little while, but then she laid down longer, and then much longer. The protracted coughing brought fatigue. The doctor in town gave her medicine, but it did not stop the coughing. After a particularly long, hard cough, she would spit thick yellow stuff into the pan at her bedside. When I went into the bedroom to see her, she would caution me not to kiss her on the mouth or to touch the pan of sputum.

"Stand far back when I cough. You don't want to catch this." I did not quite understand what "this" could be, and I wanted to get close to her, but she would keep me at arm's length. "I know what you want, but I can't help you right now." Each time I would ask what was wrong with her. She would say that she didn't know. Slowly I would walk out through the bedroom door, and, closing it gently, I would go away. The next day I would be back, "Are you better today?"

On March 22, 1945, eight of us line up in the kitchen, oldest to youngest, like stair steps, to say goodbye to Mother. Bernice is eighteen, Pete seventeen, Stan has just turned fifteen, Verna Mae is almost thirteen. Milly has recently turned ten; I am eight. Elmer is six, and Glenn has just turned five. The three oldest, Ray, twenty-three; Gladys, twenty-one; and Clarence, nineteen, are serving in the military. As we wait, we can hear Mother moving around in the bedroom preparing to leave. When she walks out of their bedroom and enters the kitchen, her winter coat seems to be hanging more loosely than usual around her shoulders and body. She is stooped forward just a little. Slowly she goes down the line, step by step, saying goodbye to each one of us. When she gets to me, the sixth in line, there are tears in her eyes. She kisses me on the cheek and lets me hug her briefly as she murmurs something indistinct, "Ach ... just too much." It seems as though she will be overcome by tears, but then she straightens up again and bends to kiss Elmer, then Glenny. She walks out through the wash porch to the stoop, down the steps, past the pump, and out the gate to the waiting ambulance. Pa carries her suitcase. They embrace and kiss; then she is helped into the back of the ambulance.

Pa talks briefly with the driver while all of us stay in the house, watching through the windows. We little kids want to run outside, but someone older has instructed us in advance to stay inside and let Mother and Pa be alone to say goodbye to each other. "Just think how hard it is for them to leave each other, even harder than for Mother to leave us." Slowly the ambulance rolls out the driveway and down the dirt road, no siren, no flashing red lights. Inside the house it is uncommonly quiet.

Going upstairs to find out what will happen now that Mother is gone, I open the door to the big girls' bedroom. Milly seems to be a quiet shadow on the wall. Bernice is sitting against the headboard on the chenille bedspread, painting her long fingernails red. What feels apparent is that she will not be able to get supper off the cookstove onto the table, and I feel worried about who will feed us now. She smiles not to worry, pulls us close, and says soft words. Not convinced, I walk down the stairs and out into the front yard where everything is quiet and nothing is happening. The air is like the eerie silence just before the tornado hit.

Life without Mother is tiring and trying. Most of the time I drag myself around the farm, waiting to see what is going to happen. What actually did happen the next couple of years is pock-marked with holes. Who cooked the meals, did the housework, and took care of the family has become fragmented into intermittent recollections easily forgotten. The Jigsaw puzzle lying on the dining room table had pieces missing. The bottom of my world had dropped out.

I often ask the adults: "When is Mother coming home?"

"I don't know. Why don't you write her a letter and ask her?" I wait, thinking, wondering. On lined paper I carefully, precisely, print in pencil each letter of each word. Each punctuation mark is perfect.

> Dear Mother,
> How are you? I am fine. What are you doing? I go to school. How is the weather? Our weather is fine.
>
> Love and Kisses,
> Irene XXX OOO

"When are you coming home?" was erased over and over again until the paper grew too thin to erase. Apparently someone had insisted "Don't ask her that, it will make her feel bad," but I persisted. In time, tuberculosis became shortened to TB, and Bethesda Sanatorium to The San. Our questioning grew angry, blaming *that San*. "Well then, when will Mother come back from *that San*?"

The sanatorium was named for Bethesda, the "spring of living waters," in Biblical Israel, but I think sanatorium means clean and sanitary— that Mother must stay there until she gets clean enough to come home.

The separation that disease makes between parent and child is something a young child cannot understand. I imagined someone, some lucky fate, or a good fairy rising up to rescue us. Burdens, as a colorless, blinding-white light, became wed in terrible ceremony to the black night. In the dungeon, disillusioned, a still, soft black invaded the many-hued windows with soulful music. The velvet silence that settled in became the great gaping hole of the well in the front yard set into the scruffy lawn. Next to the pump above the well was a bucket, usually left half full of water, ready to use. A long-handled dipper hung on the side of the bucket. If the bucket was not there, the dipper hung over the pump's long arm, its spout turned down like an elbow. If the dipper was not there, we simply cupped our hands to catch water from the spout to get a drink. The harsh squeak of the windmill, its blades twisting and turning to catch the wind, echoed the wheezing of the pump handle as it was jerked up and down to bring up water. The wheezing pump handle sounded like coughing lungs bringing up yellow spit. Abandoning the well, I go out the yard to the cornfield where a scarecrow's arms twist and turn, catching the wind. I wish they could reach out to hug me.

Uncle Sam and Aunt Mattie wrote letters and postcards about Mother's condition in Bethesda during 1946 and 1947, and sent them to the relatives in Friesland. These letter tell me about events and times that I've forgotten.

From a letter dated 26 November, 1945: "Ida herself had to go to Denver in July [March] because of tuberculosis. Since then she underwent surgery three times: six ribs were removed from her, and one of her lungs has been put out of work. Her latest surgery took place a month ago, and as far as we know, everything is going well with her. Her major surgery took all day in another hospital, and she came back in painful condition." On a postcard dated 9-8-45: "Ytje is in Denver for health reasons. Things are going reasonably well for her." From a letter dated 11-26-1945: "Fourth surgery week, but doing exceptionally well. Fred, her husband, visits her every time they perform a surgery on her."

"Ida had her fifth operation this week and is feeling pretty good. It's hard on them though; on January 27th they have their 25th wedding anniversary" (1-21-46 letter). And, in another letter to Ytje from Mattie dated 1-1946: "Ida had 12 children, and never very strong. Now she has TB, for 7 (10) months already. She's had surgery and doctor says that she should get better now, but she'll have to stay there another year or so."

In February of 1946 Aunt Mattie wrote to Ytje in Friesland, "Ida's son, Clarence, flew over Franeker in a bomber on his way to Germany. He was here last week and told us that he had seen Franeker. He's now honorably discharged from the service. He's planning to go to school in Denver where Ida is. Ida's oldest son is still in the service, and her oldest daughter too, but next month she'll get her discharge too. A girl of 19, Bernice, takes care of the household. Ida is about 500 miles from here, in the mountains."

Understandably, there are some inaccuracies in their letters. Denver is not in the mountains, but next to them, and apparently Verna Mae was taking care of the household.

Each major surgery took all day in another hospital. Then Mother would be brought back to Bethesda. She was in much pain. When Pa drove to Denver to be with Mother during her surgeries, he left the oldest of his children in charge of the farm. Usually these were Peter and Stan, who were not yet in military service, and Verna Mae, or Bernice when she was not working and living in Sheldon. Pa's car trip to Denver, then back again, would have taken about a week. Before and after those visits he would try to get the Sheldon operator on the party line to ring up Doctor Kramer at Bethesda Sanatorium. After the supper dishes were done and darkness was coming through the windows, I would see him standing at the wall phone in the kitchen yelling into the upturned mouthpiece. Apparently the operator had a hard time hearing him because of static on the line, neighbors listening in on the party line, or simply a bad connection. He would shout, "Operator!" Then wait, hang up, then try another time, ringing up the operator with one long ring.

"Fred Kooi here. I want to talk to Doctor Kramer at the San." Another wait. Perhaps the lines were busy from several calls coming into the hospital at one time.

"Ja, in Denver ... that's Colorado." Long wait.

"Ja, the San, that's Bethesda Sanatorium." Another wait.

"Ja, ja, I got the number right here." Pause. "Ja, the number is right."

"Ja, I'll wait." Pa's anxiety infected all of us within earshot, especially as darkness came on and his worry increased. He waited, then said in resignation, "Okay, ja, I'll try again tomorrow then." Although I knew it was bedtime, I would lurk in the shadows at the bottom of the stairs to listen, unseen behind the door, afraid to go up the stairs alone in the dark. No longer was anyone chanting the familiar bedtime litany that I had heard every night for so long. "Go on now, time to go up to bed."

At first, after Mother left, Verna Mae would get up early to help Bernice in the kitchen before Verna Mae had to go to school. At night she gave Elmer and Glenn their baths by standing them on the cement floor of the side porch. She used a basin of water that she carried from the kitchen pump. She recalled that, "Bernice, I believe, left in the spring of 1946. We were left alone that summer of 1946 because I recall yelling at Pa one Sunday evening. I was trying to round up you little kids for bed and you wouldn't come. I yelled 'I can't take care of all these little kids.' This was one of the few times in my life I ever yelled at him." Verna Mae was only fourteen that summer, quite young to have the entire care of the family, the house, and cooking for eight people in addition to the hired men needed during harvest.

Verna Mae gets sick and stays upstairs in bed all day long, too sick to get out of bed. A week goes by, then another. Pa goes upstairs to see what is the matter with her. We pile into the car to go see the doctor in Sioux Center. While Pa and Verna Mae go into the examining room, we four kids huddle close together on a small couch in the waiting room. We hear the doctor yelling at Pa, but what he is yelling we can't make out. They come out. Nobody says anything. We get into the car. Pa drives down Main Street, then stops. He tells us to stay in the car as he gets out to do some shopping. Aunt Gert walks by and sees us sitting there, in the back seat waiting, four little kids alone together. After a little while she comes back and hands each one of us a doughnut.

Before Mother left, we were categorized as the five little kids, the big boys, and the big girls. Mother used to warn Pete and Stan before they went upstairs to bed, "You big boys stop that rough housing up there, you hear? Or you'll break that bedspring." After Mother left, we were called the three little girls, partly, I suppose, because we did jobs together, like doing dishes after each meal. Verna Mae would ask, "Okay, who will clear the table and stack the dirty dishes?" And, after no answer from Milly or me, "Who will wash? Who will dry? Who will put away the dishes?"

There was joking, joshing, jockeying to get the easiest task, rivalry with Milly, respect for Verna Mae, arguing to get the desired job, giving in when it was clear it would have to be done anyway. A beat-up metal dishpan hung on a nail pounded into the wall in back of the stove. It was used for dishes, bread dough, popcorn, and a variety of things. After a meal, hot water from the kettle would be poured into the dishpan that was set on the table and into another pan for rinsing the dishes. Next in line on the table was the drainer. First we washed the dishes that were the least dirty, then the glasses, then the plates that had been scraped. Next we washed the serving bowls and then the forks, knives and spoons that had been soaking at the bottom of the pan. The dirty pans got scrubbed last. By this time the water in the dishpan was very dirty.

Many of our cousins, like other young people in love and facing separation because of the draft, would marry before the young man had to leave for the war. When he returned home, he would see their baby for the first time—and need a job. At the end of 1946, Pa's oldest son still at home was helping Pa in the fields, and his oldest daughter still at home was taking care of the house and little kids. When his son left for the Army, Pa realized that he needed two adults to help him run the farm, a woman in the house and a man in the fields.

During 1944, one of the many daughters of one of our many uncles and aunts fell in love with a young man. Before he left for the war, they got married in her parents' farmhouse. When he returned at the end of 1946, he saw his baby son for the first time. He needed a job and Pa needed help—both in the fields and in the house. Pa hired the couple—his niece and the new nephew. In either December of 1946 or January of 1947, the couple and their baby moved into our farmhouse and lived with us. They had two rooms upstairs, one for a sitting room and one for a bedroom. Pa asked his niece, "Why do you need two rooms?"

"Because we need a room to be alone together in the evenings."

"Why can't you be downstairs in the front room with the rest of us?" They argued about it, but she got her way. There were four bedrooms upstairs. Now, we three girls slept in the Girls Bedroom and the boys slept in the Boys Bedroom. Now, Pa had help both outside and inside, both to keep house and do the farm work. Vicki recalls that the year of 1946-1947 was not a good year:

> It was a hard winter and we didn't get out much except to go to church or school. Our cousin pretty much by-passed us kids and concentrated on fixing meals, cleaning house, and taking care of her baby. Her husband paid more attention to us, as I recall he was kind hearted and easy going. One night she talked him into taking us to a play in Newkirk, even though it was the middle of winter and the dirt roads were bad. We made it part of the way before he had to turn back because he cannot go any farther in the deep snow drifting over the road. Home again, standing in the kitchen, she turned to me and said, "I'm sorry." She looked very sorry, and I said, "That's okay."

Our cousin is in the kitchen. I am underfoot. Milly is underfoot. Nuisances, we are in her way. Dispirited, we go outside. Her husband is

360   outside. He grins at us, "You two little girls are the two cutest little girls I've ever seen." He lights a cigar and looks at us. "I can't tell which one of you is cuter." He cocks his head to one side and looks at us sideways, as though seeing us in another light will help him decide. "Guess it'll hafta be Milly." Seeing my face drop, he adds, "But it's pretty hard to tell." We tease him. Milly grins. I needle him and poke at his broad chest, trying to get him to play, but he backs away saying, "Gotta get back to work now." As he goes away, he turns around and keeps on grinning at us, repeating, "Can't tell which one of you is the cuter one." His words were a mantra of comfort that covered up an empty hole.

In the kitchen, the baby fusses. He is a year-and-a-half old and, in the spring of 1947, his mother is newly pregnant. However, we do not yet know this, so we have no clue as to why she is irritated with us. She allows me to carry her baby outside after I promise to be really careful.

"Cross my heart and hope to die, I won't drop him."

In order to carry him around the farm, I get a milk pail from the barn to put him in. However, when I put the baby into the pail and try to lift it up by its wire handle, it is too heavy. I love the way he looks, standing there in the pail, so I run into the house and get the camera to take pictures of him in the pail. Then I go find someone to take a picture of the two of us. His mother is nervous about my watching her only child. I have to convince her that he is safe with me. Finally, I manage to lift the pail and lug him around the farmyard. He is a fat baby so I cannot carry him very far without stopping to rest every few minutes. Soon I am tired out.

Vicki recalls, "One morning Pa and our cousin had a tiff. He got into his car in a huff. She grabbed the baby and said, 'Well, if he's going, I'm going too!' They were gone for a few hours—ate breakfast in town, I guess. He said later, 'Uncle Fred is not an easy person to work with.' This was true."

I was nine when the news came that Gladys had met a sailor in San Diego and fallen in love. When both of them were discharged from the military, they wanted to be married in Denver at the Bethesda Sanatorium chapel so that Mother would be able to be at the wedding. After the wedding a reception was to take place in one of the hospital's screened porches. One carload of us was to drive to Denver for the wedding. Clearly, not all of us will fit into the car. Someone decides that the two little girls will be among those who get to go. Pa, of course, will drive. We must have new dresses for the wedding, special dresses to be bought in Sheldon. Someone older explains what we can expect to happen. "Mother cannot kiss you when you see her."

"Why?"

"Because she might give you TB."

"Can't she even hug us?"

"Carefully. She's had all those operations, you know."

Of course I know. I've often heard Pa's anxious voice on the phone.

We go to Sheldon and Milly and I get new dresses in the same style, but in different colors. They have a new kind of short sleeve that I have never seen before, a flap that falls over the upper arm. Someone tells me that this is so that we will not catch TB. Believing this to be true, I examine the sleeves over and over, trying to figure out how they can stop the TB from getting into me.

The long drive to Denver takes three days. When we get there and get to see Mother, I stand very still so I won't get TB. She is teary-eyed and weak looking and barely touches me. Although I trust the dress sleeves to protect me from TB, I still feel scared. Everything is suspended, at risk, in danger, as though I must be very careful and be absolutely sure to do all the right things, or I too will get sick, get taken far away, and maybe even die. Everything is a mystery.

Gladys marries George Gritter in Denver on the same day that her cousin, Gladys Feikema, the daughter of Aunt Mattie and Uncle John, gets married in South Dakota. When the wedding at Bethesda occurs, on April 18 of 1946, all the write-ups say "Mrs. Kooi has been a patient here the past year and is making a good recovery after a series of operations." There are wedding pictures. Snapshots taken at other times show Mother sitting outdoors with groups of patients, also a group on a day trip. Ray and Mother are pictured in the Denver City Park on July 6, 1946. After the war ended, Ray was a student at the University of Denver, not too far from Bethesda Sanatorium.

This evening on the farm, Pa is tired out and lies on the davenport in the front room—what Mother used to call the front parlor. The davenport sags from age and heavy use. Pa's body dents it. His asperity softens in the twilight. Chores done, supper over, "When the cows come home" has become a metaphor for draining the ire from Pa's harsher features. No one else is in the room when I ask him where we will get the money if we have to move to Denver. He says from selling the farm. I ask how much we will get. He tells me how much per acre, and I multiply that times 160, then ask how much a year it will take to live in Denver, item by item, electricity, gas, food, clothes. I multiply, add, and then ask. "How much will a house cost?" He says that he doesn't know exactly, but he humors me along with another figure. I add it up.

"Boy, you sure can do sums fast," he says, but, however briefly I swell with importance, I will not be put off. I tell him that much money means we can live on that sum for only a certain number of years. I worry about that for a little while, and then want to know where the money would come from after the money from the sale of the farm is gone. He is relaxed and feeling good—unusual these days. He lets the newspaper he is reading fall to the floor and dismisses my concern. "I guess it will all work out okay, Irene."

Twilight falls lightly through the windows and darkens the sashes. The integument of Pa's discipline seems set aside, and I want more than anything to keep this—his brief affection—but he quickly reverts back to his usual self, dismissing me by his inattention. Almost, I can feel his love; at the same time I feel angry at him for not looking ahead, not being realistic, not doing things my way. During the next months I am persistent: asking, computing, trying to get Pa to look ahead. He continues to dismiss my interest as the ramblings of a child doing her sums. I am deadly serious, convinced the money might run out if we move; convinced he is not thinking ahead, convinced our world is falling apart. His good-natured grins, relaxed body, and off-hand answers do not mollify me. I see disaster ahead. The house feels empty. The sagging screens in the doors have bulged to breaking. Flies enter and buzz. The flypaper is curled up, dried out, long ago used up. Everyone is gone. The air is still. Where are Elmer and Glenny?

Where are Milly and Verna Mae? I walk into the kitchen. Our cousins are
not here. Who will fix supper?

Separation is quick, matter-of-fact, over and gone, nothing said afterwards. Those separated are expected to go on and forget. But that is not
the way the mind of a child works. The emotions linger, ask to be digested, regurgitated, and digested again until finally they find a safe home
to stay–until the next separation comes along, and then the feeling whim-
pers and reminds, asking to be heard. Each separation surfaces from the
bottom of some deep lake where there is no light. What did I do to make
this happen?

Whirling up are pools, ghosts, shadows on X-rays, images playing songs.
On the farmyard in August, the wind plays games with the finely-shifting soil.
Shadows leap out of the slanting ribs of empty corncribs to leave long bars of
darkness on the flat yard. The swinging door into the parlor is heavy, but above
me the hands of someone taller pushes hard to swing it open. In the front parlor
the Blue Star Banner sways in the front window. Davenport cushions sag.
Playing on the piano stool, I spin it up and down, get dizzy going round and
round, almost falling off, barely hanging on. The piano sings a melody as the
breeze picks up. At dizzying speed, circling shadows in Israel call to mind
dresses made from flour sacks, the bloomers way too big. The rag rug
here, the rag rug there, rag-tag ends used at Ladies Aid, on Wednesday
afternoons, Mother at church, Mother at home ...

"Man a livin'! Man a livin'!" someone shouts when Mother comes
home. She will stay for a week or two to see if she is able to resume life on
the farm. A snapshot shows us at the Kooi Family Reunion in the park in
Sheldon. Pa is dressed up. Mother wears a new dress. Milly is nearly as
tall as Mother. I am a head shorter than Mother and Glenny is a head shorter
than me. Two ribbons pinned on my shirt were apparently for winning foot
races or some other contest. Behind the five of us are women and children
at picnic tables. Our faces all look a little uncertain, not grim but not happy.

At night in their bedroom, Mother and Pa are overheard arguing
about the future of the farm. Apparently, Pa wants to stay on the farm, but
Mother does not. She is not able to resume the hard work. Also, she cannot
handle breathing the farm dust now that one of the lobes of her left lung is

gone. She says the older boys do not like farming. Pa argues that there are more sons growing up who will farm. Mother does not think any of the boys want to become farmers. World War II took the three oldest children away from the farm. Then Mother's tuberculosis carried her away. Gladys was married now and living far away. Bernice had left for a job in town. Mother's TB was not the only reason to consider moving off the farm. Pa needed farmhands to continue farming, and none of the boys, except perhaps Pete, wanted to do farm work.

Mother's visit home was over in a flash. In Israel, a flash flood races down a narrow wadi to block a desert road. Without warning, our car is carried away, careening toward the side of a bus. Just before hitting the bus, our car slides to a stop under the bus driver's window. He looks down at us. "You okay?"

"In shock, but okay." We wait. When the water begins to run off the road, we go slowly to dodge the debris lodging in flooded low spots. Late in Eilat, wire hoops hold doilies whirling around the bare bulb in the center of the room. The light settles on the kitchen table in Iowa, set with twelve mismatched plates. After supper, the plates will be washed, dried, and stacked in the cupboard, one on top of another.

Fine Cracks in Dinner Plates

> Among the twelve of us I am third from last
> stacked like Mother's plates, once new, now
> chipped, fine cracks showing. Mismatched, some
> missing, each old plate becomes an original no
> longer manufactured, irreplaceable at any cost
> Lost, through the swinging door into the parlor
> I go, where the Blue Star Banner sways in the
> front window and the davenport is falling apart.
> I am eight, practicing of late at being twelve
> Tattered rag doll flung across the piano stool
> spinning up and down, getting dizzy going around

Random worries grow in the undeveloped conscience of a child, like a quilt pieced together from any old material: a worn-out dress, scraps or edges from homemade curtains, a bit of this or an irregular piece of that. Without pattern, without plan, logic is abandoned, imagination not curbed by the common sense that parents possess. Emotion runs amok. The electricity of shame flashes red in the face. A crazy quilt of guilt covers the sagging cushions of the couch in the front room. Again it is evening, and again Pa is admiring how I can add numbers in my head. "You're pretty good with sums, I see." But now I am nearing age ten and I press him. I want to know what he will do to make money if we move to Denver. Soon, it is quite apparent that he is not worried about that. I leave the room worried, more than a little disgusted, and go outside to find a straw in the haystack to take to Mother, to ask her if she will make lemonade. I want to suck up lemonade through this straw—so hard to find and so easy to collapse—but Mother is not here. She has been home for a little while, but now she is back in The San.

Dumb hayseed, I mutter to myself, dumb dirty farmer's daughter. Gone is the stern gaze of Mother's blue eyes and her exasperation when once I tested her until she threatened, "Be good or I'll ask Pa to box your ears when he comes in from the field." Gone are the vague fears that cannot be shaped into words. Gone is the hopeless feeling Mother might never return. In its place is a bittersweet closeness as my heart warms to Pa's inattention and I feel protective of his vulnerability. Warmed, softened, my heart pumping hard under a flimsy summer dress, I climb the steep stairs to bed.

I was wandering around the farmyard when the big news came in May of 1947 that Gladys had given birth to a son, Robert Dale Gritter, born in Grand Rapids, Michigan, where they lived. On the farm, Pa was most likely preparing to move. What the older sisters remember is that "One rainy Saturday there was an auction of the farm machinery. It was a gloomy and wet day—miserable."

During the long drive to Denver we stayed in small motel rooms alongside the road at night. In the crowded car I fought to sit next to Pa, to convince him to let me hold the steering wheel, however briefly. We kids squabbled about anything and everything.

"It's MY turn to sit next to the window."

"Not so, it's mine, you already did."

"When do I get to look out the window?"

"You're as slow as molasses in January."

"Let's play twenty questions."

"Naw, who can get the most states on license plates?"

On the long road of winding into the Land of my Dreams and the City of Hope, Mother's rocking chair became the motion of the Chevrolet speeding along the highway. Up popped Pa's sing-song voice, reminiscent of summer evenings on the front porch as he played World War I songs on his accordion.

> There's a long long trail a-winding
> Into the land of my dreams
> Where the nightingales are singing
> And a white moon beams!
>
> There's a long, long night of waiting
> Until my dreams all come true
> 'Till the day when I'll be going
> Down that long, long trail with you

A series of signs were placed on posts and spaced to be read at the speed of a '47 Chevrolet on the two-lane highway. Around a very long curve we call out: A Curve / A Kiss / A Miss / He kissed / The Miss / And Missed / The Curve / Burma Shave. For a ten-year-old traveling thirty miles an hour, sometimes even forty, the 700 miles to Mother went by awfully slow. To pass the time Pa sang snatches from songs he knew. One of his favorites was "Waltzing Matilda." Probably he had heard Australian soldiers sing this ballad in France during World War I. Far from home, they adapted lines of Banjo Paterson's folk song to suit their mood. I never heard Pa sing the line that went, "And his ghost may be heard as you pass by that billabong," but I loved to hear his happy voice sing the lines:

Once a jolly swagman camped by a billabong
Under the shade of a coolibah-tree.
And he sang as he watched and waited till his billy boiled
Who'll come a-waltzing Matilda with me?
Waltzing Matilda, Waltzing Matilda,
You'll come a-waltzing Matilda with me.

Bill-a-bong sounds like the familiar song of bull frogs at the creek in springtime. As the car goes around another long curve, we call out the next series of signs: Spring has sprung / The grass has ris / Where last year's / Careless driver is / Burma Shave. Pa adjusts his Sunday straw hat as he mutters, "Ach, it all works out."

Author at age ten with
baby in milk bucket,
Hospers farmyard, 1947.

Gladys Kooi marries George Gritter
at Bethesda Sanatorium in Denver,
Milly on left, Irene on right, 1946.

Mother at Denver City Park
with Ray, 1946.

On Sunday visit to farm of Kooi cousins: Irene, Milly,
Renzella, Kenny, Glenn, Elmer, 1946.

Mother home briefly from "The San" at reunion in Sheldon Park.
L-R: Glenn, Pa, Irene, Mother, Milly, 1946.

Sister of Fred and friend of Ida, Bertha (Kooi) Vander Lugt turned 100 on June 14, 1996, at the Lebanon Christian Reformed church. Six of Fred's and Ida's adult children traveled to Iowa to be at Aunt Bertha's birthday party.

Appendix

Epilogue

In the Westside Hills of Central California above the San Joaquin Valley is a canyon called 'Ospital by the Basque sheepherders who once tended their flocks here. They built a simple wooden refuge at the site of a spring, and in this green oasis they left sick or crippled wild animals to recover in the shade during the long, hot summers when all other water holes had dried up. A photograph from that day spent in 'Ospital Canyon became the springboard for a poem. Willow Place, a farm on a creek seen through six lines of barbed wire, became the six lines of a poem, "Images of Iowa."

Willow Place, 'Ospital Canyon in Westside Hills, California, 1986.

Glossary

ach heiden: oh dear, oh well. Och heiden was a slang expression, "attention pagan" in Friesian, but Mother used it as an expression of futility or of understanding, much like "Heavens to Betsy."

ach ja: oh yes

dominie: preacher, pastor, minister

geboren: born in Dutch, berne is born in Friesian

gulden: dollars

huis or **huizen:** house

huis bezoek: home visitation

huisvrouw (huisfrou): housewife

Intifada: a war between Israelis and Palestinians.

jaar: year

keuken kinderen kerk: Dutch for kitchen, children, church. In German it is kinder, kuche, kirche, the province of women

kleine beetje: little bit, i.e., little child, a term of endearment. "Ik kan Hollandse verstann een klein beetje" means "I can understand Dutch a little bit."

kleine kinderen or **kinder:** dear child, little or slender child

klompen: wooden shoes. Mother kept small, painted, souvenir wooden shoes on the fireplace mantel in Denver. Although she said wooden shoes were uncomfortable, Pieter de Boer was comfortable in his well worn klompen.

koffie klets: coffee-drinking group. Dutch women enjoying a leisurely cup of coffee became enshrined in what two researchers called the three k's of Dutch women's lives: krant, kachel, koffie (newspaper, stove, coffee).

oliebollen: kind of spice doughnut with raisins eaten in Holland during holidays

oorijzer: ear iron or cap. Began as a band to hold back the hair. Some still say it is a crown of thorns gradually glorified into the golden casque.

opa: grandpa

oud: aged

overleden: died

polder: comes from the word, pol, meaning stake. Early dikes were staked off by poles an the enclosed land became known as a polder.

schoon: beautiful and at the same time clean, neatness raised to the dignity of a virtue

spek: pork fat, bacon fat. Immigrants sometimes termed their letters "spekbrieven," literally bacon letters, because little could convey their success as well as reports of eating lots of fat pork.

tante: aunt

terps: earthen mounds built centuries ago for protection from flood waters before dikes were built

vies (Dutch) or **fiis** (Friesian): dirty, soiled, filthy, puritanical in Pebesma's "Nederlands-Fries en Fries-Nederlands Woordenboek," (dictionary of Dutch to Fries and Fries to Dutch), includes the words, "vies" (Dutch) and "flis, smoarch" (Fries).

List of Photographs

PART II: DUTCH ANCESTORS

List of Maps

Annotated Bibliography

Herbert, Zbigniew. <u>Still Life With A Bridle</u>. New Jersey: The Ecco Press, 1991. Polish poet's essays on Dutch 17th century art show the incisive depths made by paintings and the sacred life of objects into the Dutch psyche, and prompts a sense of wonder about its effects on contemporary Dutch life. "The artist's work was a mere substitute...for a faraway and unreachable lost reality. Similarly, lovers doomed to separation must be content with the likeness of a beloved face."

Jager, Ronald. <u>Eighty Acres, Elegy for a Family Farm</u>. Boston: Beacon Press, 1990. Described is the securely regulated life of the author's childhood on a Michigan farm. Life was orderly, square, and spare and insulated from the outside world.

Jakes, John. <u>Homeland</u>. New York: Doubleday, 1993. Novel traces German immigrant boy's journey and subsequent family life in Chicago, events and politics in the Midwest during last half of the 19th century.

Jellema, Rod. <u>The Sound That Remains: A Historical Collection of Friesian Poetry: a Bilingual Edition</u>. Grand Rapids, Michigan: Eerdman's Publishing Company, 1990. Collection of a hundred poems spans three and a half centuries, 1603-1959. The poems portray religious and daily life, the pastoral and practical, with directness and lyric beauty.

Jungman, Nico. <u>Holland</u>. Text by Beatrix Jungman. London: Adam and Charles Black, 1904. Costumes and customs of the turn-of-the-century Dutch in 75 color plates, all illustrations by English artist, Nico. His wife, Beatrix, faithfully recounts her impressions of the life among the Dutch. Both text and art provide fine views of 1904 Holland, at the time Ietje Sybesma lived there.

Nieuwenhuis, G. Nelson. <u>Siouxland: A History of Sioux County, Iowa</u>. Orange City, Iowa: Sioux County Historical Society, 1983. Comprehensive history includes maps of townships in Sioux County in 1875 and 1887. Photographs include the peddle wagon of Carmel mounted on a 1923 Model T, and the Middleburg peddle wagon has doors open to show goods, barrel with spout roped to joints of stove pipes.

Schaap, James C. <u>Sign of a Promise</u>. Sioux Center, Iowa: Dordt College Press, 1979. 383
Fifteen stories based on fact dramatize the lives of Dutch immigrants settling
into Midwest farming communities at beginning of 20th century. Author passes
on his ethno-religious heritage with stories told from a Dutch Calvinist Christian
Reformed viewpoint. Particularly engaging are "The Mocker," "Snowstorm,"
and "Courting Dame Justice."

Schama, Simon. <u>The Embarrassment of Riches - An Interpretation Of Dutch Culture
In The Golden Age</u>. Berkeley: University of California Press, 1988. Cultural
historian explores the paradoxes of being Dutch in terms of social beliefs
and behavior in social process and habits. Domestic and community life of
the well-fed and housed is his subject. Seventeenth century art is seen as
descriptive literalism or a photographic documentation of beliefs.

Schuchart, Max. <u>The Netherlands</u>. Great Britain: Walker Publishing Company, Inc.,
1972. Overview of the Dutch people, their history, nature, politics and arts
by a Dutch poet; forces that shaped the national character; Dutch religion,
mentality and temperament. Written in the postwar Holland of 1945 with
notes added for 1972 revision.

Singleton, Esther, ed. <u>Holland</u>. New York: Dodd, Mead Company, 1906. Essays on
history, manners, art and customs, description of polders, dykes, canals,
mills collected by an American guide book writer at the turn of the 19th to the
20th century.

Sitwell, Sacheverell. <u>The Netherlands</u>. New York: Hastings House Publishers, 1945,
1974. English art historian's account of Holland's arts and decoration in
buildings and appearances, especially in the north, is linked to landscape,
history, and the first "Golden Age" in 16th and 17th centuries.

Vanden Bosch, Mike. <u>Pocket of Civility, A History of Sioux Center</u>. Sioux Falls, South
Dakota: Modern Press, Inc. 1976. Celebrates Sioux Center's 85th year (1891-
1976), describing the town's life through the people's lives on the surrounding
land and their organizations, notably the Christian Reformed Church.

Genealogy Sources

Genealogy sources for both Sybesma and Kooi

- International Genealogical Index, 1994 Edition, Version 3.05, 9-26-96, from computer records at Modesto LDS church with help of Don Sanford, Modesto, California.

- Dutch Immigrant Records 1835-1880, "Ship Sailings Records," page 26, Dordt College Archives and Dutch Memorial Collection, Sioux Center, Iowa. Individual Records from Dr. Robert Swierenga's Dutch Immigrant Records, 1835-1880.

- "Our Family Register" by Gladys Kooi Gritter, 1981.

- "A People With Convictions—A History of Sioux Center 1870-1991," compiled for Centennial of Sioux Center, contains histories and pictures of scores of relatives. Book is in Sioux Center, Iowa, Public Library. See pp 235-6, 242-53, 403-404, 616.

Sybesma Sources

- Documents and records came from Mattie Sybesma Feikema, Sam Sybesma, Ida Kooi Sybesma and their cousins in Friesland. For many years the three immigrants corresponded with their Friesian cousins Brand and Sybe, and added family data from these letters to their own records. Data also came from scribbled names, places, and dates on the backs of pictures and photographs.

- "Sybesma Oral History: Things Mother Told Me," by Gladys Kooi Gritter, Grand Rapids, Michigan, 1984.

- Records in the Family Bible kept by Clarence and Elaine Sybesma in Platte, South Dakota.

- Genealogie van het geslacht: Sybesma. Family Trees and charts in several letters from Grace Anne Sybesma, Kalamazoo, Michigan, to Gladys Kooi Gritter, 1984.

- Begraafplaats (Cemetery) Pietersbierum. Genealogysk Wurkferban Fryskeakademy. Documents with explanatory letters and photographs from second cousin, Rinske de Boer, Amsterdam, 1995.

- Letters and postcards in Dutch between Sam Sybesma in Platte, South Dakota, and his cousin, Brand Sybesma, in Friesland were loaned by Peter R. and Tietje de Groot, Sint Jacobiparochie, Friesland.

- "Dutch Family Heritage Society," Mary L.S. Parker, Ed., 1995 quarterlies loaned by Don Sanford, "Naamsaannemigen or Name Adoption," vol. 8, no. 2, pp. 44-45, no. 1 p. 3, 1995.

- "Louis Bonaparte En Hollande D'pres Ses Lettres" 1806-1810, Avec Un Portrait En Heliogravure, Editeur Andre Duboscq, Emile-Paul, Paris, 1911. Three hundred letters written by Louis Bonaparte, King of Holland.

- "The Life and Times of Catherine Feikema De Bie," no date. Received from her in June, 1995.

- LDS Film #107542, Nederland Hervormde Gemeente, Film section Ea, Engwierum, Oostdongeradeel Marriages—Vol 10, 1664-1772 Baptisms—Vol 8, 1659-1772. Translated from Friesian by Janice Riemersma, Ripon, California. Also, Bill and Francis Alta, Escalon, California, translated Friesian words in genealogy documents.

Kooi Sources

- Most of the source documents and records came from Aunt Jennie Haverhals in Sioux Center, Iowa, between 1986 and 1996. Letters, visits, phone calls, photographs and oral history also came from visits to other siblings of Fred Kooi in Iowa: Bertha, George, Ellis, and from John's son: cousin Bill Kooi and his nephew, Terry Kooi. Aunt Bertha's grand daughter, Kathy Schreurs, also gave data and photographs.

- "Kastein Ancestors of the Nymeyer-Haecks" (pp 107-119) by Fred Nymeyer, (FN) loaned by Aunt Jennie Haverhals in Sioux Center, Iowa. Kastein cousins, Fred Nymeyer (1897-1987) and his sister, Grace N. Haan, provided a great amount of information and research on the Kasteins and Ten Brinks from way back, gathered during travels to Europe and Wisconsin.

- "Kooi Book" is a family record of several generations compiled and updated annually by Kooi family members. Grada Kastein Kooi was the genealogist who kept a good record of Koois, Kasteins and Ten Brinks.

- Pieter and Geertje Kooi Bible is now with grand nephew, Terry Kooi, and wife Julie, in Inwood, Iowa. When Peter and Geertje Kooi died, 1873-4, Uncle John Kooi, 1858-1926, oldest brother of Remko Kooi, evidently had it in his possession. Then his son, Elmer Kooi, 1883-1978, passed it on to Robert Kooi, 1922-91, and on to Robert Haverhals, who sent it to Jennie Kooi Haverhals with other mementoes in 1983.

- "Birth Certificate" of Great Grandfather Pieter Reuben Kooi, in Friesian language, translated by my second cousin Sientje de Boer in Amsterdam, 1996. Second cousin, Willie Gert Dekkers, Grace Haverhals' daughter, did a search, and got the birth registration at the local bureau in Oldenzyl, The Netherlands.

- "Psalm Book" of Geertje Abbenga Kooi, Chicago, passed down several generations, from Barbara Kooi Smithson, Hollywood, to Gertie Kooi Haverhals, Lebanon, then to her daughter, Anne Dekkers of Sioux Center, who intends to pass it on to her oldest daughter.

- Abstract of title to farm was a temporary loan from Artie Haverhals Bonnema, Sioux Center, Iowa. Abstract has legal and financial data on homeplace (Remko Kooi farm), lists owners, details of inheritance.

Data from the above sources was collected between 1984 and 2003 by the author, Irene Kooi Chadwick, tenth child of Fred Kooi and Ida Sybesma. Both genealogy charts were made by Don Sanford, Modesto, California.

Genealogy Notes

Klaas Sybesma

Jan Cornelis and Affka Sijbes were married in 1721 and their first son was born in Nijwier in 1723. Sijbe Jans was baptized at Oostdongeradeel. Our first knowledge of Sijbe Jans is as a farmer in Nieuw Cruisland, where he died. He served as guardian over many children, including those of a brother. His first marriage was to Akke Botes in 1748. Sijbe Jans married a second time, apparently to Jantsen Atses (Johannes), of Tjallebird, and they had a daughter named Antie Jans. His third marriage was in 1784, in Kollum, to Baukjen Brants and the children included Brandt Sijbes, who was the grandfather of Ietje's Friesian father, Klaas Sybesma.

In the Friesian language, Brand means fire. Years later, in Sioux Center, Iowa, Bertha Bierma Geels related that "During the Dutch church service one Sunday, when I was quite young yet, the janitor smelled smoke coming from the basement. He calmly stood up and said, 'Er is brand,' [there is fire], and everyone calmly walked outside and watched the church in which I was baptized go up in flames."

Brandt Sijbes married Maaike Rinzes Keegstra, the daughter born to Rinze Hessels and Pietje Kornelis, in 1795. Both had been baptized in the Nederlands Hervormd [Reformed] Church. To this union were born eleven children within twenty-four years. The first born was a son, Sybe, who died at age four, a month before the next son was born and given the same name, Sybe. Their eighth child, Cornelis, died the day he was born, and the son born five years later was given the same name. Brandt Sijbes lived to age 99, Maaike to 63, both dying in Sexbierum, Barradeel, where the last seven children had been born.

At Barradeel in 1843, the son of Brandt Sijbes, Sijbe Brandts (1817-1866) married Metje Jans Pols (1822-1892) from Lidlum, daughter of Jan Ernst Pols (Polstra, son of Pol, taken after Napoleon's rule) and Jeltje Anskes Meijer. In the Sybesma Family Bible, Sybe's name appears as Sijbe Brants," but Brandt Sijbes is how Dutch genealogy lists it, and as simply "Sybe," third in the list of kinderen. His brother, Bote, on December 12, 1811, took Sijbesma for a surname on a marriage document. Bote was born "under the rule of the city of Anjum," about two miles from Metslawier, where Brandt was born.

Now also, for the first time, the surname, Sijbesma, appears in all the names of the five children born between 1844 and 1859 to Metje and Sijbe Brandts. Metje and Sijbe named their oldest child Brand. The next one was named Jeltje. Then came Maaike, then Jan, and the last-born was Ietje Sybesma's father, Klaas. The same named-after pattern continues. All five were born in either Dongjum or

Oosterbierum. Sijbe and his wife, Metje, cared for the infant son of his brother, Jan Brandts, of Sexbierum, when his wife died. Sijbe's wife, Metje, was born in Lidlum. She outlived him by twenty-six years. Klaas Sybesma was the youngest of five children.

Bregtje Sybesma

The names of my grandmother, Bregtje Syne Kroeze, come from her father's side of the family. His parents were Gerrit Synes Kroeze (1791-1868) and Brechtje Sjoerds Kramer (1794-1863), both of Pietersbierum. On old maps of Friesland, the towns of their ancestors are near to each other. Bregtje's parents were Sijne Gerrits Kroeze and Gettje Aukes Dijkstra, both of Pietersbierum. They had seven children. Gettje is an old Friesian name that became Geertje and was passed down through the generations, to become Gertie and Gertrude in America. Bregtje married Klaas Sybesma and they named their first-born daughter Geertje, the Aunt Gertie I came to know in Iowa. Several cousins are named Gertrude, and my next-older sister's middle name is Gertrude. My mother, Ida Sybesma Kooi, said Gettje Dijkstra had a lot of sisters. She died of smallpox when her youngest child was six months old. She was preceded in death by one of the seven children, Auke, who died as a small child in 1857. Her husband brought up the remaining small children. The parents are buried in Pietersbierum, as are five of their seven children: Ytje, Gerrit, Auke, a second Auke, and Bauke. Bregtje was buried in Franeker, and Rensche in Wyjnaldum near Harlingen. My interest is in the three sisters who were Great Aunt Ytje, Grandmother Bregtje, and Great Aunt Rinske. However, for others who may be interested, I will pass on what little information I have about all six siblings of Bregtje Syne Kroeze.

The oldest, Ytje, married Enne Gerritsma. Ytje died at age fifty and is buried in Pietersbierum. They had three children: Aukje Terpsma, of Lynden, Washington; Geertje, who married Jan Medema and lived in Holland; and Syne Gerritsma, who married Ida Fiekema and lived in Sioux Center, Iowa. These three, Mother's only cousins in America, came to Sybesma family reunions when my oldest sister, Gladys, was young.

The next sibling was Gerrit, the oldest son, who did not marry and died at age 74. The third child, Auke, died as a baby. According to custom, the next child of the same sex received the same name, Auke. He died at age 20. Either he died while in service to his country or in an accident while shooting ducks. In Amsterdam, my second cousin, Rinske de Boer, says, "I have been told that this brother died because he was homesick when he had to go in National Service."

Pieter and Geertje Kooi

Pieter Kooi married Boukje Burg and they had a son named Remge Willems Kooi, in Oldenzijl, Groningen. He became a tailor and married Bouke Pieters Groenhius, a housewife also born in Oldenzijl, Groningen. The handwritten birth certificate of their son, Pieter Reuben Kooi, was translated into English by my second cousin, Rinske de Boer, who lives in Amsterdam, and also by an official of the gemeente of Uithuistermeden in 1982, who says that "Oldenzyl on current maps is spelled Oldenzijl and is located some five miles south of the extreme north border of the province of Groningen." A letter dated 9 August 1982 to Jennie Haverhals from John and Betty Vander Heide includes copies of Pieter Kooi's 1823 Birth Certificate, Report of Service Record, and his Dutch Passport, with translations of each document.

Pieter was born May 25, 1823, in Oldenzijl, Groningen, in house Number 11. In addition to the father, three witnesses signed the certificate. Officially, it is registered under number 38 in the Province of Groningen, Town of Appingedam, Gemeente of Uithuistermeden. Pieter used this registration and his Service Record to get a passport on February 17, 1847. His passport describes him as five feet five inches tall, with blue eyes, a long nose, small mouth, round chin and forehead, blond eyebrows and hair, and no unusual markings. He entered military service in April of 1842 and was mustered out in October of 1845. The passport is issued by the "Kingdom of the Netherlands." The florid signatures of P. R. Kooi and a Dutch official appear after: "All civil and military authorities are requested to permit P.R. Kooi to go freely and unhindered and to give him assistance and support if needed." Confirmation of these records exists in the U.S.A.

At age thirty-one, Pieter emigrated as a Dutch Reformed blacksmith's hired hand to Chicago. The Dutch Psalm Book records that "PR Kooi & GP Abbenga came to U.S.A. on same boat, married in Chicago, Illinois, 1854." Ship Sailing Records show that Geertje Pieters Abbenga emigrated at age twenty-one, in 1854, from the same place as he did. She is listed on the ship records as Dutch Reformed, a farm servant girl, bound for Chicago. Her reasons for emigrating were religious freedom and economic improvement, while his reason is listed only as economic improvement. Dutch Immigrant Records show that Pieter Kooi crossed the Atlantic with three children and a woman in 1854. He is listed as less well-to-do, as was his father. His destination was "NA3" which was South Chicago in 1855, coming from School, North Holland. The woman was Geertje Abbenga, and the three children with them probably were her younger siblings, the orphans, Anna, Bena, and Hessel. Geertje's other three siblings had died in the Netherlands, as had her parents, Pieter Hessels Abbenga (1790-1852) and Jantje Jans Barghoven (1800-1853). The trip took three months.

Two funeral notices are attached to the inside front cover of the "Geertje Kooi" Family Bible (1870). The first is for Hessel P. Abbenga, 1842-1911, who was a younger brother of Geertje Abbenga (Kooi). The 1880 United States census for Chicago, Cook County, shows a Hessel P. Abbenga at age 38 to be a retail grocer, his wife's name as Anje (Anna Dykema), a housewife. All four of their parents were from Holland. Aunt Jennie Haverhals felt that evidence of living in the U.S.A. was shown in the more American type of names of the spouses and of their children.

The second funeral notice is for Frank Pilgrim, 1834-1911, husband of Anna Abbenga, 1840-1912, who was the mother of eight daughters and two sons. Anna and Bena Abbenga, born in 1841, were still young, perhaps ten and twelve, when their parents died in Holland in 1852 and 1853. Two brothers and a sister died in 1854 at ages sixteen, seventeen, and twenty-seven, ending the Abbenga family line in The Netherlands. In South Chicago, Bena Abbenga married John Evenhuis. Geertje Kooi recorded these names and dates in two places; the Kooi Family Bible and her Psalm Book.

A NOTE ON THE AUTHOR

Irene Kooi Chadwick lives on a creek in the San Joaquin Valley of California. She is a poet, published in magazines, literary journals and anthologies. A book of poems, *Dawn Pearl*, was published in 1994 and remains in print. Before writing this book she was a travel writer. Her stories and photographs from Timbuktu, Tashkent, Nassau, South Africa and USA locations have been published by periodicals in the USA and Canada. During the past decade she has been gathering images, researching, and writing this book.

Ancestors and Siblings of Frederick Kooi

elckinck

lckinck

Hendrik Oostendorp

Aaltjen Brunsink

Berent Rademaker

Hendricken Huijs

Dirk De V

Wendele Oostendorp
b. 13 Nov 1728
at Dinxperlo, Gelderland, Neth.
d. 12 May 1797
at Dinxperlo, Gelderland, Neth.

Jan te Beest

Geesje DeGelink

Geert Damkot

Jan Rademaker
b. 18 Aug 1695
at Dinxperlo, Gelderland, Neth.

Grietjen D

Hendrika Bruggink
b. circa 1755

d. 29 Jun 1805

Hendrik te Beest
b. 9 May 1745

Janna Gertrude Damkes

Berend Rademaker
b. 23 Apr 1730
at Dinxperlo, Gelderland, Neth.
d. 29 Jul 1805
at Dinxperlo, Gelderland, Neth.

a Duenk
782
Gelderland, Neth.
836
, Gelderland, Neth.

Hendrik Willem te Beest
b. 16 Nov 1766
at Dinxperlo, Gelderland, Neth.
d. 5 Oct 1846
m. circa 1805
at Dinxperlo, Gelderland, Neth.

Hendrika
b. 10 Jan 1
at Dinxperlo
d. 5 Oct 18
at Dinxperlo

Elizabeth te Beest
b. 19 Apr 1809
at Dinxperlo, Gelderland, Neth.
d. 6 Dec 1876
at Fox Lake, Dodge Co., WI

Benart Kastein
b. 7 Oct 1836
at Dinxperlo, Gelderland, Neth.
d. 16 Sep 1917
at Conrad, Pondera Co., MT
m. 11 May 1868
at Varsseveld, Gelderland, Neth.

*Paternal
Grandparents* ←

*Maternal
Grandparents* →

Jantje (Jennie) Kooi
b. 1871
d. 1872
at Chicago, Cook Co., IL

William Kooi
b. 1873
d. 1873
at Chicago, IL

Grada Wilhemina Kastein
b. 15 Feb 1869
at Varsseveld, Gelderland, Neth.
d. 13 Feb 1935
at Lebanon, Sioux Co., IA

Dina Kastein
b. 15 Jun 1871
at Fox Lake, Dodge Co., WI
d. 6 Oct 1942
at Sioux Center, Sioux Co., IA
m. 1894, Steven Campagne

Elizabe
b. 4 Nov 1
at Fox La
WI
d. 23 Feb
at Hull, S
m. 1895,

Frederick Kooi
b. 19 Apr 1894
at Lebanon, Sioux Co., IA
d. 5 Feb 1986
at Denver, Denver Co., CO
m. 27 Jan 1921
at Lebanon, Sioux Co., IA

Bertha Jeanette Kooi
b. 14 Jun 1896
at Lebanon, Sioux Co., IA
d. 7 Apr 2002 - age 105 yrs
at Sioux Center, Sioux Co., IA

John Kooi
b. 18 May 1898
at Lebanon, Sioux Co., IA
d. 9 Oct 1992
at Sioux Center, Sioux Co., IA

Dreaka Helena Kooi
b. 19 Feb 1901
at Lebanon, Sioux Co., IA
d. 19 Jun 1927

Ietje Ida Sybesma
b. 6 Sep 1899
at Franeker, Friesland, Netherlands
d. 2 Feb 1984
at Denver, Denver Co., CO

Gerrit Van der Lugt
b. 31 Aug 1896
d. 9 Jan 1968
m. 27 Jan 1921

Gertie Van der Lugt
b. 21 Sep 1900
d. 31 Jul 1966
m. 10 Feb 1921

Sebrecht Cornelius Haver
b. 2 May 1898
at Netherlands
d. 15 Nov 1943
m. 30 Jan 1923

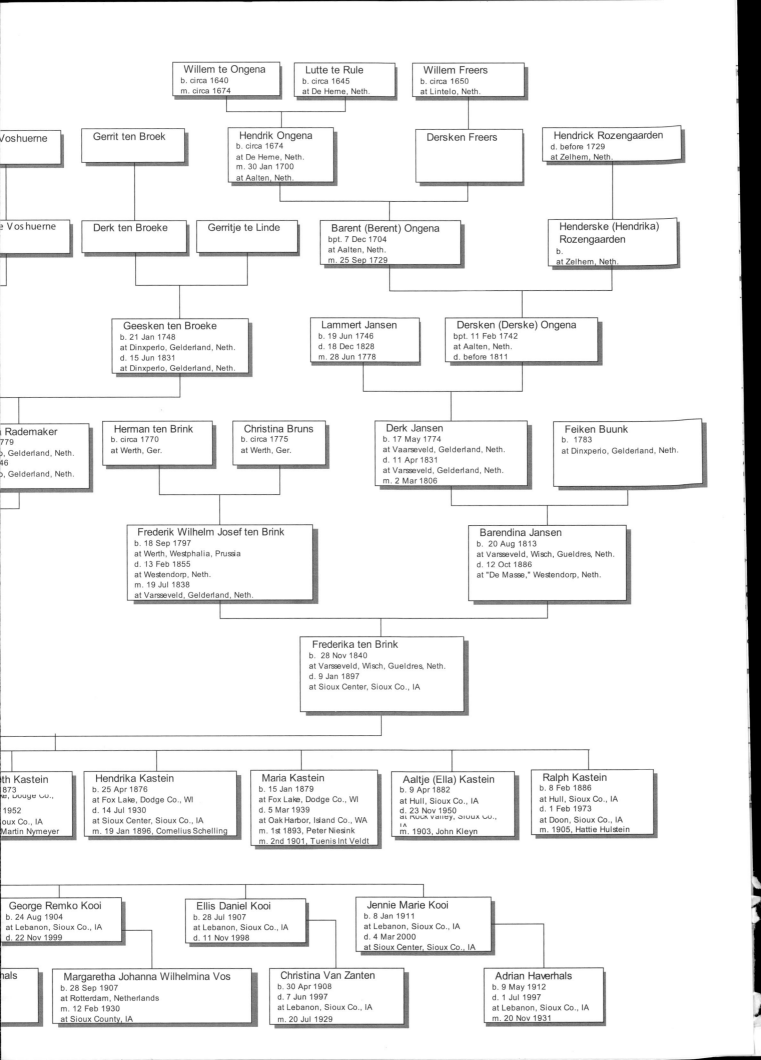

Willem te Ongena
b. circa 1640
m. circa 1674

Lutte te Rule
b. circa 1645
at De Herne, Neth.

Willem Freers
b. circa 1650
at Lintelo, Neth.

Voshuerne

Gerrit ten Broek

Hendrik Ongena
b. circa 1674
at De Herne, Neth.
m. 30 Jan 1700
at Aalten, Neth.

Dersken Freers

Hendrick Rozengaarden
d. before 1729
at Zelhem, Neth.

e Voshuerne

Derk ten Broeke

Gerritje te Linde

Barent (Berent) Ongena
bpt. 7 Dec 1704
at Aalten, Neth.
m. 25 Sep 1729

Henderske (Hendrika)
Rozengaarden
b.
at Zelhem, Neth.

Geesken ten Broeke
b. 21 Jan 1748
at Dinxperlo, Gelderland, Neth.
d. 15 Jun 1831
at Dinxperlo, Gelderland, Neth.

Lammert Jansen
b. 19 Jun 1746
d. 18 Dec 1828
m. 28 Jun 1778

Dersken (Derske) Ongena
bpt. 11 Feb 1742
at Aalten, Neth.
d. before 1811

Rademaker
779
, Gelderland, Neth.
46
, Gelderland, Neth.

Herman ten Brink
b. circa 1770
at Werth, Ger.

Christina Bruns
b. circa 1775
at Werth, Ger.

Derk Jansen
b. 17 May 1774
at Vaarseveld, Gelderland, Neth.
d. 11 Apr 1831
at Varssveld, Gelderland, Neth.
m. 2 Mar 1806

Feiken Buunk
b. 1783
at Dinxperio, Gelderland, Neth.

Frederik Wilhelm Josef ten Brink
b. 18 Sep 1797
at Werth, Westphalia, Prussia
d. 13 Feb 1855
at Westendorp, Neth.
m. 19 Jul 1838
at Varsseveld, Gelderland, Neth.

Barendina Jansen
b. 20 Aug 1813
at Varsseveld, Wisch, Gueldres, Neth.
d. 12 Oct 1886
at "De Masse," Westendorp, Neth.

Frederika ten Brink
b. 28 Nov 1840
at Varsseveld, Wisch, Gueldres, Neth.
d. 9 Jan 1897
at Sioux Center, Sioux Co., IA

th Kastein
873
e, Dodge Co.,

1952
oux Co., IA
Martin Nymeyer

Hendrika Kastein
b. 25 Apr 1876
at Fox Lake, Dodge Co., WI
d. 14 Jul 1930
at Sioux Center, Sioux Co., IA
m. 19 Jan 1896, Cornelius Schelling

Maria Kastein
b. 15 Jan 1879
at Fox Lake, Dodge Co., WI
d. 5 Mar 1939
at Oak Harbor, Island Co., WA
m. 1st 1893, Peter Niesink
m. 2nd 1901, Tuenis Int Veldt

Aaltje (Ella) Kastein
b. 9 Apr 1882
at Hull, Sioux Co., IA
d. 23 Nov 1950
at Rock Valley, Sioux Co.,
IA
m. 1903, John Kleyn

Ralph Kastein
b. 8 Feb 1886
at Hull, Sioux Co., IA
d. 1 Feb 1973
at Doon, Sioux Co., IA
m. 1905, Hattie Hulstein

George Remko Kooi
b. 24 Aug 1904
at Lebanon, Sioux Co., IA
d. 22 Nov 1999

Ellis Daniel Kooi
b. 28 Jul 1907
at Lebanon, Sioux Co., IA
d. 11 Nov 1998

Jennie Marie Kooi
b. 8 Jan 1911
at Lebanon, Sioux Co., IA
d. 4 Mar 2000
at Sioux Center, Sioux Co., IA

hals

Margaretha Johanna Wilhelmina Vos
b. 28 Sep 1907
at Rotterdam, Netherlands
m. 12 Feb 1930
at Sioux County, IA

Christina Van Zanten
b. 30 Apr 1908
d. 7 Jun 1997
at Lebanon, Sioux Co., IA
m. 20 Jul 1929

Adrian Haverhals
b. 9 May 1912
d. 1 Jul 1997
at Lebanon, Sioux Co., IA
m. 20 Nov 1931